WHOSE

WORLD ORDER ?

WHOSE

WORLD ORDER ?

Russia's Perception
of American Ideas
after the Cold War

ANDREI P. TSYGANKOV

University of Notre Dame Press

Notre Dame, Indiana

Manufactured in the United States of America

Library of Congress Cataloging-in-Publication Data
Tsygankov, Andrei P., 1964–
Whose world order?:Russia's perception of American ideas after the
Cold War/Andrei P. Tsygankov.
p.   cm.
Includes bibliographical references and index.
ISBN 0-268-04228-4 (cloth : alk. paper)
ISBN 0-268-04229-2 (pbk.: alk. paper)
1. World politics—1989–   2. Fukuyama, Francis. End of history.
3. United States—Foreign relations—2001–   4. United States—
Foreign public opinion, Russian.   5. Russia—Foreign relations—
United States.   6. United States—Foreign relations—Russia.
7. Public opinion—Russia.   I. Title.
D860.T78   2004
327.73'009'049—dc22

2003024970

∞ *This book is printed on acid-free paper.*

. . . the question whether we belong to a larger community
is answered in terms of whether our own action calls out
a response in this wider community, and whether its response
is reflected back into our own conduct.

George H. Mead

For my Russian and American teachers and friends

CONTENTS

ACKNOWLEDGMENTS

The events of September 11 reinforce the need to develop a better cross-cultural understanding among the various peoples of the world. This book attempts to understand why some Western ideas, whose authors defend their visions of global freedom and peace, are often rejected outside the West. Its central argument is that in today's increasingly global circumstances, we scholars share responsibility for how our ideas are perceived in the outside world. Social science is not neutral in global political debates; we shape reality, as it shapes us. Judging by the reactions of Russia to two prominent American visions of a post–cold war order, ours is a global world; what we say in one of its parts is echoed and (re)interpreted elsewhere. Judging by the same reaction, we must work harder on improving our ideas of world order and moving beyond excessively ethnocentric perspectives.

This book is a tribute to my Russian and American teachers and friends. I began to understand the politics of ideas back in Russia—first as a student at Moscow State University during Gorbachev's era, and then as an activist helping a prominent intellectual to be elected to the Russian Duma. I am grateful to Gorbachev and his era for all its illusions and insights. My teachers and friends at MGU, MGIMO, and *Voprosy filosofiyi* encouraged me to think in terms of measuring our words against standards of political consequences.

In the United States, the University of Southern California School of International Relations has provided an intellectually stimulating environment. I am most grateful to Hayward Alker and Ann Tickner for their inspiration and support. Ann encouraged me to write about Russian International Relations in her theory class, and she subsequently provided important feedback on this project. Hayward's vision of International Relations as a globally pluralistic body of knowledge pushed me to ask questions about Western intellectual engagements with the outside world. It urged me to study the conditions under which such engagement can be mutually enriching, rather than alienating. On several occasions, Hayward asked me to brief him on how Russians perceive particular Western ideas, and it was during one of these brainstorming sessions that I came to think of this project. I am also indebted to John Odell and Jeff Knopf for their methodological advice. Although none of them is responsible for the content of my ideas, I greatly benefited from their training in research design and foreign policy analysis.

Outside USC, many friends and colleagues were generous with their help and encouragements. Among them, I should like to mention Sanjoy Benerjee, Juliana Budjevac, Eileen Crumm, Luba Fajfer, Lee Ann Fujii, Gerry Gendlin, Larry Helm, Peg Hermann, Andrzej Korbonski, Alan Kronstadt, Laura Neack, Daniel N. Nelson, Martha Merritt, Guillermo O'Donnell, Boris Pruzhinin, and Thomas Schmalberger. Special thanks to the College of Behavioral and Social Sciences and Dean Joel Kassiola at San Francisco State University for providing partial financial support for editing and indexing the book.

Parts of several chapters draw on my previously published articles "Pluralism or Isolation of Civilizations?" *Geopolitics* vol. 4, no. 3 (2000); "Rediscovering National Interests after the 'End of History,'" *International Politics* vol. 39, no. 4 (2002); and "The Irony of Western Ideas in a Multicultural World," *International Studies Review* vol. 5, no. 1 (2003). I thank the publishers for permission to publish these revised materials in this book.

At University of Notre Dame Press, I was fortunate to receive outstanding comments of two anonymous referees. I hope to have been able to benefit from these comments and to satisfy the referees' expectations. I am grateful to Christina Catanzarite and Barbara Hanrahan for their faith in this project and helpful feedback. I also would like to thank Carole Roos for editorial assistance and smoothing out my English.

As always, I thank my wife, daughter, and parents for simply being who they are.

NOTE ON THE TRANSLITERATION

In transliterating names from the Russian, I have used "y" to denote "Ы", ' to denote "Ь" and "Ъ", "yu" to denote "Ю", "ya" to denote "Я", "i" to denote "Й" and "ИЙ", "iyi" to denote double "И", "e" to denote "Э", "kh" to denote "Х", "zh" to denote "Ж", "ts" to denote "Ц", "ch" to denote "Ч", "sh" to denote "Ш", and "sch" to denote "Щ". I have also used "Ye" to distinguish the sound of "e" (such as "Yevropa") in the beginning of a word from that in the middle of a word (such as "vneshnei"). Everywhere, I did not distinguish between "E" and "Ё". Spelling of Russian names varies by author in quotations.

TABLES

CHAPTER 1

INTRODUCTION

Whose World Order?

In 1936, John M. Keynes wrote, "the ideas of economists and political philosophers, both when they are right and when they are wrong, are more powerful than is commonly understood." Recently, political scientists have taken the role of ideas seriously and produced a voluminous literature on how ideas impact policies and institutional orders.[1] Where our knowledge remains quite limited, however, is in understanding why ideas formulated in one society tend to be perceived differently, even negatively, in other social contexts. What are the conditions under which a potentially harmful negative perception occurs? And, no less significantly, who should be held responsible for such a perception?

For our purposes, a negative perception is defined as interpreting an idea as threatening to world peace and order. One example of a negative perception is how non-Western cultures understand Western ideas of world order.[2] While in the West there is growing acceptance of the universal viability of Western market democracy and a human rights–centered world, the non-Western parts of the globe remain wary and skeptical of this view. In various parts of the globe, Western-centered world order projects have often been perceived as unable to promote a just and stable international system because of their exclusively Western orientation and lack of empathetic understanding of other cultures. Some scholars have argued that rather than promoting the dialogue necessary for finding an appropriate international system, these projects contribute to further isolationism and hostility among international actors.[3]

In an attempt to contribute to our understanding of the cultural perception of ideas, this book proposes to trace the impact of two prominent American visions of a post–cold war order—Francis Fukuyama's "end of history" and Samuel Huntington's "clash of civilizations"— on Russia's intellectual and political discourse. Both ideas were widely discussed in non-Western parts of the world, particularly in Russia. Fukuyama's thesis, which emerged in the conservative Western context of the late 1980s, argued the case for a global ascendancy of the Western-style market democracy. Huntington, on the other hand, drew the attention of scholars and the policy community to the elements of global disorder, which in mid-1990s were perceived to be increasingly dominant. Russia received both ideas critically. Despite the intentions of Fukuyama and Huntington to contribute to the development of freedom and stability in the world, Russia viewed their intellectual projects as limiting social and cross-cultural creativity at best, and as a war-prone justification of a global West-centered dictatorship at worst. A central reason for such perceptions has to do with the ethnocentric or culturally exclusive nature of these two ideas and the inability of their authors to appreciate fully the historical, geopolitical, and institutional distinctness of Russia.

The perspective developed in this book is rich with implications for scholarship and policy inside, as well as outside, the Eurasian region. It raises several important explanatory and normative questions for the field of International Relations (IR). In explanatory terms, this work points toward further investigations of how American world order ideas and practices are perceived by non-Western worlds. It implies the need for scholars to study cultural perceptions in world politics and to map the progress and the obstacles on the way to developing a truly global society. Normatively, the book raises the issue of the moral responsibility of intellectuals for the ideas they produce and what implications this responsibility may have for IR theory. Several ways are suggested to overcome ethnocentric bias and to move beyond culturally exclusive realist and cosmopolitan discourses toward embracing the development of various communitarian projects.

1. FUKUYAMA, HUNTINGTON, AND WESTERN WORLD ORDER PROJECTS

Fukuyama's and Huntington's world order projects emerged in the particular context of the West's perceptions of the post–cold war international environment. Each in its own way reflected distinct visions dominant in Western policy circles.

Fukuyama's "end of history" thesis emerged out of the intellectual and policy tradition of Western conservative internationalism. By the end of the 1980s, conservatives had been in power for a good decade and, with the decline of Soviet power, they became convinced of the West's victory in the cold war struggle. For example, 1989 saw the unification of Germany and further meltdown of the Soviet Union, which some characterized as "the best period of US foreign policy ever."[4]

Several other prominent Western projects defended the idea of the West's supremacy in the post–cold war era. For example, President Jimmy Carter's former national security advisor Zbigniew Brzezinski envisioned the upcoming victory of the West by celebrating the Soviet Union's "grand failure."[5] In his view, the Soviet "totalitarian" state was incapable of reform. Communism's decline was therefore irreversible and inevitable. It would have made the system's "practice and its dogma largely irrelevant to the human condition," and communism would be remembered as the twentieth century's "political and intellectual aberration."[6] Other commentators argued the case for a global spread of Western democracy. Marc Plattner declared the emergence of a "world with one dominant principle of legitimacy, democracy."[7] Still others, such as Charles Krauthammer, went so far as to proclaim the arrival of a "unipolar moment," a period in which only one superpower, the United States, would stand above the rest of the world in its military, economic, and ideological capacity.[8]

For a short time in the early 1990s, even fewer conservative commentators both in Europe and the United States expressed similar Western democratic triumphalism. In Europe, theorists of civil society and "participatory democracy" such as Andrew Arato, Ralf Dahrendorf, and Timothy Garton Ash saw the Soviet decline and the Eastern European revolutions as the catalyst for a revival of civic norms of plurality and publicity.[9] British journalist Timothy Garton Ash forcefully stated the mood by maintaining that the European revolutions "can offer no fundamentally new ideas on the big questions of politics, economics, law or international relations. The ideas whose time has come are old, familiar, well-tested ones"—liberal ideas about the rule of law, parliamentary government, and an independent judiciary.[10]

Fukuyama's vision was a bold summary of these optimistic feelings in Western policy circles as expressed by some leading intellectuals. The "end of history," in this sense, was not accidental in its appearance. Politically as a Bush Administration strategist and intellectually as an ardent proponent of modernization theory,[11] Fukuyama was well positioned to defend the worldwide ascendancy of Western-style liberal capitalism. His main intellectual target was the realist emphasis on international anarchy and cyclical development.[12] Influenced by Hegel and Kojève's interpretations of the end of history, he insists that power politics is hopelessly ahistorical and that liberalism and liberal institutions such as the rule of law, representative democracy, and the market economy are acquiring a truly universal significance. In a famous passage, Fukuyama asserted, "what we may be witnessing is not just the end of the Cold War . . . but the end of history as such: that is, the end point of mankind's ideological evolution and the universalization of Western liberal democracy as the final form of human government."[13] Fukuyama projected a future of Western values for the non-Western parts of the world and argued that other nations have no choice but to develop and modernize exclusively in the manner of Western societies. In a Nietzsche-inspired pessimistic spirit, he insisted that while the liberal capitalist order is not perfect, it could not be improved upon.

Next came Huntington's "clash of civilizations" vision, which was fundamentally different from that of Fukuyama. Huntington's theory reflected different social circumstances, emerging in the early 1990s out of anxiety over the West's growing inability to preserve peace and stability throughout the globe. The new ethnic conflicts in Europe and the former USSR, the perceived threat from the non-defeated regime of Saddam Hussein, and environmental and demographic pressures from Asia and Africa seemed to pose great risks. Several other prominent intellectual projects emerged to reflect the rising pessimism among U.S. policy makers about the future of the world order and to reject Fukuyama's rosy picture.

Many perceived the rise of various ethnic and religious identities as especially worrisome. In 1992, Benjamin R. Barber, writing in the influential *Atlantic Monthly,* summarized the feelings:

OPEC, the World Bank, the United Nations, the International Red Cross, the multinational corporations . . . often appear as ineffective reactors to the world real actors: national states and, to ever greater degree, subnational factions in permanent rebellion against uniformity and integration—even the kind represented by universal law and justice. The headlines feature these players regularly: they are cultures, not countries; parts, not wholes; sects, not religions; rebellious factions and dissenting minorities at war not just with globalism but with the traditional nation-state. Kurds, Basques, Puerto Ricans, Ossetians, East Timoreans, Quebecois, the Catholics of Northern Ireland, Abkhasians, Kurile Islander Japanese, the Zulus of Inkatha, Catalonians, Tamils, and, of course, Palestinians—people without countries, inhabiting nations not their own, seeking smaller worlds within borders that will seal them off from modernity.[14]

Barber went on to argue that the dangers of technology, communication, and commerce-driven globalization—McWorld—increasingly generate a powerful response from Jihad or forces of primordial nature such as religion, tribe, and ethnicity. These forces of Jihad and McWorld operate "with equal strength in opposite directions," and the global future is unlikely to be democratic.[15] The solution, in his view, might come from global civic activism, but he saw little chance of such activism developing. Barber concluded on a pessimistic note, "for democracy to persist in our brave new McWorld, we will have to commit acts of conscious political will—a possibility, but hardly a probability, under these conditions."[16]

Robert D. Kaplan, writing in the same *Atlantic Monthly,* went even further.[17] Drawing on impressions from West Africa, he described the emerging world as characterized by demographic, environmental, and social stress. In this neo-Malthusian world, Kaplan argued that "disease, overpopulation, unprovoked crime, scarcity of resources, refugee migrations, the increasing erosion of nation-states and international borders, and the empowerment of private armies, security firms and international drug-cartels," will eventually take over forces of peace and stability.[18]

It was within this context that Huntington's vision emerged. Just as Fukuyama expressed the West's optimism, even euphoria, about the future world order, Huntington expressed the growing feelings of anxiety and frustration. Huntington was convinced that the West as a civilization was unique, not universal, and, instead of expanding globally, it should go on the defensive and prepare to fight for its cultural values in coming clashes with non-Western "civilizations." In his view, civilizations are meaningful cultural entities, separated by clear boundaries, and differentiated from each other by history, language, tradition, and, most importantly, religion.[19] With the end of the cold war, civilizations were replacing nation-states and fighting for power, rather than adopting Western values. In fact, Western values, such as rule of law, social pluralism, representative government, and individualism,[20] were in danger, and Huntington asserts that the West must strive for power to protect itself effectively.

2. RUSSIA'S NEGATIVE PERCEPTION OF AMERICAN POST–COLD WAR ORDER PROJECTS

Fukuyama's "end of history" vision became the first test for Russia's post–cold war perception. The vision implied that, with the end of the cold war, the last viable alternative to Western liberalism had been exhausted, and the non-Western world would eventually modernize in the manner of Western societies. In Russia, however, the idea of such modernization was contemplated only briefly and by only a narrow group of pro-Western political elites. The Russian intellectual and political spectrum criticized the idea as insensitive to the Russian domestic context and even aimed at perpetuating and expanding Western hegemony. Some intellectuals condemned Fukuyama's vision as demonstrating degradation of the Western liberal discourse because it assumed the absence of alternatives.[21] Others pointed to the thesis's role in justifying a Western temptation to "play geopolitical games."[22]

In a similar way, the Russian intellectuals were critical of Huntington's "clash of civilizations" vision. For Russia, Huntington's "clash" scenario assumed the need to side with the West against the identified threat, especially from China and the Muslim world. Many Russians refused to perceive other cultures as potentially threatening to their well-being and security. Instead of encouraging cooperation and stability in Eurasia, Russians argued, Huntington's project pushed for war and mutual hostilities in the already vulnerable region. It also played into the hands of Russia's extreme nationalist politicians, as noted by scholars of Russian far right movements.[23]

Outside the discourse, Russia's institutional practice did not conform to the visions of Fukuyama and Huntington. In the ten years that have passed since the end of communism, Russia has developed a set of political, economic, security, and cultural institutions that are distinct from the expectations of the two American visions. Russia's super-presidential system, oligarchical capitalism, and a renewed perception of the West as a potential threat[24] are hardly in agreement with Fukuyama's image of a pro-Western liberal democracy. Nor do Russian cultural institutions conform to the image of a "clash of civilizations." Despite its domestic and peripheral ethnic diversity,[25] Russia does not seem to face a major threat to its cultural cohesion and territorial integrity. However serious Chechnya's secessionism is, it remains an isolated example in Russia's postcommunist development.[26]

Outside Russia, other non-Western cultures perceived the "end of history" and the "clash of civilizations" at least as critically, if not more so, than did Russia. China and Iran are cases in point.[27]

China's intellectuals rejected Fukuyama's notion of linear and pro-Western modernization following Chairman Deng Xiaoping's critique of the Western model of democracy and capitalism. Many Chinese scholars were also critical of the theory of the "clash of civilizations." Those of a more nationalist bent often perceived the theory as a misrepresentation of the post–cold war world and as an encroachment on China's "cultural sovereignty."[28] More liberally oriented scholars, while relatively less influential, were also critical of Huntington's image. In their view, the image was a misrepresentation of increasingly globalized international politics, a misleading intellectual trap of realpolitik with the potential for becoming a self-fulfilling prophecy.[29] To prevent Huntington's view from becoming such a prophecy, Chinese scholars proposed to adopt a wider definition of politics that would include working to build "double-win" situations beyond traditional security alliances.[30]

In Iran, the leading school of thought[31] is reformist and is associated with President Mohammed Khatami. The president is advocating far-reaching political reforms toward a more secular society and away from theocratic principles of authority, but building on Iran's own cultural tradition.[32] In foreign affairs, his vision of the world is that of pluralism and a dialogue of civilizations moving toward commonalities, mutual understanding, and ultimately the "emergence of a world culture." In Khatami's own words,

> World culture cannot and ought not to ignore characteristics and peculiarities of any particular local culture with the aim of imposing its own upon them. Cultures and civilizations that have naturally evolved among various nations, in the course of history, are constituted from elements that have gradually adapted to collective souls and to the historical and traditional characteristics. . . . From an ethical perspective, the paradigm of dialogue among civilizations requires that we abandon the will-to-power and instead pursue compassion, understanding, and love. The ultimate goal of dialogue among civilizations is not dialogue in and of itself, but attaining empathy and compassion.[33]

Internationally, Khatami's call for "the dialogue among the civilizations" was endorsed by the United Nations, and the year 2001 was called the Year of Inter-civilizational Dialogue by the 53rd session of the U.N. General Assembly. In and of itself, this is a powerful response to both Fukuyama's pro-Western expansionism and Huntington's isolationism.[34]

3. WHY THE NEGATIVE PERCEPTION?

Two interrelated factors must be explored for understanding cultural perception: the degree of ethnocentrism embodied in the ideas or ideology of world order (the sender's side) and the structure of local culture (the receiver's side). Negative perception is most likely to occur when an external idea and its assumptions, substances, and implications are formulated in ethnocentric terms. Various forms of resistance from local cultural contexts may further complicate a positive perception of an idea.

Ethnocentrism, defined as the belief that one's own culture represents the natural and best way to do things,[35] is rooted in certain institutional, societal, and civilizational structures and discursive assumptions.[36] Typically, ideas that are most easily perceived as being ethnocentric are those advancing either a Cosmopolitan or a Realist vision of the world. These two visions tend to advance mutually exclusive images of the world by neglecting the dialectical nature of global vs. local interactions and overemphasizing either local or global sources of moral authority. Cosmopolitan writers view the increasingly globalized character of world politics as a movement toward a culturally homogeneous global society. For conservative cosmopolitans such as Fukuyama, this homogeneous cultural development is often linked to the progression of Western civilization. For cosmopolitans of a more radical orientation, Westernized modernity may mean regression and enslavement, but is equally homogeneous and identity-insensitive. Realists, on the other hand, advance a highly particularistic vision of the international system, in which local cultures compete for power and resources under the condition of anarchy. For cultural realists, such as Samuel Huntington, this competition means an inevitable "clash" that often pits the "West against the rest."[37]

Local culture is another important factor for understanding how ideas are perceived. For an idea to be received by a local culture, it must go through stages of initial interest, persuasion, and socialization. At the first stage, a local culture develops an initial perception of its similarity to, rather than difference from, another culture and initial interest in an external idea. At the stage of persuasion, an idea is actively debated and distributed within the leadership and political elite. Finally, at the stage of socialization, reception of an idea reaches the point of distribution to the larger society. It is worth emphasizing, however, that the process of ideas' social incorporation is never predetermined. Local cultures typically differ in their historical experiences and present concerns.

4. WHO IS RESPONSIBLE?

My present argument is, in part, normative, and raises the question of the *responsibility* of intellectuals for the ideas they produce and the effects these ideas have outside their immediate cultural contexts. Throughout the book, I argue that Fukuyama's and Huntington's engagements with Russia and its national discourse can only be evaluated as a moral failure. Clearly, these American scholars do not bear the full burden of responsibility for Russia's negative cultural perception; several domestic and international developments contributed to Russia's interpretation of their ideas. Yet, to the extent of the "end of history" and "clash of civilizations" theses' involvement with Russia's domestic intellectual development, their authors are responsible for the rise of isolationism and anti-Western hostility in Russian discourse. These ideas were widely exploited by radically anti-Western forces in Russia as the only voices of the West. Fukuyama's and Huntington's overall contributions to and direct participation in Russia's debates were anything but helpful to the country's painful process of self-definition.

In non-Western cultures outside Russia, the "end of history" and "clash of civilizations" had a similar effect. In China, these arguments reinforced the position of nationalists, for whom Fukuyama and Huntington were but a façade of power politics waged by the West against non-Western nations, including China.[38] Iranian nationalist-oriented thinkers also perceived these two American ideas as the covert efforts of a morally inferior Western civilization to destroy the unity and cohesiveness of their own.[39] Other Muslim scholars made the point that "when it is in the hand of politicians, military officers and thinkers such as Samuel Huntington or Francis Fukuyama, [the argument about civilizational identities] becomes a means of propaganda for violence and the instigation of nations and civilizations for greater clashes."[40]

The argument about the moral responsibility of scholars runs, of course, both ways: it is not only Western thinkers who are capable of empowering anti-Western nationalists in other cultures, but scholars in Russia, China, Iran, and elsewhere, too, have the potential for reinforcing hegemonic thinking and policies in the West. For example, consider the case of Russian hard-line Eurasianism, the theory that portrays Russia as a culturally anti-Western, independent unit responsible for maintaining stability and control in the post-Soviet Eurasia. The hard-line Eurasianists often advocate the restoration of the Russian empire in the former Soviet borders and interpret Russia's interests as resisting Western economic, political, and cultural influences.[41] Eurasianism draws support from Russia's procommunist sympathizers and alarms everyone in Russia and the West concerned with the preservation of political dialogue in the world.

Cultural nationalists in both Russia and the West need each other. By developing theoretically essentialist arguments and recommending tough unilateral policies to their governments, they perpetuate each other, as well as the familiar world of violence and power politics. Western intellectuals and politicians with hegemonic mindsets need those hard-line arguments outside the West. Capitalizing on this essentialist aspect of Russia's cultural and geographic distinctness, they present Eurasianism as reflecting uniform anti-Western thinking across the entire Russian political spectrum and of cloaking a Russian drive for imperial restoration.[42] This reading of the Russian intellectual discourse is self-serving and helps to justify Western hegemony and unilateral policies in dealing with post-Soviet Russia. Russia's hard-line intellectuals do disservice to their own country and bear a direct responsibility for feeding Russophobia and anti-Russian policies in the outside world.

Fukuyama's and Huntington's arguments were chosen because of their worldwide significance. Both arguments sold millions of copies and were translated into dozens of foreign languages. Disseminating experiences of the (currently) most dynamic and internationalist culture, these two scholars found themselves in a position of influencing the world's discourse significantly more than representatives of Russian or any other culture. The main moral lesson of Fukuyama's and Huntington's engagement with Russia is that an intellectual producing a world order idea should be held responsible for how his or her idea is perceived outside its immediate cultural context. Because we continue to live in a multicultural world, a certain degree of negative perception is inevitable, but it is in our power to reduce it. Intellectual ethnocentrism, by definition, produces negative reactions across cultures, but we are the ones who design and think through our projects, and it is our responsibility to minimize the potential harm and maximize the potential good.

5. ALTERNATIVE EXPLANATIONS

Our account of perception of world order ideas can be objected to on at least two substantive grounds, rationalist and culturally essentialist. *Rationalists* might argue that the approach taken in this book overstates the role of a social context and understates actors' interests and political calculations. To scholars working in this tradition, the negative perception of ideas is not cultural; in fact, the perception of an idea might well be positive, if it were not for the actors' political interests. If rationalists were to raise the responsibility question at all, they would place responsibility for the negative perception on the receiving side of the idea, rather than on the producer.

For instance, rationalist studies of nationalism[43] downplayed the role of cultural environment—both domestic and external—and, instead, concentrated on nationalists' potential loss having to do with their fear of risking already acquired status and privileges. If so, nationalist interpretations of various aspects of Western civilization (religion, institutions, social science, literature, etc.) as "alien" and not applicable to their local context are nothing more than the use of politically convenient rhetoric to create the image of an enemy and consolidate public opinion around desired goals. The West then has a small role to play in putting down the fire of anti-Western behavior and interpretations. Responsibility lies entirely with local nationalists.

With regard to the present discourse analysis, rationalists might assert that it was the Russian elites, not Fukuyama or Huntington, who were responsible for how these two Western visions of world politics were received. Russia's rejections of Fukuyama's and Huntington's visions of the post–cold war world order were then purely political and interest maximizing, and not cultural. Russian elites might have simply more success in presenting themselves as guardians of "national interests" against the "encroaching" and "hegemonic" West when they have a specific target. The "end of history" and "clash of civilizations" theses could usefully serve as such a target. Presenting these ideas as cloaks for Western intentions to weaken, exploit, and conquer Russia is appealing politics if one is motivated purely by preserving power.

This explanation is unsatisfactory for at least two reasons. First, presenting the Russia's elites as "rational" in calculating power benefits has its limits. Whereas Russian National Communists certainly benefited from the arguments of Fukuyama and Huntington, Russian Liberals and Social Democrats did not. Intellectually and politically, these latter two groups had little to gain by creating a threatening image of the West, yet they, too, were highly critical of both visions. Indeed, Russian Liberals view the West as a potential partner, not a threat. The rejection of Fukuyama's and Huntington's ideas across the entire intellectual spectrum suggests that the perception was of a cultural, and not merely political, nature. Second, Russia's ruling elite became more nationalistic and anti-Western toward 1993 with the failure of the first wave of reforms and as a reflection of the fact that the Russian public had become less receptive to Western ideas and models of society. According to one poll, public support for the American model of society fell from 32 percent to 12 percent over the period from 1990 to 1992.[44] Under Gorbachev, the domestic elite had no interest in viewing the West and its ideas as a scapegoat; on the contrary, it hoped to benefit from a "strategic partnership" with the West and strove to sell an image of the country's international openness. Before the Soviet collapse, it was Fukuyama's ideas that were undermining the political credibility of the West, not the Russian elite's. The rationalist argument is, therefore, deceptive: it conveniently diverts responsibility for ideas from the intellectuals who produce them and implies that such responsibility rests with the ideas' recipients.

The alternative, *culturally essentialist* perspective would advance an argument that is just the opposite of the rationalist view. Culturalists view the world as inherently multicultural and emphasize the role of factors of essentialist nature, such as ethnicity, language, and religion.[45] Rather than placing the emphasis on actors' political interests, culturalists might argue that local cultural values and social contexts are resistant to external ideas. This perspective downplays the question of intellectuals' responsibility for the ways in which their ideas are perceived by the outside world by presenting such ideas as loyal and accurate messengers of their cultures. In the cultural account, the Russian elite's rejection of Western ideas would be natural because Russia's worldview is based on a different set of cultural values reflecting their distinct religion, language, and ethnicity. So long as Fukuyama's and Huntington's visions reflected the values of Western civilization, they could not possibly be persuasive to peoples of cultures and civilizations with non-Western origins. The responsibility of those producing the ideas is limited here to their immediate cultures, and not extended to the broader cross-cultural context.

The cultural perspective is curiously similar to that of Huntington. A major problem for this perspective is its essentialism: the rejection of ideas that are transported from one culture to another is natural, even inevitable. This essentialism does not take into account the fact that perception is a variable rather than a constant. In reality an idea—though a cultural product—never represents culture adequately or loyally; instead, it represents one aspect of a culture, while denying and reshaping others. Local cultures are not homogeneous, once and for all fixed entities; people within them may react differently to similar ideas across time. Fukuyama's ideas, for example, generated a stronger nationalist critique after 1992 than before the Soviet disintegration. The political elite's rejection of the "end of history" idea was, indeed, cultural, but it was neither inevitable nor essentialist. Different schools among the Russian elite reacted to the idea differently, and their reactions evolved over time as their cultural identity changed.

As a result, neither rationalists nor cultural essentialists are able to adequately interpret the phenomenon of the perception of ideas. If we are to make progress, we need a perspective that offers a more nuanced classification of ideas, on the one hand, and a more time specific and less essentialist account of local cultures, on the other. This is what the present study attempts to accomplish.

6. THE STUDY'S DESIGN, METHODOLOGY, AND ORGANIZATION

This study is a combination of political theory and empirically focused comparative research. Our first goal is to introduce theoretical arguments resulting from the engagement of Fukuyama's and Huntington's visions of world order with Russia's foreign policy discourse. If these arguments have any merit, they will continue to arise in IR debates and contribute insights to the discipline's development. We also want to consider how generally applicable the argument about ethnocentrism and cultural perception in international politics is and to what extent it holds up in regions outside Russia and Eurasia, as well as in regard to ideas beyond the two currently under consideration.

I selected Fukuyama's and Huntington's ideas for several reasons. Both of these visions qualify as examples of highly influential ethnocentric ideas,[46] an obvious target for arguing that ethnocentric beliefs are responsible for negative cultural perceptions.[47] Yet these two also represent different poles or "ideal types" (to borrow an expression from Weber) of Western thinking about world order. Fukuyama's vision is hegemonic and expansionist, whereas Huntington's is defensive and isolationist. Such a combination of ethnocentrism and intellectual diversity creates the necessary analytical space for constructive engagement with these ideas and for the search for a better alternative. However diverse these two visions are, they were both negatively perceived, and rejected, by Russia. This helps to sustain the argument that the reason for the negative perceptions was these visions' shared ethnocentrism, rather than their particular substance.

Russia is an appropriate case for testing the argument about cultural perceptions. First, it is a non-Western culture that represents a special point of reference for both Huntington and Fukuyama. Huntington explicitly identifies Russia as one of the eight major civilizations,[48] and it is tempting to see whether his argument withstands scrutiny in the indigenous context. For Fukuyama, Russia's reaction must be especially interesting because, of all other international events, it was primarily the failure of the Soviet institutions that shaped the analyst's belief in an "unabashed victory of economic and political liberalism."[49] Second, because of the influence of these two ideas in the West, the Russian intellectual and foreign policy communities discussed both of them in depth.

In order to trace the impact of Western ideas on Russia's cultural community, we must learn about this community's structure and dynamics. Methodologically, we undertake what can best be referred to as a "school of thoughts" analysis of political and intellectual discourse. In this tradition, discourse is understood as a cultural space in which different beliefs and ideas interact, clash, and interweave, without being able to form an ultimate unity.[50] Although discourse analysis does not lead to cumulative knowledge after the manner of natural science,[51] it provides valuable insights into the nature of foreign policy debates and their policy implications. Following Martin Wight's conceptualization, we first identify several distinct schools of thought that emerged in Russia since the beginning of Gorbachev's Perestroika (Globalists, Nationalists, and Expansionists). We then trace their reactions to Fukuyama's and Huntington's visions across the schools' spectrum and over time. We also identify hegemonic and recessive visions and analyze the main dynamics of Russia's discourse as shifting from one hegemonic state to another. This sets the terms for tracing how Western ideas participate in Russia's domestic discourse, are perceived by this discourse, and contribute to its changes.

In addition to the theoretical study of social discourse, the analysis is significant for policy reasons as a study of how mental constructions, subjective and inter-subjective, can teach us a great deal about foreign policy making and states' international behavior. For example, the debate about Huntington is linked, in its own way, to Russia's foreign policy–making process. On the level of discourse, major currents of Russia's foreign policy thinking about Huntington—Globalists and Nationalists—at the same time represent major currents of Russia's thinking about other contemporary issues of world politics such as European stability and NATO expansion, the future of the Middle East, the role of the United Nations, or Russia's relations with its immediate periphery. In addition, most of Moscow's intellectuals who were engaged in debating Huntington's thesis are intrinsic parts of Russia's foreign policy community, often linked to the decision-making process directly or via various epistemic ties.[52]

Finally, the discourse analysis is supplemented with an analysis of actual institutional changes in Russia since the Soviet collapse. The discussion is structured in terms of Fukuyama's and Huntington's used categories and falsifiable expectations. It provides an extra test of the validity of these expectations and further substantiates my argument about the low cross-cultural receptivity of ethnocentric ideas.

Ethnocentric ideas and actions are likely to undermine global peace and stability in the post–September 11 world. Russia's and the world's engagement with American military interventionism is a case in point. President George W. Bush's decision to intervene in Iraq without the United Nations' approval spurred a rise of anti-Americanism worldwide. Although many in Russia were sympathetic to America following the September 11 terrorist attacks and had little support for Saddam Hussein, Russian public opinion turned sharply against Washington's intervention in Iraq.[53] Russian Globalists viewed the war in Iraq as yet another dangerous precedent jeopardizing the role of the United Nations.[54] Nationalists, predictably, saw it as George W. Bush's drive for global hegemony and warned of his appetites for Russia's resources and territory.[55] Russia's criticism came at a price—indeed, as some pro-American intellectuals argued, Putin's move strained the "strategic partnership" with the United States and diminished Russia's economic role in Iraq.[56] However, the decision to oppose the war rested on firm social support at home and abroad. Aside from France and Germany, the world overwhelmingly—as the Pew Global Attitudes survey demonstrated[57]—holds a negative image of America and its actions in the post–September 11 era. Increasingly, American actions and the worldview behind them are viewed as insensitive of local cultural conditions and as undermining the potential for cultural dialogue across the globe.

The study is organized in five parts. The next chapter suggests a theoretical framework for understanding the question of ideas' perception in a multicultural world. Chapter 3 discusses the structure and dynamics of Russia's foreign policy discourse as it emerged in the aftermath of the cold war. The chapter identifies several domestic currents of Russia's international thinking. Chapters 4 and 5 deal with Russian discursive and institutional reactions to Fukuyama and Huntington, respectively. The concluding chapter summarizes the main findings of the project. It also provides an extension of the argument to the post–September 11 world order and draws implications for both theory and policy making.

CHAPTER 2

WORLD ORDER

Ideas, Perception, and Responsibility

1. IDEAS OF WORLD ORDER

1.1. IDEATIONAL PERSPECTIVE OF WORLD ORDER

In the 1970s, the prominent scholar Hedley Bull defined world order to mean "those patterns or dispositions of human activity that sustain the elementary or primary goals of social life among mankind as a whole."[1] Since then scholars have emphasized the critical roles played by the military capabilities of the most powerful states, economic transnationalization, cultural identity, and social technology in the emergence of various world orders.[2]

While these economic, political, and cultural factors certainly contribute greatly to shaping "patterns or dispositions" of global human activity, the role of ideas in establishing regularity in worldwide social life should not be underestimated. Ideas, understood as normative beliefs and worldviews held by individuals, groups, and societies, are crucial in the functioning and maintenance of world orders. For example, imperialism as a politically and socially institutionalized idea has been defining the shape of the world since at least the seventeenth century, whereas socialist and liberal ideas were behind many institutional

19

developments in the nineteenth and twentieth centuries. Recent constructivist scholarship has established the proposition that social life is, in fact, "ideas all the way down" until "you get to biology and natural resources"[3] and that world order can be understood as practices of an ideological or discursive nature.[4]

In the early 1980s, John Gerard Ruggie pioneered the claim that ideas provide purpose and imbue meaning to world orders, without which world orders cannot exist and successfully function. Responding to Kenneth Waltz's familiar formulation,[5] Ruggie revealed that the neorealist view of world polity had no transformational logic, only a reproductive one, precisely because that view had no concept of a social context or a social purpose.[6] Richard Ashley further argued that neorealist anarchy was, in fact, a discursive principle, and not something given.[7] Other scholars have convincingly critiqued the materialist bias and reductionist nature of neorealist thinking.[8]

World order ought not be viewed as a product of mainstream discourse alone—such an approach would also reflect a status quo bias and deprive us of the same transformative logic that Ruggie found missing in static neorealist thinking.[9] Instead, within every separate order, there is a diversity of perspectives; there is and will always be an uneasy coexistence and a dialectical competition of various visions of the global polity.[10] At least since the French Revolution, various world orders have arisen and fallen in part as a result of a fierce competition between fundamentally different ideas of social systems. Before World War I, the newly emerged liberal European vision confronted that of the conservative and authoritarian old regime, which eventually led to military conflict. During the interwar period, three idea-based systems—Liberalism, Nazism, and Communism—competed to shape the world order. The cold war, too, was far from being merely a power competition between two "units" or "superstates" (to borrow from the rationalist language); it will likely be remembered as the confrontation of communist and liberal ideas. The post–cold war order, rather than being a triumph of an exclusively defined Western civilization, reveals new lines of future hierarchical and non-hierarchical relationships within that order.[11]

Therefore, there can be more than one vision of world order at the same time. Such visions can be overlapping or subsumable under larger visions.[12] Because of the diversity of relationships within every world order, each world order project is a complex visualization of

Self in its interaction with significant Other(s). There can be no universal or all subsuming Self, as Self exists only in the process of identifying the Other.[13] One way or another, each world order project visualizes the relevant cultural community (the Self) and the one that is left outside this community (the Other). Each world order vision contains the notion of the appropriate moral action of the Self toward the Other.

To sum up, following Hayward Alker and his collaborators I propose that world order is best viewed as dialectical and multicultural, with a diversity of ideas and social visions coexisting and often competing for hegemonic influence. To quote from Alker, Amin, Biersteker, and Inoguchi,

> World orders are patterned human activities, interaction regularities or practices evident on a world scale. . . . Within their cultural, structural, and behavioral dispositions and motivations, world orders are multidimensional and typically have a normative, political, directional aspect. They are intentional, and their politically contested goals, norms and values are grounded in widely (and intersubjectively) shared beliefs, worldviews, historical missions, cosmologies or modes of thought. They contain ideas of governance and tend to be based on common, underlying (slowly changing) modes of thought, cohesive systems of ideas, world views or cosmologies. . . . Different world orders coexist, at times with mutual incomprehension of one another. [14]

Only by adopting such an ideational perspective will we be able to adequately address the phenomenon of cross-cultural perception of world order theories. This perspective is methodologically different from the "world culture" tradition, which studies the culture of modernity and traces how one particular set of ideas spreads from one part of the world (the West) to others.[15] By not exploring ideas and ideational systems outside the West, the "world culture" approach emphasizes only one side of the "modernization" process at the expense of many others and, therefore, tends to remain blind to the rich diversity of cross-cultural relations, perceptions, and interactions. To compensate for the weaknesses of the "world culture" tradition, I propose that we study world order as a dialectical competition of various global visions and scholarly projects.

1.2. WORLD ORDER PROJECTS:
ETHNOCENTRIC AND CULTURALLY SENSITIVE

The nature of world order projects affects how they are perceived outside their societies. Such projects can be analyzed along two main dimensions: power and values. While visualizing world order, each theorist develops a concept of the world's *political* or power organization by viewing it in more or less hegemonic terms. The more hegemonic power organization assumes the existence of a most powerful center, from which the world is politically controlled and stabilized. Such a "top down" vision of global polity is different from the less hegemonic, or "bottom up" view, which visualizes the world as politically multipolar. Conceptualizing world orders along the power dimension is common in International Relations.[16] Much less common is analyzing various world orders along the dimension of *cultural values.*

In addition to being viewed as uni/multipolar, world orders can be conceptualized as *uni/multicultural.* The unicultural approach assumes a values-exclusive or ethnocentric vision of global order that represents the belief that there is only one natural and best way to do things. Conversely, multicultural accounts present the world as a coexistence of various cultural systems, which may or may not come to a common agreement. Although all ideas are generated in a certain social context and can never be entirely neutral, multicultural projects are typically less ethnocentric.

Each world order idea theorizes the relationships between Self and Other, but ethnocentric ideas do so differently from those that are more culturally sensitive. What makes an idea ethnocentric is how strongly it proclaims its commitment to the exclusively defined values of its own environment and how closed it is to possible dialogue with and fertilization from the external environment. Ethnocentric projects are based on three main assumptions: superiority of the Self and its moral community; inferiority of the Other; and the legitimacy of hegemonic actions of the Self toward the Other. The authors of ethnocentric ideas are willing to promote their visions outside their social universe because they are firmly committed to their concept of "virtue" and "good." In contrast to ethnocentrism, culturally sensitive visions define the Self and its moral values as something open to negotiation, rather than absolute, exclusive, and essentialist; they view the Other as different, but morally equal and, for that reason, as a source of potential learning;

and in case of conflict, they promote negotiation as a practice that seeks to establish mutually acceptable norms and is strongly preferred to hegemonic actions. Table 2.1 summarizes the content of ethnocentric ideas by comparing them to ideas that are culturally sensitive.

In International Relations, as in other disciplines,[17] most debates reveal various degrees of ethnocentrism expressed in the ideas of the participants. To illustrate this point, let us briefly consider three well-known debates in the discipline (the list can certainly be continued and extended beyond Western IR).[18]

In International Political Economy, a prominent example is the old hegemonic stability debate. In this discussion, the two sides clashed over the degree of economic openness and cooperation among advanced capitalist countries, highlighting the role of a hegemonic leader or of multilateral institutions, respectively.[19] If we apply the above-specified criteria of ethnocentrism, the hegemonic idea would be characterized as more ethnocentric than the idea of cooperation based on multilateral institutions. This is so because it is the former school that puts the strongest emphasis on values of the Self (economic openness), assumes these values to be superior, and promotes their advancement as "necessary" for accomplishing the goal of international economic cooperation. The other side is less ethnocentric as it insists that cooperation requires a shared understanding of what is involved among the participants, and that hegemony itself will work only when the involved parties accept it. This debate is coming back in

TABLE 2.1. The Content of Ethnocentric and Culturally Sensitive Ideas

	Ethnocentric Ideas	*Culturally Sensitive Ideas*
How the cultural community is defined	As morally superior, defined in exclusive and essentialist terms	As inclusive and open to renegotiation
How the Other is viewed	As morally inferior, a potential threat to values of the Self	As morally equal, a source of potential learning
How the Self should act toward the Other	Advance or defend its values and interests	Negotiate mutually acceptable norms

the age of globalization, with more ethnocentric schools pushing for West- or even U.S.-centered globalization, and more culturally sensitive scholars arguing that such globalization cannot be sustainable.[20]

In the field of Security Studies, the "democratic peace" debate may be illustrative of various degrees of intellectual ethnocentrism. In a development akin to that of hegemonic stability, proponents of democratic peace are often perceived as demonstrating a pro-Western ethnocentric bias. One critique has been that the social structures in which democratic orders take root vary considerably. In some cases, such social structures are far from conducive to promoting peace and stability. For example, in the postcommunist context, democratization may become a permissive condition allowing the re-emergence and rise of a previously dormant militant ethnic nationalism. As a result, not only do some of the newly established democracies go to war against each other, they may do so in part as a result of their moving away from authoritarianism.[21]

As a final example, the debate over the virtues of humanitarian intervention likewise demonstrates a similar pattern in scholarly thinking and perception. Here, the contested concept has been that of "humanitarian," and one of the critiques has suggested that the discovered norm of humanitarian intervention bears an excessive imprint of Western culture.[22] Documenting this bias, scholars have demonstrated how unilateral Western interventions can generate highly negative reactions outside the West.[23]

1.3. WORLD ORDER PROJECTS: CLASSIFICATION AND ILLUSTRATIONS

If the identified dimensions of political power and cultural values are brought together, we arrive at four distinct classes of world order projects. The classification of world order projects described below is summarized in table 2.2.

The first class includes projects of a globalist ethnocentric nature. The authors of such projects advance a vision of the world that is both unipolar and unicultural. Fully aware of the increasingly globalized character of world politics, they often maintain an image of a progressively culturally homogeneous global society and overlook the forces of identity and diversity. For Western representatives of this approach, homogeneous cultural development in global society is often linked to the progression of Western civilization. Fukuyama's "end of history"

TABLE 2.2. World Order Projects: Political versus Cultural Dimensions

POWER		Ethnocentric	Multicultural
	Unipolar	FUKUYAMA (liberal expansionism)	BULL–WATSON (expansion & learning)
	Multipolar	HUNTINGTON (defensive realism)	COX (dialogue & learning)

CULTURAL VALUES

project as well as the entire tradition of Western modernization think-ing illustrates the approach well. Fukuyama's argument about an "un-abashed victory of economic and political liberalism"[24] and a global expansion of the Western-style market democracy is a justification of the West's political and cultural hegemony in the post–cold war era. Behind the claim of universal applicability is the ambition of some rep-resentatives of Western civilization to shape the non-Western worlds by providing financial aid, technology, and advice. Outside the West, the globalist ethnocentric vision is often defended by cultural nationalists and has its proponents in Russia, China, Iran, and elsewhere.[25]

The second class includes projects that are also ethnocentric or cul-turally exclusive, but less hegemonic in their vision of power organiza-tion. The projects of this type emphasize a local, rather than global, source of political authority, but they are similarly unicultural. They too tend to neglect the dialectical nature of global vs. local interactions and view the world through the lenses of one culture. Huntington's vision of a "clash of civilizations" fits well with this thinking. It did not advocate a politically unipolar world, but it perceived other cultures with fear, as a source of potential threat to the West. The Huntingtonian West is a local, not universal, civilization and, instead of expanding globally, it should go on the defensive and prepare to fight for its cul-tural values in coming clashes with non-Western "civilizations."[26]

The third group theorizes world order as global and yet multicul-tural. Hedley Bull and Adam Watson's edited collection *The Expansion of International Society* may serve as an example of this kind of think-ing about world order. The authors traced the emergence and various stages of development of a universal society of states and peoples. They viewed the world as being still considerably controlled by one pole, Europe, and describe the relationships between Europe and the world as "Eurocentric."[27] Although in such emphasis on the "Europeanness" of international society, Bull and Watson displayed some elements of ethnocentrism, their approach was not as culturally exclusive as those of Fukuyama and Huntington. Instead they acknowledged both the global and their own European community without unequivocally committing themselves to one or the other. They also appreciated the tensions between the Self (Europe) and the Other (non-European world) and the existence of elements of mutual learning in their relationships. For example, they recognized, albeit rather implicitly, that during the process of international society's expansion, Europeans had to adjust their rules and values and did not merely export them to the rest of the world.[28]

The fourth class of world order projects views the world as both non-hegemonic and multicultural. The scholars working in this tradition begin with local cultures as units that dialectically interact, overlap, and learn from each other through various economic, technological, and political encounters. The Self is therefore not separated from the Other; instead, the Self and Other(s) dialectically relate to and constitute each other. Political or power arrangements on a global scale come "from below" in order to legitimize and facilitate the already existing cross-cultural encounters. Unlike Huntington's claim that power precedes culture,[29] in this tradition power is neither separated from nor preemptive of culture; instead, power is a dimension of culture, and cross-cultural interactions can only take the form of a dialogical multipolar political order.

Robert W. Cox is an articulate defender of such a multicultural and non-hegemonic vision of world order. Like Huntington, Cox views civilizations as key units of world order. However, Coxian civilizations overlap and learn from each other, rather than clash over power and resources. "Civilizations are ways of being, ways of understanding the world" that can coexist within a state and even an individual.[30] They are products of "collective human action, an amalgam of social forces and ideas that has achieved a certain coherence but which is continually changing and developing in response to challenges both from within and from without."[31] Pleading for "recognition and the acceptance of difference" of the Other, Cox drew attention to the encouraging cross-ethnic developments in South Africa, which had been obscured in the media by the prominence of more discouraging events in the former Yugoslavia and Rwanda. His way of forging a non-hegemonic world and a common ground points to the development of common concern for avoiding major conflicts, maintaining ecological balance, and facilitating cross-civilizational dialogue on human rights which "would not be seen as the imposition of one civilization's values over those of another."[32]

The elements of the four identified visions can also be found in today's policy world.[33] President George H. W. Bush's view of an emerging world order in the aftermath of the Persian Gulf war is an example of a hegemonic and ethnocentric vision. Following a demonstration of overwhelming post–cold war American military and economic power, he spoke of a "new world order," which was coming to replace "a world of barbed wire and concrete block, conflict and cold war" and in which "freedom and respect for human rights find a home among all nations."[34] The view echoed Fukuyama's "end of history" idea and later evolved into President George W. Bush's view of terrorism as "pure evil" directed at freedom-loving people throughout the world. This view translated into Bush's preemption strategy[35] and subsequent foreign policy interventions in Afghanistan and Iraq.

Mainstream Chinese political discourse can be identified as an approximation of a multipolar ethnocentric vision of the world. The tone was set by Chairman Deng Xiaoping, for whom nationalism and globalization were not incompatible, but existed in a virtuous relationship.[36] Deng wanted China to integrate with the international community, but only by preserving its essence of a "socialist spiritual civilization" and the Chinese Communist Party dictatorship. After the Tiananmen Square and Soviet Perestroika-related upheavals of 1989, Deng's vision of world order became more pessimistic, and he concluded—not unlike Huntington—that the cold war would be followed by new violent conflicts. In this picture, the developed states will encourage conflict between the developing states and will continue to bully them. The other conflict will be against socialism, with the liberal West trying to foment chaos in the socialist states.[37]

Soviet President Mikhail Gorbachev's New Thinking may be an example of an expansionist and multicultural view of world order. Not unlike Bull and Watson, Gorbachev envisioned some global unity emerging, in part, from European values of political democracy and market economy. At the same time, Gorbachev remained a committed socialist and believed that the whole world was and would continue to be influenced by the socialist experience.[38] By advancing his New Thinking vision "for our country and the world,"[39] the leader of Perestroika meant to preserve and, in a modified form, further advance what he referred to as "socialist values." In the process of expanding this liberal socialist vision, Gorbachev was prepared to learn from other systems and other nations.[40]

Finally, the vision of Iranian President Mohammed Khatami seems to have been on a less expansionist and more multipolar side. It may be illustrative of a multicultural and multipolar world order. Echoing the Coxian view, Khatami defended the notion of pluralism and dialogue of civilizations in world affairs that were to "abandon the will-to-power and instead pursue compassion, understanding, and love."[41] Speaking at the U.N.-sponsored Conference of Dialogue among Civilizations, he argued that the "ultimate goal" of such dialogue was not to be "dialogue in and of itself," but to attain "empathy and compassion."[42] Khatami only advocates Islam domestically, moving cautiously and arguing consistently for the need to modernize on the basis, rather than at the expense, of Iran's own cultural tradition.

2. CULTURAL PERCEPTION

Cultural perception can be defined as the interpretation of the assumptions, substances, and implications of external ideas across a local society. Negative perception involves the interpretation of ideas as threatening world peace and order. Although being an understudied aspect of international politics,[43] cultural perception remains the most deep-seated obstacle to establishing robust institutions of world peace. In a world that is multicultural and discourse-sensitive, a negative social perception is often at the heart of conflicts, and political decisions are at best incomplete if they are made without considering conflicts' cultural "externalities." Military conflict is a case in point. Most of the currently existing conflicts such as the India-Pakistan, the Arab-Israeli, the Russia-Chechnya, and the Ethiopia-Eritrea disputes have long histories of the participants' mutual mistrust. Without seriously considering the social side of mistrust and negative perception, these conflicts cannot be adequately understood, much less resolved. If peace is to be understood as an institution rather than merely the absence of war, the remaining ultimate challenge is to find an idea of a settlement that would be broadly compatible with the participants' locally grounded visions of the world.

2.1. THE PROCESS OF CULTURAL PERCEPTION

Ideas rarely travel without meeting resistance. Because they are born as particular expressions of various cultural contexts, ideas spread at various speeds and through different channels, overcome various forms of institutional resistance, and function differently in different cultural contexts. Quite often ideas are perceived negatively, and, in alien cultural contexts, they may be transformed almost beyond recognition. Arguably, this is what happened with Marxism in its Leninist interpretation in Russia, which is why Georgi Plekhanov, Julius Martov, and many other social democrats stopped their political collaboration with Lenin in the early twentieth century. In a similar way, an originally defensive and inclusive nationalism traveled to nineteenth-century Germany and elsewhere as racist, exclusive, and hate-filled. The spread of liberal ideas at the end of the twentieth century, too, as this study intends to show, has its own peculiar paths.

For understanding how ideas are perceived outside their societies, we now turn to the role of the receiver's side or *local culture*. Even when an external idea is formulated in relatively neutral, or nonethnocentric terms, the process of its perception and social incorporation is never linear or predetermined, as local cultures may differ from one another in fundamental ways. Typically, these cultures differ in their historical experiences and present concerns, which shape local social perceptions and often remain the key barrier to openness to external ideas.[44]

Local cultures are not homogeneous and should not be viewed in essentialist terms. Even if "shared" in some important sense, cultures remind us more of an "open-ended text," than a "closed book."[45] They can be usefully viewed as existing at multiple levels and in varying attitudes. First, they exist among three distinct and mutually interrelated groups—leadership, political elite, and larger society—each with their own attitude and internal structure or institutions.[46] Second, domestic attitudes can cut across the elite and society levels and represent some larger patterns of discursive agreement or dispute. Here I follow the tradition of studying discourse as incorporating both hegemonic and recessive trends, rather than being able to form an ultimate unity.[47] For example, national discourse can be viewed as the competition of globally and nationally oriented visions. Similar to the old IR distinction, globalists support cooperation in world politics, whereas nationalists emphasize national interests and a struggle for power.[48]

If we adopt the distinction between nationalist and globalist attitudes, we may describe the general process of cultural perception as one that incorporates the nationalist-globalist dispute over the substance of an externally proposed idea of world order. Such dispute can be crucial for determining whether an idea will remain relatively marginal or may eventually become part of a collective understanding or even obtain a socially hegemonic status. One can further hypothesize that a less ethnocentric idea has a better chance to be perceived favorably by a local culture and eventually supported by this culture's leadership, because, other things being equal, such an idea tends to strengthen the discursive position of globalists. On the other hand, a more ethnocentric idea has less chance to be culturally accepted, as it tends to strengthen the nationalist discourse. Even if the ruling elite finds the idea useful, such an idea is likely to get rejected by the larger social strata (see table 2.3 for a summary of this reasoning). Ultimately, for an idea to be received by a local culture, it must become successfully socialized by the larger society beyond the leadership and political elite.

For understanding the process of cultural perception, it is also important to appreciate the fact that external ideas and local cultures interact dialectically and therefore cannot be fully separated from one another. An external idea's ethnocentrism and a local community's openness are then, to some extent, *relational*: what may seem ethnocentric to some cultures is not so to others. For example, the Western

TABLE 2.3. Cultural Perception: Process and Discursive Consequences

Initial Effect ⟶	Domestic ⟶ Contestation	Discursive Consequences
Ethnocentric idea	Globalists versus Nationalists	Nationalists strengthened / Globalists weakened
Culturally sensitive idea	Globalists versus Nationalists	Globalists strengthened / Nationalists weakened

idea of liberal economic reform or shock therapy was received differently across the postcommunist world. The idea of reform often recommended by Western economic organizations (e.g., the IMF) implied the need to "liberalize as much as you can, privatize as fast as you can, and be tough in fiscal and monetary matters,"[49] rather than to proceed with more evolutionary approaches to economic regime transition from communism. Despite the proclaimed benefits of adopting the idea and its availability, some of the postcommunist nations perceived it as liberating and stabilizing, while others condemned it as threatening or inappropriate.

To the Baltic states, the shock therapy strategy did not seem to be too ethnocentric. Pro-Western feelings in Latvia, Lithuania, and Estonia were quite strong, and the political class became committed to the idea of implementing the IMF and World Bank recommended approach. Other postcommunist societies, such as Ukraine and Russia, had mixed feelings about shock therapy, and pro-Western and anti-Western political factions could not agree on the virtues of the idea. While some forces perceived the idea as generally favoring domestic economic stability and prosperity, others insisted shock therapy was designed to ruin the national economy and impoverish the countries' populations. Still other societies, such as Belarus, Kazakhstan, and some other Central Asian countries, rejected shock therapy as entirely inappropriate for solving their nations' problems and proceeded with more gradual approaches.[50]

In addition to varying cross-nationally, cultural perception of external ideas can vary *over time*. As a result of some new historical practices,[51] a local culture may become more receptive to an idea that was produced in a different cultural setting and previously seemed alien. For example, the above-mentioned originally Eurocentric idea of international society, referred to as "a commonwealth divided into several states" by Voltaire and as a "diplomatic republic of Europe" by Edmund Burke, was received differently across time. Gradually, it ceased to be exclusively European and expanded far beyond the continent.[52]

2.2. TYPES OF CULTURAL PERCEPTION

The above discussion suggests that negative perception and the rejection of external ideas may not be inevitable.[53] Whether or not an external idea is rejected or accepted depends on how ethnocentric such an idea is and how open a local society is to receiving it.[54] Cross-cultural learning then is a product of several variables, and one can formulate at least four distinct types of cultural perception (summarized in table 2.4).

In *less open* cultures, nationalist attitudes dominate, and the society is likely to reject external ideas, whether or not such ideas are formulated in ethnocentric terms. In this type of perception, the predominant language is that of power and domination. Nationalistic factions might argue that external ideas are irrelevant for "us," but they are also likely to argue that such ideas represent a conscientious attempt by an "alien" culture to undermine the cohesiveness of "our" values and to establish its economic and political supremacy.

An example of a relatively closed society may be China. Chinese experience with the idea of political democratization can help to illustrate this point. Although Chinese nationalism is of a defensive, rather than aggressive, nature, it has been generally successful in silencing more globalist voices and controlling the policy agenda. Recently China has joined some international organizations, such as the WTO and the regional Shanghai forum, but it is the issues of political control and military security that continue to shape the domestic discourse. The ongoing conflict with Taiwan, the military modernization program,

TABLE 2.4. Nationalist and Globalist Types of Perceiving External Ideas

Domestic Discourse		Low	High
	Nationalists	Rejected as irrelevant	Rejected as a threat to national identity
	Globalists	Accepted as a contribution to world dialogue	Rejected as a threat to world pluralism

Degree of Idea's Ethnocentrism

and the suppression of domestic opposition movements dominate the political arena, and it is this context that shapes the nation's perception of the idea of democratization. When the idea is formulated in less ethnocentric terms—as a need to reform the existing political system to keep up with changing society and the economy—it often gets dismissed as inappropriate for Chinese conditions. The communist party dictatorship continues to be viewed as essential for preserving the essence of a "socialist spiritual civilization."

Chinese nationalists react even more nervously to the more ethnocentric proposal that China ought to democratize by terminating communist party rule and adopting a Western-style multiparty system. They perceive the proposal as reflecting the will of the liberal West to establish its domination over China. Such domination would allegedly come as a result of a multiparty system's likely disintegration into chaos, which would weaken the country in the face of a possible foreign invasion. China therefore continues to preach a relative isolation from the world. Such isolationism is rooted in the country's officially pronounced Five Principles of Peaceful Coexistence, which include mutual respect for territorial integrity and sovereignty, mutual nonaggression, mutual noninterference in internal affairs, equality and mutual benefits, and peaceful coexistence.[55]

Alternatively, in local cultures that are *more open,* globalists are more influential and capable of defining the political discourse. Unlike nationalists preoccupied with relative power and control, globalists' main concern is peace and security in the world as a whole. Their language is that of international/intercultural cooperation, and they are more likely to be open to the influence of external ideas. When such ideas are relatively non-ethnocentric, they are likely to be perceived by globalists as having a potential for contributing to world dialogue and, therefore, worthy of serious consideration. An idea with a strong dose of ethnocentrism, however, may generate an entirely different reaction and be viewed as threatening that very same dialogue and peace in the world. At least some globalists are likely to perceive such an ethnocentric idea as undermining democratic principles in the world, among which are respect for cross-cultural pluralism and creative diversity.

Iranian society today is more open than that of China, and Iranian experience with the idea of political democratization may help to illustrate the difference in cultural perception. Although Iranian discourse is quite heterogeneous, even polarized, the country is in a process of reform that is more akin to Gorbachev's Perestroika than the Chinese economy-centered modernization. Iran's globalist spokesmen, such as President Khatami, are not dismissive of the democratization idea. Khatami himself was publicly elected in a relatively free and fair election, and the Iranian parliament and media are increasingly free of centralized control by the religious authorities.

However, even globalist, let alone nationalist, factions in Iran are not supportive of some more ethnocentric versions of the democratization project. For example, many globally oriented intellectuals and politicians reject the idea of a far-reaching secularization that might lead to the complete separation of Islam from state institutions. The Khatami-advocated project views reform as synthesizing rational modern values with those of a traditional Islamic nature and does not attempt to completely eliminate religion from public life.[56] In reacting to some West-centric proposals, even Khatami's supporters sometimes proclaim that "the West has no objective other than driving the world of Islam to extremes."[57] As Sohail H. Hashmi writes, for many Muslims today, the notion of an international society founded on principles of human rights, religious tolerance, and democracy, is "seriously threatened not by cultural pluralism or religious diversity, but by the equivocation shown by Western powers in enforcing them."[58]

3. SOCIAL RESPONSIBILITY

If some ideas are capable of generating conflict-prone perceptions in the world, one must go beyond "how and why" questions and ask those of a "who is responsible" and "what to do" nature as well. In the social sciences, the tradition of posing normative questions goes back to Aristotelian social and moral thought, in which the social scientist is ethically involved in continuing reflection on urgent practical issues.[59] In attempting to build on this tradition, I raise the question of intellectuals' responsibility for the ideas they generate and for how these ideas are received outside their primary social context.

3.1. SOCIAL RESPONSIBILITY IN A MULTICULTURAL WORLD

First, the notion of social responsibility assumes that individuals are not merely self-interest seekers, but have obligations to their larger cultural community.[60] Such a view of responsibility puts the social *before* the individual and, therefore, is principally different from the individualist "what's good for me is good for society" concept. Social responsibility should also be distinguished from the Weberian "ethic of responsibility," in which a charismatic leader acts primarily out of the power of his *inner* calling and strength, rather than from outer obligations.[61]

Social responsibility is vitally important in the increasingly globalized world. The ever-growing power of modernity and technology make the world "smaller," but also more vulnerable. Such global humanists as Sun Yat-sen, Vladimir Vernadski, Jawaharlal Nehru, Albert Schweitzer, Hans Jonas, and Andrei Sakharov warned us about the potentially destructive power of technology and argued for a new sense of global responsibility in order to avoid a human catastrophe. For example, in his highly influential *The Imperative of Responsibility,* Hans Jonas, a German philosopher and a pupil of Rudolf Bultmann and Martin Heidegger, argued that modern technology fundamentally disturbed the balance between humanity and nature. The scale of this disturbance is long-range, cumulative, irreversible, and planetary and has created a situation of "freedom without values" and the demand for a new vision of responsibility for maintaining human life.[62] In line with this thinking, the Russian scientist Vladimir Vernadski has formulated the idea of *Noosphere* (as opposed to the biosphere of the earth) or global Reason responsible for solving problems common to all humankind.[63] Many others have warned that without developing such global responsibility the world, burdened with military conflicts, poverty, disease, and ecological destruction, will fall victim to its own inventions.[64]

The second key dimension of social responsibility concerns the relationships among different cultures in global society. The sense of global obligation does not imply that we are relieved of responsibility to our local cultural communities. The global society is a complex interaction of Self(s) and Other(s). It is not uniform, and the historically determined diversity of local cultures (groups, nations, civilizations) in no way guarantees that the process of developing global responsibility will go smoothly. Nor can such responsibility be imposed in a unilateral fashion. Unilateralism is no answer to global dilemmas and has a strong potential for generating resentments, provoking new conflicts, and delaying genuine solutions. As some post–cold war developments demonstrate, the unilateral Western responses to global economic inequality in Seattle, ethnic conflicts in Yugoslavia, or world-wide terrorist threats are capable of generating powerful backlashes among some non-Western cultures.

Both Western and non-Western philosophers have developed powerful insights for understanding social responsibility as global yet culturally sensitive. In the West, the tradition of communitarian thought in the humanities has been long engaged in debates about inclusiveness and recognition in building order and community.[65] The principal accomplishment of these debates has been the justification of the ethics of responsibility to or for the Other(s) and distinguishing these ethics from a laying down of rules and regulations for pre-given, autonomous subjects.[66] Non-Western thinkers have also generated important ideas about dialogue, mutual engagement, and responsiveness in our words and actions. For instance, one might mention the Russian religious philosophical tradition of acknowledging guilt/responsibility by intellectuals for contributing to a discourse of social violence. In the early twentieth century, a group of former Marxist sympathizers responded to the Revolution of 1905 by publishing the collective volume *Vekhi* (Landmarks) and calling for the Russian intelligentsia to be constructive, rather than "nihilist," in its social criticism. The authors of the volume held the Russian radical intelligentsia responsible for the revolutionary violence,[67] giving a new turn to the old tradition of intellectuals' reflections on their engagements with social reality.[68]

To summarize, if we are to adequately address challenges of a global multicultural world, we need a notion of responsibility that is social in two senses, local and global. A responsible member of global society is someone who is aware of his *dual obligations,* to his local community and to the wider global society. He or she must be able to view such obligations as equally significant and work on reconciling and bridging their differences. The local and global sources of social authority are equally significant and equally insufficient in their rights. In this global multicultural world, we must sustain a discourse of constructive tensions in which "local" and "global" both conflict and cooperate for the purpose of dialectical engagement and for negotiating mutually acceptable norms and solutions. This is no easy task, and to solve it we need a better understanding of morally responsible action/theory in a global multicultural world.

3.2. Morally Responsible Action/Theory

A morally responsible action should incorporate this duality of social obligations and be free of the false dichotomy of *either* local *or* global sources of moral authority. Such action implies the need for everyone to be aware of and ready to synthesize from diverse cultural influences across the world.

Theory, too, is a form of social action;[69] any theory/project of world order must be constructed as ethically sensitive and socially responsible. Building on the insights of communitarian thought, we should construct our theories to view the relationships between the Self and the Other in non-exclusive, dialectical, and mutually constitutive ways. Based on the above discussion of ethnocentric versus culturally sensitive ideas, one could recommend that scholars of the world order be conscientious in developing their vision of the world, of the source of moral authority, and of appropriate moral action toward the Other.

First, a morally responsible world order theory views the world as a multicultural global society in which global and local forces coexist, interact, interweave, and are mutually dependent. Second, searching for moral authority, such theory does not didactically choose in favor of local or global community. Instead, it assumes that the two sources of moral authority are equally significant and sustain a discourse of constructive tensions for the purpose of the common good. Finally, in the same dialectical spirit, such communitarian theory approaches the Other as a source of learning, rather than a threat, and argues against self-advancement or self-defense as appropriate modes of moral action toward the Other.

Such *Communitarian* world order vision[70] is based on a concept of knowledge that is dialogical and dialectical, rather than didactic and ethnocentric. In producing such knowledge, intellectuals ought to be guided by at least three questions: Who is the Other that may react to their scholarship? How different is the Other from the Self in its previous experience? And how distinct is the Other in its present concerns? For example, if the scholarship is the familiar West-centered theories of hegemonic stability, democratic peace, or clash of civilizations, one should not be surprised by a highly critical reaction to it from the non-Western Others, such as Russia and China. If, on the other hand, such world order scholarship theorizes nationalist resistance to the West, then its authors are likely to be confronted with estrangement from, rather than involvement with the West in the non-Western worlds.

Such Communitarian world order vision should be distinguished from Realist and Cosmopolitan schools of thoughts (these differences are summarized in table 2.5). For *realists,* the image of anarchy and competition remains the key metaphor in describing the nature of world order. Although some realists appreciate the role of culture in international politics,[71] most of them consistently deny that the world is becoming more globalized.[72] This group is explicit in defining its cultural community as local,[73] and its vision of responsibility is therefore highly reductionist. Realists perceive the rise of alternative cultural communities as a threatening development and recommend that the West prepare to defend itself and its values. Rather than trying to make room for dialogue with various visions and approaches, realists advance a particular and a particularistic vision of world order.

The *cosmopolitan* writers are fully aware of the increasingly globalized character of world politics, but they maintain an image of a progressively culturally homogeneous global society and overlook the forces of identity and diversity. Most typically, this homogeneous cultural development in global society is linked to the progress of Western civilization. Both conservative and radical cosmopolitan writers tend to view cultural development as a worldwide spread of Westernized

TABLE 2.5. Three Moral Visions: Realism, Cosmopolitanism, and Communitarianism

	Realism	*Cosmopolitanism*	*Communitarianism*
Vision of the world	Cultural Anarchy	Westernized global society	Multicultural global society
Source of moral authority	Local	Global	Local & global
Appropriate moral action	Self-defense	Self-advancement	Mutual learning

modernity and its norms of nation-states, market economy, political democracy, etc., rather than as a dialectical interaction of diverse local communities.[74] Whether supportive or critical of the Westernization process, cosmopolitans trace how the norms of a dominant civilization transcend the values of different cultural communities, rather than studying problematic receptions of "dominant" values by local cultures and emerging dialectic syntheses of the global and the local.

Realism and cosmopolitanism are therefore unfit to offer a coherent view of responsible action/theory in a global multicultural world. They have a strong tendency to view the "local versus global" dichotomy in absolute or mutually exclusive terms and tend to favor unilateral approaches. The two traditions are also deeply ethnocentric in their unwillingness to learn from those with differing perspectives on the world and moral authority. Often, realist and cosmopolitan ethnocentric projects have hidden agendas and serve some narrow political interests. Such ethnocentrism becomes an insurmountable barrier to developing a genuine progressive world order scholarship. The culturally sensitive perspective developed in this book seeks to uncover such hidden ethnocentrism in the realist/cosmopolitan projects. Condemning the ethnocentrism of some world order scholarship has nothing to do with a form of "political correctness": the purpose of this book is to uncover cultural biases in the search for truth, not to inhibit that search by invoking "culture."[75]

In today's increasingly globalized world, the eighteenth-century European view that other cultures could be committed to different values without being incomprehensible to one another regains its currency and obtains a new meaning.[76] Yet, sustaining and advancing a communitarian vision of responsible action in a world of territorially divided nation-states is no easy task. The old Westphalia-generated borders continue to encourage thinking in mutually exclusive categories, along the lines of defending or advancing "our values." To be sustainable, the vision of communitarianism must therefore have a useful dose of illusion and idealism. Indeed, ethical ideas almost always do. What Giambattista Vico called "fantasia," what Isaiah Berlin called an "imaginative leap," what Richard Rorty called an "imaginative acquaintance" with another's value system, what Michael Smith called "relevant and constructive illusions," and what Edward Tivnan referred to as "moral imagination" is precisely what is required if we are to move beyond exclusionary and didactic ways of thinking and acting.[77]

CHAPTER 3

RUSSIA

*The Foreign Policy Community
and Schools of Thought*

This chapter undertakes what can be referred to as a "schools of thoughts" analysis of political discourse. In this tradition, discourse is understood as a cultural space, in which different beliefs and ideas interact, clash, and interweave, without being able to form an ultimate unity.[1] No discourse is homogeneous or entirely hegemonic; instead, it is always composed of both hegemonic and recessive trends. Nor is discourse a simple sum of its parts/schools of thoughts; rather, it should be viewed as a combination of various intellectual influences that is fluid, interactive, and dialectical.[2]

1. RUSSIA'S RECEPTIVITY TO WESTERN IDEAS

Western post–cold war thinkers are certainly not the first nor the last in generating ideas capable of influencing Russia's domestic debates and identity formation. Russia has always been relatively open to ideas from the West. Western ideas traveled to Russia through different channels. Depending on the substance of those ideas, they were diffused to Russia as normative beliefs and worldviews, expert policy-relevant knowledge, and various individual experiences.[3]

At least since Czar Peter the Great, the West has figured as the significant Other in Russia's debates about its identity and policy vis-à-vis the external world. As a result, Russia's responses to challenges posed by the West were typically met with the use of ideas that had been originally generated in the West.[4]

Before the Bolshevik Revolution the major intellectual debate in Russia was between Westernizers and Slavophiles about whether Russia could and should become a part of the Western world. Westernizers supported Peter the Great's efforts to modernize Russia and went on to advocate a widespread application of European institutions on Russian ground. Influenced by the French Revolution, Westernizers were highly critical of the Russian autocratic tradition and produced a variety of arguments in favor of social reform. The Decembrists of the early nineteenth century, for example, followed the lead of people like Speransky and advocated constitutionalism and the abolition of serfdom. Later, in the aftermath of Russia's defeat in the Crimean War, Westernizers split into several distinct currents. One group—Cadets, or constitutional democrats—continued to advocate liberal reforms and constitutional development.[5] Other Westernizers emphasized the need for the country's industrialization. Minister of Finance Sergei Witte argued, for example, for a more radical break with the country's rural tradition and for monarchy-led "energetic and decisive measures" to develop the industrial base and satisfy the needs of Russia.[6] Unlike Slavophiles, who often saw the industrialization of Russia as a sell-out to Europe, this group advocated rapid economic development. Still others, like Alexander Herzen, proposed not to discard Russia's communal cultural features, but instead, build on those features in order to take a development shortcut and "catch up" with the West. In an extreme way, the "catching up" line of thinking found its continuation in Bolshevism.

In contrast to Westernizers, Slavophiles thought of Russia as a unique culture, rather than as an offspring of European civilization.[7] Beginning with Ivan Kireyevski and Alexei Khomyakov, they advocated Russia's indigenous tradition, which they visualized as a genuine religious and social community. Even for Slavophiles, however, the West (Europe) remained the significant Other, and they continued to make sense of Russian development by contrasting it to that of Europe.

Like Westernizers, Slavophiles were thoroughly familiar with Western religious, social, and political traditions, but they were convinced that the West had finished its role and that Russia must now become the capital of world civilization.

After the Revolution, Marxism, a stepchild of Western civilization, became the official ideology of Soviet Russia and, for many years ahead, dictated the shape and form of domestic debates. Yet even while maintaining its Marxist identity Russia remained susceptible to the influence of Western ideas. Although Bolsheviks were unimpressed by Western constitutionalism and democratic freedoms, they wanted to borrow Western technology in order to catch up with the West economically. Throughout the Soviet era, a debate within Bolshevism existed between radicals and moderates, with radicals advocating forceful methods of industrialization and moderates arguing for a more gradual process of development. The latter group was more open to Western ideas and proceeded from the late-Lenin's notion of "co-existence" with the "capitalist world."

In the post-Stalin era, the intercourse with Western ideas grew even stronger. Soviet leader Nikita Khrushchev's famous de-Stalinization speech at the XXth Communist Party Congress broke many taboos of isolationism and was meant, among other things, to bring Soviet Russia closer to Europe. Khrushchev saw Russia as culturally close to Europe, and at one point he proposed the mutual disbandment of NATO and the Warsaw Pact accompanied by a withdrawal of American military forces from the continent.[8] After Khrushchev's removal, hawks in the Soviet leadership attempted to reverse the de-Stalinization tide and restore the emphasis on "irreconcilable contradictions" between socialism and the capitalist West. But the impact of the post-Stalin reform efforts proved to be irreversible—a considerable part of a new intellectual generation referred to themselves as the "children of the XXth party congress" and worked within and outside the establishment to undermine the Stalinist thinking.[9] The post-Stalin period saw, in particular, the growth of specialized institutions, in which researchers carefully analyzed Western mainstream ideas, such as those generated by American IR scholars.[10]

Slavophiles or more nationalist thinkers did not entirely disappear from the public discourse and continued to influence the Marxist-Leninist regime. Stalin at times appealed to Russian, rather than Marxist, slogans and symbols and, in his own way, continued the indigenous tradition of nationalist thinking.[11] After the end of Joseph Stalin's terrorist rule, the Soviet regime became more susceptible to nationalist ideas.[12] The debate between Westernizers and Slavophiles continued although it was often set on the regime's terms and phrased in Marxist terminology.[13] Many of Russia's new nationalists opposed the Soviet regime, but, following the old Slavophile tradition, continued to be highly critical of the West and visualized Russia as socially and culturally superior. Therefore, despite the relative autarchy of the Soviet system, the outside influences continued to matter in shaping Russia's domestic debates.

Russia's openness to ideas from outside reached its highest point after Soviet leader Mikhail Gorbachev proclaimed a new era in relationships with the West. Symptomatically, the "New Thinking" was not quite new to the extent it was influenced by the domestic tradition critical of the Soviet anti-Western nationalism. In addition to Khrushchev's policies of de-Stalinization and peaceful coexistence, Gorbachev drew from ideas of major Russian scientists, such as Vladimir Vernadski, Pyotr Kapitza, and Andrei Sakharov.[14] The leader of Perestroika was also building on European social democratic ideas as well as American theories of transnationalism and interdependence.[15] The Soviet disintegration brought about a new fundamental change in Russia's intellectual and political discourse.

2. RUSSIA'S POST–COLD WAR DISCOURSE

2.1. IDENTIFYING RUSSIA'S SCHOOLS OF THOUGHT

The old IR distinction between realists (those supporting the view that world politics is a struggle for power) and idealists (those emphasizing cooperation) was further complicated by Martin Wight's triple conceptualization.[16] Wight observed that there were three, rather than two, theoretical traditions among scholars studying international relations: those who emphasized international anarchy and control (the realists), those who concentrated on international interactions as a civilizing force in world politics (the rationalists), and those who focused on various transformations of the international system (the revolutionists).

An examination of what scholars, foreign policy analysts, bureaucrats, and the media are writing about security issues in contemporary

Russia yields the following five groupings: Westernizers, National Democrats, Statists, National Communists, and Eurasianists. These five loosely fit Wight's typology: the Globalist (Westernizers and National Democrats) or "mutual security" school, the Nationalist (Statists and National Communists) or "balance of power" school, and the Expansionist (Eurasianists) or "security through expansion" school.[17] The five groupings also fit the identified patterns in Russian historical thinking about the world. Globalists represent Russia's Westernizers' aspirations to belong to the larger world, whereas Nationalists and Expansionists reflect the old Slavophiles' beliefs in Russia's cultural uniqueness, spirituality, and separate path of development. Although each of the intellectual currents grows out of and is reflective of national culture, none can be viewed as its ultimate representative or the ultimate authority to speak on this culture's behalf.

Before describing each of the contemporary schools in more detail, a caveat is in order. While the typology offered here serves an important analytic purpose, the schools represent "ideal types." The materials that were studied indicate these clusters of ideas even though no one writer was a perfect fit to what is described below. Following Wight's observation that even Machiavelli was not in the strictest sense a Machiavellian,[18] the persons linked to the various schools expressed ideas more in line with that school than with the others.

Westernism and National Democratism broadly belong to Russia's "mutual security" school of thinking. Both traditions are rooted in Gorbachev's New Thinking, which was particularly influential in Soviet Russia from 1987 to 1990. In accordance with this worldview, captured in such phrases as "values common to all mankind," "global problems," and "interdependence," a new conceptualization of national security arose, one that gave first priority to international cooperation. Security, Gorbachev argued, must be mutual, especially in the context of U.S.-Soviet relations, because if one side was insecure, the other side would be, too. The presence of large nuclear arsenals and the threat of mutual destruction also contributed to this view, but were not the only reasons for pursuing the notion of "mutual security." Increased economic interdependence demanded such a focus as well.[19]

Immediately after the collapse of the Soviet Union, the leaders of the new Russia accepted the general premises of New Thinking and developed them in a more sweeping philosophy of liberal Westernism. In the Westernizers' design, Russia was not only supposed to cooperate with the West in a broad range of international issues, as Gorbachev had planned. In addition to the international dimension, the new leaders also viewed Russia as increasingly domestically pro-Western. Russia's president Boris Yeltsin and Russia's new foreign minister Andrei Kozyrev, stated that, with the end of the cold war, Russia would engage in a strategic partnership with the West based on such shared values as democracy, human rights, and a free market. The Western countries, it was claimed, were "natural allies of Russia."[20] The underlying logic was that the main challenges to the country's security were internal. To cope with domestic challenges Russia must build a modern economy and democratic political system, and these necessitated a partnership with the West.[21]

As a result of the country's disillusionment with its economic and political reforms, the view of Westernizers—still influential in some policy circles—became increasingly marginalized in Russia's foreign policy discourse. The old pro-Western liberal philosophy was increasingly criticized by more comprehensive philosophies sensitive to Russia's culture. The National Democratic thinking is one of these philosophies. It shares with the Western liberal philosophy a commitment to community-based views of the world and Russia's "good citizen of global society" identity, but the new Democrats disagree with their pro-Western counterparts over universally acceptable rules. Similarly with Gorbachev's socialist thinking, they argue that basic human rights should not be the product of Western civilization alone. Rejection of a view of the world in terms of a dichotomy between a "progressive" civilization and other, yet-to-become civilized nations, led the new school to rethink the old Gorbachev-introduced maxims about "interdependence" and "mutual security."[22] Their picture of Russia's identity and the world in the post–cold war era is more complex and dialectical.

Statism and Neo-Communism are representatives of "balance of power" or "relative security" thinking. Like Western realists, Russia's Statists and National Communists are committed to the identity of "great power," rather than that of "good citizen," because they do not see the forces of international cooperation as shaping the nature of world politics. Security, they argue, results from balancing rather than cooperation; it is based on a state's individual strength more than on collective efforts; and its major goals are the maintenance of the existing balance of power and geopolitical stability rather than upsetting these for the purpose of transformation.[23] "One power's security is another power's insecurity. . . . Security is . . . a relational concept: security against whom?"[24]

The balance-of-power focus has been traditionally strong in Russia since pre-Soviet times. In a certain sense, Russia has always had elements of balancing as well as expansion in its foreign policy behavior. For example, Joseph Stalin's doctrine of "socialism in one country" was in some ways a recognition of the fact that the country did not have sufficient material capabilities for undertaking the earlier planned geopolitical expansion. Under Stalin's leadership there was an increased focus on developing military and economic capabilities rather than sacrificing them for world revolution or world socialism. The Soviet doctrine of "correlation of forces" was a continuation of this policy and focused on balancing and containment.

With the decline and the subsequent collapse of the Soviet Union, the National Communists emerged as particularly active critics of liberal policies and assumptions. They are on the right-wing side of the political spectrum (see table 3.1) and formed a hard-line opposition to both Gorbachev's and Yeltsin's reforms, attacking them as servants of the West and traitors to Russia's national interests. National Communists are aggressive in their nationalism and want the Soviet Union to be restored because for them this is the only way to maintain the global balance of power, or equilibrium. The most active promoters of National Communist aggressive nationalism are those intellectually and politically close to the Communist Party of Russian Federation (CPRF).[25]

Statism as a school of thought emerged later and as a reaction to Kozyrev's liberal foreign policies. While conceptually similar to National Communism in terms of defining security, there are several important distinctions between the two philosophies. Most importantly, while viewing the world primarily in terms of disparities and a competition among great powers, Statism is not anti-Western and can be quite critical of Soviet foreign policy. For example, in evaluating the cold war, Statists proceed from the thesis of mutual and equal responsibility, rather than putting all the blame on the West.[26] In fact, several Statists were originally supportive of Gorbachev's New Thinking as it was emerging in 1986–1987. Another important distinction is that, while sharing with National Communists an interest in exercising control over the former Soviet territory, Statists disagree that such a control should be implemented by the use of force. Politically, this group is

TABLE 3.1. The Political Spectrum of Russia's Foreign Policy Discourse

Globalists ("Mutual security")		Nationalists ("Balance of power")		Expansionists ("Security through expansion")
Westernizers	National Democrats	Statists	National Communists	Eurasianists

West ⟵————————————————————————⟶ Anti-West

neo-conservative, because they generally defend conservative principles in the post-Soviet period.[27] Statist philosophy is associated with the post-Kozyrev foreign minister Yevgeni Primakov, and it has dominated the intellectual debates in Russia and played a major role in shaping foreign policy.

Finally, Eurasianism views Russia and the world in terms of classical geopolitics and geopolitical struggle between land-based and sea-based powers. Much like Statists and National Communists, most Eurasianists are committed to relative security thinking.[28] However, they carry this line of argument to the extreme and advocate a widespread external expansion as the best means of ensuring Russia's security. The need to expand is explained by the geopolitical vacuum that was created by the end of the cold war. Eurasianists' historical influences might be traced back to the Lenin-Trotsky call for world revolution. Theoretically, the school takes its inspiration from traditional geopolitical theories, both Western and domestic. Politically, Eurasianists are on the extreme right-wing side of the political spectrum. Unlike supporters of "balance of power" who portray themselves as adherents to conservative beliefs such as the call for cultural, religious, and social stability,[29] Expansionists argue that to be conservative is not enough and advocate the notion of a "conservative revolution."[30] Despite the attraction to Eurasianists' language across Russia's political spectrum,[31] their political influence remains marginal. (Table 3.1 summarizes the political structure and the political spectrum of Russia's foreign policy discourse.)

2.2. IMAGES OF RUSSIA'S IDENTITY AND EXTERNAL THREATS

Westernizers, including politicians such as Yegor Gaidar and Andrei Kozyrev, contend that during the cold war Russia acted against its own interests and must now do everything necessary to become an integral part of the West. The West is perceived as the only viable and progressive civilization in the world. Main threats to Russia's "true" identity come from its economic backwardness and its association with non-democratic countries, especially with some of the former Soviet allies. Only by incorporating Western institutions and joining the coalition of what is frequently referred to as the community of "Western civilized nations" will Russia be able to respond to its threats and overcome its economic and political backwardness.

From the National Democratic perspective, Russia is an independent civilization, but also a part of international society. In the emerging post–cold war era Russia and other major actors are redefining their roles and identities, and are learning how to live in an increasingly interdependent, yet diverse world. In this world the main threats come from two directions: the violation of basic human rights and the disrespect for cultural pluralism. The challenge is to establish a "unity in diversity" regime, in which different nations and cultures might be able to maintain intense dialogue and cooperation by observing certain globally acknowledged rules, yet still follow their own internally developed sets of norms. The challenge for Russia, then, is not to copy the Western pattern but to find an appropriate culture-sensitive path to a world economic and security system. In attempting to do so, Russia must activate its own cultural legacy.[32] Some National Democrats define this legacy as that of a borderland nation, which puts Russia in a position of being able to learn from a variety of geographic, religious, and ethnic influences. If rightly reformulated, this legacy of a borderland nation can help to mobilize societal support for reform and produce domestic social and political institutions suitable for living in the twenty-first century.[33]

Whereas National Democrats emphasize the role of cultural factors in world politics, Statists are committed to viewing the world primarily in terms of power disparities and competition between states. Prime Minister Yevgeni Primakov and his supporters argue that the main threat to the international system comes from those interested in destabilizing the world's geopolitical equilibrium. In order to maintain equilibrium, at least in Eurasia, Russia must remain a sovereign state and a great power capable of resisting hegemonic ambitions anywhere in the world. As with Westernizers and National Democrats, Statists do not see Russia as inherently hostile to the West. They maintain that, although Russia is an independent civilization and its interests and values differ from those of the West, it has historically interacted with the West, and this interaction had not threatened Russian sovereignty or cultural distinctness.

The National Communists continue traditional Soviet thinking and merge some old communist assumptions with those of Statists. They, too, argue that Russia is an independent civilization and a great/superpower and should be maintained as such. But they take this line of reasoning a step further. In the National Communists' view, most frequently articulated by the leader of Russia's communists, Gennadi Zyuganov, Russia is not only culturally distinct from other civilizations, it differs from them fundamentally and should not be mixed with "alien"—especially Western—cultural, economic, or political institutions. Instead, Russia ought to remain an independent socialist civilization that is autarchic, has a self-sufficient economy, and is generally isolated from "alien" influences. Russia's interests are incompatible with those of the West, and its main threat comes from the West and its imperialist intentions.

Influenced by classical geopolitics, Eurasianists view Russia as first and foremost a land-based geopolitical empire, the main threats to which come from sea-based powers and their ideologies. Like National Communists, this group views Russia's interests in mutually exclusive terms with those of the West, particularly the United States and Britain. But unlike the more status-quo oriented Statists and National Communists, Eurasianists advocate constant territorial expansion as the only way to survive in a world that is characterized by an eternal struggle for geopolitical power. The ultra-nationalist Zhirinovski was one of those who advanced, and consistently advocated, the vision of Russia as being a self-expanding territorial empire. (Table 3.2 summarizes visions of Russia's identity and its external threats.)

2.3. IMAGES OF WORLD ORDER

The vision of Russia espoused by the five schools of thought is consistent with their respective visions of world order. Westernizers maintain that the ideal world order is one based on democratic values and the respect for human rights as articulated by Western civilization. Accordingly, the key division in the world, overriding all other divisions, is the one between democratic countries and those in the process

TABLE 3.2. Visions of Russia's Identity and Its External Threats

School of thought	Vision of Russia's identity and its external threat	Principal proponent
Westernizers	Russia is a part of the West and should integrate with Western economic and political institutions; the main threats to Russia's identity come from non-democratic states.	Andrei Kozyrev
National Democrats	Russia is an independent civilization, but also a part of international society; it has its own specific interests, but also shares some common interests with other civilizations; the main threats to Russia come from the violation of basic human rights and disrespect for cultural pluralism.	Michail Gorbachev
Statists	Russia is a sovereign state and a great power with its own specific interests in maintaining the stability of the international system; the main threats to Russia come from state-revisionists seeking to change the existing balance of power.	Yevgeni Primakov
National Communists	Russia is an independent socialist civilization and a great/superpower; Russia's interests are incompatible with those of the West and include the preservation of a balance of power between socialism and capitalism and the spread of the influence of Russian civilization; the main threats to Russia come from the West and its imperialist intentions.	Gennadi Zyuganov
Expansionists	Russia is a land-based geopolitical empire; Russia's interests are mutually exclusive with those of sea-based powers and include the preservation and expansion of Russia's geopolitical sphere of influence; the main threats to Russia come from sea-based powers.	Vladimir Zhirinovski

of democratic transition, on the one hand, and those that are still prac-
ticing authoritarian forms of government, on the other. The West and
its supporters have the right to push their human rights agenda and
even intervene anywhere in the world when a gross violation of human
rights takes place. With respect to the agencies that are to enforce a
human rights–centered world order, it is best if human rights interventions are sanctioned through the United Nations Security Council.
If this is not possible, regional security organizations are to carry out
the intervention without U.N. authorization, as happened in Kosovo.[34]
Westernizers also supported the United States' military intervention in
Iraq and argued that Russia should side with America.[35]

The attitude of National Democrats toward the design of a world
order is more complex than that of Westernizers. In their view, the
international system should function as a "unity in diversity" regime,
which implies that human rights are important, but are not to be
enforced at the expense of cultural pluralism. Rather, for the international system to be stable and legitimate, human rights should be
defined in culture-sensitive terms. The key players in such a world order
are various cultures that maintain a diversity of economic and political
institutions within which they negotiate the respect for and the enforce-
ment of basic human rights. To negotiate the definition and ways of
enforcing basic human rights is difficult, but it must be done through
the existing institutions of the United Nations, and possibly through
their reformation.

The Statists' worldview is a familiar realist picture of power competition between sovereign states, with domestic policies largely unaf-
fected by external influences. This group's vision of the international
system is reminiscent of nineteenth-century European politics, i.e., the
world is not inherently hostile, but it does consist of selfish power-
seeking state actors whose interests must be balanced in order to maximize peace and stability. Statists think about the international system in
terms of power poles and favor the U.N. as the key institution for
maintaining a multipolar balance of power, particularly among great
powers.[36]

The Neo-Communist school, too, displays some respect for the
United Nations, but only as an institution suitable for regulating peaceful coexistence between two superpowers, Russia and the United States,
and their respective client states. This group appreciates the fact that
Russia is currently weak, and can only become stronger if it concentrates

on mobilizing its internal resources and abstains from direct involvement in global military conflicts. Yet it maintains a loyalty to and a fascination with the cold war international system, and longs for its possible restoration in the not so distant future. It also generally continues to view the world as a struggle between the Russian socialist-oriented civilization and American-led Western imperialism.

Finally, the Eurasianists' image of the international system is also bipolar, except that the international system is viewed as being divided mainly by a struggle for territory. According to this view, the key players are empires that build and expand their spheres of influence using their natural territorial advantages, such as open access to the sea or control over vast landmasses. Eurasianists are silent on the issue of international institutions; they seem to believe that the true balance of geopolitical power between sea- and land-based powers can only be achieved through a process of military competition.

2.4. ALTERNATIVE STRATEGIES FOR THE POST–COLD WAR WORLD

Westernizers advocate that Russia stop worrying about external threats to its security and its great power status and concentrate on resolving a number of domestic problems, such as creating a healthy economy and a democratic political system. In the contemporary interdependent world, Russia does not need ultra-powerful military arsenals to protect itself. Instead, it should invest its resources in the creation of a modern economic and political system for the purpose of gaining full-scale membership in international organizations, and not in the realm of military power and geopolitics. Rather than pursuing its "greatness," Russia should be prepared for a relative decrease in its status in a non-confrontational world and try to solve its problems by entering the existing Western international institutions such as the European Union, NATO, and the WTO.

National Democrats, while in general being supportive of Russia's "going global" strategy, are more skeptical of the Westernist "adjustment" strategy. They believe that, because of their cultural differences, both Russia and the West must work hard to improve existing international institutions. Globalization or internationalization represents, National Democrats maintain, a two-way street. Russia must become closer to the international society by building more open (though not necessarily pro-Western) domestic institutions, but the West should likewise change and abandon the belief that it is the only viable and progressive civilization in the world. Instead of trying to integrate with the existing West-centered world, Russia should exercise caution and creativity in the process of adjustment, by learning from the world and by bringing in its own cultural experience.

Statists argue that Russia is and must remain a great power. It should be motivated primarily by its own interests, not by the demands of international institutions, and should pursue power accumulation and the maintenance of its significant global geopolitical role. At the same time, Statists warn against overextending Russia's currently limited material resources and insist that the country mobilize its diplomatic resources for security purposes. Statists are convinced that isolation is not an option and, unlike National Communists, believe that limited, pragmatic cooperation with the West is both feasible and necessary.

Such cooperation is, of course, viewed in a very different way from that envisaged by the two liberal schools. There can be a variety of economic and security reasons for engaging in cooperation, Statists claim, but in each instance absolute power equality must exist between the parties involved in the cooperative acts. Rather than trying to accept Western values and develop some common values, Russian cooperation with the West must be motivated by common interests. Because of Russia's presumed responsibility for maintaining world equilibrium and the balance of power, its cooperation with the West cannot be as deep and far-reaching as the schools advocating the "good citizen of global society" identity have proposed. Existing in a multipolar world, Russia must be able to prevent the formation of an opposing coalition by using balancing tactics in relating to all its foreign partners—Western, Eastern, and Southern. When necessary, it must capitalize on the potential conflicts that already exist in world politics, for example, those between the Western and Muslim or Asian countries.

Unlike Globalists and Statists, National Communists take external threats to Russia very seriously and advocate a restoration of the Soviet empire as the only way to address those threats and restore the lost balance of world power. Despite Russia's current weakness, this goal is too important to be abandoned. It is also quite feasible, National Communists maintain, because Russia is potentially strong and can become even stronger if it concentrates on mobilizing its internal resources and temporarily abstains from involvement in global military conflicts. The West and the United States, on the other hand, are believed to be confronting the experience of their own imminent decline.[37]

Finally, Eurasianists offer yet another foreign policy strategy, the most extreme and ambitious of all. Unlike nationalists of Statist and National Communist orientation, they advocate Russia's immediate geopolitical expansion, in particular expansion into China and the Muslim world. They are not overly worried about Russia's social and technological weaknesses and believe that the country will restore its strength in the process of creating a geopolitical empire. Some among the Eurasianists propose the geopolitical strategy "Pax Eurasiatica," which is a focus on the strategic unity of Eurasian geopolitics and geo-economics, the formation of a "neo-totalitarian" community. Others go so far as to advocate the need to absorb France, Germany, China, India, and the Muslim world within the borders of such an empire. (The identified alternative visions of Russia, world order, and security strategy are summarized in table 3.3.)

TABLE 3.3.   Russia's Alternative Visions

	Russia's Identity	*World Order*	*Security Strategy*
Westernizers	Citizen of the West-centered world	Global, West-centered world	Adjustment (borrowing)
National Democrats	Culturally distinct citizen of the world	Global, multicultural world	Creative adjustment (learning)
Statists	Independent state, great power	Multipolar, sovereignty-based	Combination of cooperation and balancing
National Communists	Independent socialist civilization, great power	Bipolar, competition of socialist and Western worlds	Balancing and limited expansion
Eurasianists	Land-based geopolitical empire	Bipolar, competition of geopolitical empires	Widespread expansion

3. THE EVOLUTION OF RUSSIA'S POST–COLD WAR DISCOURSE

Having identified the main currents of Russia's discourse, we must now answer the question of the discourse's development. Over the years of Russia's postcommunist transformation, the national discourse has not been static. It has progressed in three main stages. During these stages, competition among the schools of thought identified above revolved around the notions of the New Thinking (Gorbachev), the Strategic Partnership with the West (Kozyrev), and the Multipolar World (Primakov), respectively. These three notions and their respective foreign policy advocates mobilized and shaped the country's political discourse in competition with alternative visions. As these notions or metaphors were replacing each other, the country was progressing to a new hegemonic philosophy and the entire discourse was undergoing change.

3.1. GORBACHEV: PERESTROIKA AND THE NEW POLITICAL THINKING

The philosophy of Perestroika and the New Thinking introduced by Gorbachev became the cornerstone of Russia's policy discourse in the late 1980s. In foreign policy, the philosophy was based on the notion of the two superpowers' mutual responsibility for the cold war and the subsequent "crisis of human civilization," of which the main expressions were seen as the nuclear arms race, environmental destruction, and world poverty. The concept of the New Thinking diagnosed the crisis of civilization as being of a global nature and, therefore, capable of being resolved only through global efforts. In particular, the former cold war enemies were expected to acknowledge the futility of class and narrowly viewed national values and to develop, by the way of compromises and multilateral negotiations, values "common to all humankind."[38]

The New Thinking emerged out of Nikita Khrushchev's attempts to revise the Stalinist world outlook and grew stronger in the context of the rising economic and political power of the West. Over time, domestic supporters of moderation and accommodation in foreign relations were able to consolidate their positions and, through Gorbachev, to express their deep dissatisfaction with the old system.

Gorbachev's philosophy did not go unopposed, however. From the conservative side, he was attacked for "betraying" the principles of

Marxism-Leninism and Soviet patriotism. But the New Thinking seized the initiative in shaping the discourse, whereas its critics were defensive and had few ideas to offer as alternatives. The conservative attacks had only a limited force, and the old system was gradually losing its domestic support.

A more serious challenge to Gorbachev's vision arose from critics of a radical liberal orientation. Led by Boris Yeltsin, a long-time communist who converted to a liberal and populist, the new opposition attacked the leader of Perestroika because it viewed him and his supporters as unable to catch up with rapidly changing domestic and international developments. The fact that Gorbachev kept insisting on the reform's "socialist" character disappointed those who believed he had dressed his vision in socialist clothes for purely tactical purposes. Originally sympathetic to Gorbachev's agenda, many of these people now felt that he was too slow and inconsistent in his policies. The domestic elites and the ethnic republics, too, were growing impatient with the lack of practical results and were attracted to the "Western" model of development. The idea of communism, on the other hand, was largely discredited, and after the failed coup of August 1991 the liberal opposition was in a position to set the terms of the political discourse.

3.2. KOZYREV: RADICAL REFORMS AND STRATEGIC PARTNERSHIP WITH THE WEST

The idea of liberal Westernization was now moving to occupy center stage in the country's political discourse. Radical liberals finally found themselves in a position to move from actively challenging Gorbachev's moderately liberal ideas to setting their own agenda. Not surprisingly, the newly emerged hegemonic idea was formulated as that of Russia's strategic partnership with the West. The argument implied that Russia had exhausted the list of alternative development projects and had no other choice but to follow the lead of Western economic and political development.[39] The argument had both domestic and foreign policy dimensions. In foreign policy, the main task was formulated as the need to join Western or transatlantic economic and security institutions, such as the European Union, NATO, the IMF, G–7, and so on. Domestically, the new Russian leaders planned to implement a strategy of radical economic reform, the so-called "shock therapy," so that

Russia's transition to a Western-style system would be both fast and irreversible. The idea of strategic partnership was in part a purposeful calculation; Andrei Kozyrev saw no reasons to hide that he viewed foreign policy as a "tool for advancing Russia's reforms."[40]

However important liberal Westernism was in Russian policy and discourse, it did not last long as an official philosophy. In 1993–1994, as a result of several international and domestic developments, the philosophy of radical reform and strategic partnership with the West became seriously undermined. The arrival of Yevgeni Primakov in 1995 completed the process and marked a new turn in the national political discourse. Domestically, Russians experienced the failure of shock therapy and a drastic decline in living standards. Externally, the prospects of NATO expansion toward Russia's borders and military conflicts in the Russian periphery also undermined the efforts of Russian Westernizers. Their grand strategy involving the development of a deep, multisided partnership with the West was now perceived as flawed. Social support for liberal domestic and foreign policy reforms decreased substantially, as was convincingly demonstrated by the December 1993 and 1995 parliamentary elections.

As a result, other foreign policy schools of thought challenged Kozyrev's philosophy. Gorbachev's supporters began to recover from their previous defeat and attempted to reformulate their alternative to Westernism as a more nationally sensitive liberalism.[41] However, the defeat was serious, and the hardships the Russians suffered during the early Yeltsin era were devastating. The public widely perceived former Gorbachev supporters and the new Russian leaders as parts of the "same crowd" and refused to trust them. The impact of the hard-line opposition of National Communists and Eurasianists still remained relatively marginal. Within this vacuum, Statism, a new school of thought, emerged and began to rise rapidly to prominence.

In the new geopolitical and economic situation, Statists presented themselves as the true defenders of Russian national interests. Influenced by both liberals and nationalists, Statists were able to respond successfully to public need by bridging together polarized supporters of both the "old" and the "new" Russia. A large part of the country's political class also seemed to feel comfortable with the self-proclaimed "centrism" of Statist political views. Considerable numbers of former Soviet industrialists, state bureaucrats, and military leaders supported the Statist philosophy in part because its emphasis on a strong state promised some protection from the more painful effects of economic reform without necessarily implying the restoration of the Soviet-like control.

3.3. PRIMAKOV: STABILITY, PRAGMATISM, AND THE MULTIPOLAR WORLD

Statist-oriented intellectuals, bureaucrats, military officials, and industrialists prepared the ground for the next turn in Russian discourse. This turn away from Kozyrev's and the early Yeltsin's pro-Western philosophy was officially completed with the appointment of Primakov as Russia's next foreign minister (and, subsequently, prime minister).[42] In foreign affairs, the new course proclaimed the vision of a multipolar world. According to this perspective, excessive liberalism has a tendency to become dependence and, to avoid such a development, Russia must pursue the goal of becoming an independent power pole. It must clearly define its own national priorities and be pragmatic in pursuing them, using a combination of cooperation and balancing policies.[43] In domestic affairs, Primakov's vision assumed the need to be selective about the country's scarce resources and to pursue a model of reforms that would command a broad social support.

The newly emerged philosophy of multipolarism was challenged from both the liberal and the nationalist/expansionist ends of the political spectrum. Nationalists and Expansionists attacked the new official vision for not going "far enough" in restoring traditional Soviet foreign policy ties and Russia's "Eurasianist values."[44] In their turn, liberals warned that multipolarism is nothing but another example of unwarranted power ambitions. In their opinion, pro-Western orientation remained the only viable option, however difficult the West might be as a partner. With Vladimir Putin's presidency, Russia in part has re-experienced the philosophy of stability, pragmatism, and multipolarity.[45] As far as the other schools of thought are concerned, they are in a weak position to challenge seriously the hegemonic Statist philosophy. Westernizers are somewhat more active and influential than other schools, partly as a result of this school's previously hegemonic position, and partly due to the reflection of the West's world influence.

The Russian discourse therefore was far from homogeneous or unified and evolved as a competition of various schools of thought. More

TABLE 3.4. The Dynamics of Russia's Discourse:
Stages and Schools' Relative Status

	Schools' Relative Status: Hegemonic vs. Active vs. Marginal*			
Stages	Westernizers	National Democrats	Statists	National Communists/ Eurasianists
1986–1990	Active	HEGEMONIC	———	Marginal
1990–1995	HEGEMONIC	Marginal	Active	Marginal
1995–2000	Active	Marginal	HEGEMONIC	Marginal

* Estimated

⟶ Direction of the discourse's development

specifically, it progressed from one organizing metaphor or hegemonic idea to another: from the New Thinking to the Strategic Partnership to the Multipolar World. (Table 3.4 summarizes the dynamics of the Russian foreign policy discourse.) These changes, however, were never isolated from the external ideational influences. In order to appreciate fully the nature and scope of these changes, we now turn to Russia's discursive engagements with the outside world and the contribution of outside ideas to Russian debates and intellectual developments.

CHAPTER 4

THE TRIUMPH
OF LIBERALISM?

Debating Francis Fukuyama's
"End of History" Thesis

1. FUKUYAMA'S THESIS

1.1. THE SOCIAL AND INTELLECTUAL CONTEXT OF FUKUYAMA'S THESIS

The sociology of knowledge teaches us that ideas do not emerge merely out of intellectuals' personal agendas and aspirations. Instead, they come as reactions to various social contexts and circumstances. It follows that, being interested in ideas, we ought to go beyond studying their analytical content and form of presentation in order to learn what it is about ideas that makes them socially possible and attractive. We must understand what message a certain idea attempts to convey to a society, and we must realize to what extent this idea has a chance of affecting a society in a positive or a negative way.

Since Fukuyama's thesis remains influential in some Western circles and in the world at large, we examine this vision of a post–cold war world order with questions inspired by sociology of knowledge. Following Karl Mannheim's original focus on the "social or existential determination of actual thinking,"[1] we will look at the social circumstances from which Fukuyama's thesis emerged.[2] It is important to ask to what extent (to use Mannheim's language) the ideology of West-centered globalization can obtain qualities of utopia, or acquire the dynamism of transforming the world reality into its image.

Because Fukuyama's thesis has implications far beyond the United States, or even the West, it is important to explore both Western and non-Western social contexts of the idea's appearance and reception.[3] The social contexts in the West (United States) and outside it (Russia) were fundamentally different. In the West, the thesis grew out of the intellectual and policy tradition of conservative internationalism. In Russia the mainstream tradition was only marginally affected by Western liberal politico-economic ideas. As open as the country became to Western influences since Gorbachev, Fukuyama's thinking could not resonate with prevailing mental structures and found little support in the Russian foreign policy community. Only Russian Westernized intelligentsia have shown some sympathy with the "end of history" thesis.

The Western social context of the late-1980s was shaped by the fact that, for at least a decade, conservatives were in power and had ample opportunities to influence international public discourse. The arrival of Mikhail Gorbachev as General Secretary of the Soviet Communist Party and his pioneering ideas of Perestroika and New Thinking were originally received in the West with suspicion and, later, as an obvious sign of Soviet defeat in the cold war struggle. With the passing of time, the dominant policy communities in the United States and Europe became convinced of the Western victory and came to share three main assumptions about the nature and future of world politics.

The first assumption concerned the origins of the cold war international system and the identity of its main participants. According to this assumption, the system emerged as a struggle between good and evil. The West was perceived as morally and technologically superior and the East, to borrow President Ronald Reagan's memorable phrase, as the evil empire. Although each side was assumed to have its own concepts of good and evil, "ours" was superior and could not be compromised.

A second and related proposition argued the upcoming victory of the West over the Soviet "totalitarianism." Communism was proclaimed "the grand failure."[4] Optimism, even euphoria, quickly captivated the Western media and policy circles. The "democracy won!" mood[5] seemed so widespread that even a usually skeptical Samuel

Huntington wrote in 1991, "the contrasts in outlook between the mid-1970s and the late-1980s on the future of democracy could hardly have been more dramatic."[6] The leading policy establishment journal *Foreign Affairs* pronounced that

> The Soviet system collapsed because of what it was, or more exactly, because of what it was not. The West "won" because of what the democracies were—because they were free, prosperous and successful, because they did justice, or convincingly tried to do so.[7]

Finally, the dominant Western policy community came to believe that the West was now in a position to teach the rest of the world about economic and political institutions as well as moral standards. It seemed only logical to draw this third assumption from the previous two: "we" won because of our original strength and moral superiority.

These three propositions turned out to be widely accepted because they grew out of the dominant intellectual and policy tradition associated with modernization theory. In its mainstream version, modernization theory was firmly rooted in assumptions of the West's moral and institutional superiority. The theory was known precisely for projecting Western views and values across the globe and for offering ethnocentric, context-insensitive policy advice to non-Western societies.[8]

Although rooted in modernization theory, the assumptions were yet to be theoretically articulated and politically justified for the post–cold war world. Fukuyama's piece fit the bill in both intellectual and policy terms and, in this sense, was far from accidental in its appearance. At the time, Fukuyama worked as a Bush Administration strategist, deputy director of the Department of State's Policy Planning Staff. He was also an ardent proponent of modernization theory.[9] By the virtue of his intellectual and policy background, Fukuyama was well positioned to formulate the "end of history" vision and defend the worldwide ascendancy of Western-style liberal capitalism.[10]

In the Russia of the late-1980s, optimism also prevailed. The fact that, after decades of confrontation with the West, Soviet leaders were able to initiate the New Thinking was widely seen by Russians as a crucial step toward stable peace and cooperation in the world. But it was a different kind of optimism, and the earlier posed questions about the nature and the future of the cold war were answered differently.

Gorbachev and his supporters did not see the cold war in terms of the moral superiority of one system over another. Instead, they advanced a vision of mutual responsibility for what they saw as the "crisis of human civilization" that put humankind on the verge of nuclear, ecological, and moral catastrophe.[11] The question "Who won the cold war?" was explored differently as well. Instead of viewing the end of the cold war in terms of a victory of Western civilization over the inferior Soviet state, Soviet intellectuals and policy makers emphasized the opportunities that were lost by both sides for developing a true dialogue across countries and continents, and for building a more peaceful and sustainable world. Finally, the policy solution to post–cold war problems was seen, in the Third Way spirit, not in merely borrowing Western values and institutions, but in finding appropriate culture-sensitive paths to a world economic and security system and maintaining a "unity in diversity" regime. To Gorbachev's supporters, accepting mutual responsibility for the "crisis of civilization" and trying to act in concert in the future seemed appropriate to meet the new challenges of the post–cold war era.

Although never articulated in its specifics—in part the result of Gorbachev's communist party habit of speaking in generalities—the Russian vision presented a distinct challenge to both Western and Soviet ways of thinking about modernity and modernization. Modernity and access to world citizenship were no longer viewed predominantly in terms of power and competition; instead, a more dialogical, bottom-up approach was proposed. In Gorbachev's own words,

> The development of a new mode of thinking requires dialogue not only with people who hold the same views but also with those who think differently and represent a philosophical and political system that is different from ours. For they also carry the historical experience, culture and traditions of their peoples; they are all part of world development and are entitled to their own opinion and to an active role in world politics.[12]

When Fukuyama's article was published, leading Russian intellectuals were in the midst of debating how national, class, and common human values could be combined for the sake of building a better world. By the time of the article's appearance in Russian,[13] the Russian national community had come close to formulating its own answers to the set of tough questions posed by the approaching disintegration of the familiar international system.

1.2. THE CONTENT OF FUKUYAMA'S THESIS

Taking the sociology of knowledge technique one step further, we see that Fukuyama's thesis was not only a typical product of the West, it had crucial social repercussions for the non-Western world. By inheriting the cultural ethnocentrism of modernization theory and sharing all the complexities and biases of its cold war background, the "end of history" project served the purpose of solidifying Western cultural hegemony in the post–cold war world. Fukuyama's ethnocentrism becomes clear when we ask three ethical questions about his thesis. First, what is the cultural community on behalf of which Fukuyama speaks and whose values and views on world order he seeks to uphold? Second, what is his definition of alternative cultural communities? Finally, what are some of the practical implications of Fukuyama's thesis, and which particular responsible actions does he recommend to those who share his worldview? This framework allows us to reconstruct Fukuyama's definitions of the Self and the Other and is broadly consistent with the methodology of social constructivism.

As far as the cultural community is concerned, Fukuyama is an ardent advocate of Western values. However, his defense of the West is analytically different from that of realists. Unlike realists, who emphasize international anarchy and cyclical development, Fukuyama argues for the global and progressive ascendancy of Western-style liberal capitalism:

> What we may be witnessing is not just the end of the Cold War, or the passing of a particular period of postwar history, but the end of history as such: that is, the end point of mankind's ideological evolution and the universalization of Western Liberal democracy as the final form of human government.[14]

Influenced by Hegel's and Kojeve's interpretations of the end of history, he insists that power politics is hopelessly ahistorical and that liberalism and liberal institutions such as the rule of law, representative democracy, and the market economy are acquiring a truly universal significance. To Fukuyama, realism is blind to the fact that no other social organization such as fascism, nationalism, or communism is capable of challenging the establishment of the Liberal idea.

In defining alternative cultural communities, Fukuyama is not much different from realists, however. While emphasizing the truly global nature of liberalism and the Liberal idea, he remains strikingly parochial in defending Western values as exclusively defined. In his eyes, the West is the community with supreme institutional and moral authority, and it is this community's values that must be promoted globally whether or not they are welcomed by other members of the international system. Fukuyama views the non-Western areas of the world as the site for a future projection of Western values and tailors his analysis to demonstrate the "total exhaustion of viable systematic alternatives to Western Liberalism."[15] The "end of history" implies that the Other can no longer make a creative contribution to world development; all that is left for it at this post-historical point is to patiently and passively wait to be absorbed by the Self.

What about practical implications of the "end of history" thesis? Quite obviously, the vision implies that the world should abandon experiments with social and political forms and settle for what Western liberalism has to offer. The liberal triumph is not necessarily optimistic, however. As observers rightly pointed out, Fukuyama's determinism should not be confused with optimism.[16] In addition to being influenced by Hegel, Fukuyama is a student of Friedrich Nietzsche, and his Nietzsche-inspired pessimism is meant to discourage independent social energy and creativity. The liberal capitalist order is not perfect, but neither can it be improved. Other nations have no choice but to develop and modernize exclusively in the manner of Western societies. Fukuyama is explicit in his attempt to revive the old modernization theory and laments elsewhere that, although the theory collapsed in the 1970s, "it should not have."[17] The fact that within the West there is a great deal of variation in types of representative democracy and in the level of planning that accompanies markets is not something that Fukuyama is comfortable discussing.[18]

In sum, Fukuyama's thesis implies solidification of the cultural hegemony of the West and limitation of the participation of non-Western cultures in building a post–cold war order. Culturally exclusive projects are hardly news in Western intellectual development, and Fukuyama's project, characterized by one scholar as an "intellectual response to the fear of change,"[19] fits a long tradition of Western theorizing, including the works of Georg Hegel, Oswald Spengler, Alexandre Kojève, Arthur Koestler, Daniel Bell, and others.[20] This kind of project assumes the cultural superiority of the West and serves as the moral justification of Western intervention in the affairs of the rest the world.[21]

2. THE LATE-SOVIET RECEPTION

2.1. SOCIAL DEMOCRATS

In Russia, one school of thought advanced the agenda of Soviet liberalization and was supportive of Gorbachev's vision of reforming the system. Indeed, the very emergence and initial cohesiveness of the school was largely the result of its efforts to put the new policy agenda on a firmer theoretical ground and to defend it against attacks from its opponents. The school was broadly committed to the vision of mutual responsibility of the East and West for the cold war confrontation and to searching for a "Third Way" alternative to both Western liberal capitalism and Soviet national communism.[22] I will refer to supporters of this school as Social Democrats with the understanding that this umbrella incorporates a diversity of views.[23]

Inspired by Gorbachev's Third Way philosophy, Social Democrats remained critical of the idea that the West provides the best model for world development and Soviet reform, and they advanced a more sophisticated and less Westernized vision. For our purposes, it is useful to outline how this school viewed the morally authoritative community (the Self), the alternative community (the Other), and the practice of their communication (the Self versus the Other).

First, for Social Democrats, the authoritative cultural community is that of global humanity or civilization. Although the West is an important part of civilization, it is not the defining part. Some key Western values and institutions were adopted by non-Western societies, but in the process of their adaptation these institutions were culturally modified and transformed. For example, it was the West that first introduced and approbated the market economy and political democracy.[24] However, during the time since this introduction, these institutions have acquired the status of common human values creating the institutional fabric of a common human civilization. In contrast to what Fukuyama asserts, these values are no longer purely Western; they are of global significance and contribute to the consolidation of the global world order.[25]

The fact that the world has adopted some of the originally Western institutions does not mean the "end of history" has arrived. The present and the future of the world are not homogeneity and boredom, but a continued diversity and competition. This is so because local societies have arrived at their currently intense global interactions by way of diverse historical paths. As the result of diverse histories, local cultures persist and will continue to impact how societies learn from each other. In a typical expression of this idea, one Social Democrat suggested that the "world continues to remain culturally heterogeneous. Culture is the code, or the matrix of the human civilization that allows a person—through his or her actions—to continually reproduce the civilization."[26]

Furthermore, Social Democrats do not view the relationship between Self and Other in a zero-sum way where one is clearly superior to another. Neither the West nor the East should be viewed as the final moral authority, and therefore neither of them should be viewed as the alternative moral community. Rather, both of them are alternatives, each with potentially rich and creative experience to offer. Whereas Fukuyama views non-Western societies as passive learners of the Western experience, Social Democrats insist that both Western and non-Western cultures contribute to the development of the global civilization. For example, the West invented institutions to limit the role of the state (the market economy and political freedom), whereas the non-West introduced ideas of state responsibility and group values in social development.[27]

Gorbachev's persistent emphasis on the creative potential of each local culture served important political and intellectual purposes. Politically, emphasis on the socialist origins and character of Perestroika was helping Gorbachev to neutralize the growing resistance from Politburo Member Yegor Ligachev and other communist hard-liners. But this was not just good politics; intellectually, Gorbachev was a firm believer in the path-dependent character of Soviet development, which, for him, meant the necessity of staying the essentially socialist course of Perestroika.[28]

Finally, because both West and non-West are viewed as capable of creative contributions to world development, they should communicate in a regime of mutually advantageous learning. Social Democrats identified two forms of such learning: mutual borrowing and cultural adaptation.

Mutual borrowing assumes that different societies do not exist in isolation, but constantly borrow from each other various technological and institutional features in order to successfully meet new challenges. For example, one such challenge emerged in the interwar period and had to do with the world depression and the need to provide stronger social protection by the state. Social Democrats argue that, during this critical period, the capitalist state borrowed some of the regulative features that had already been introduced in Soviet Russia. The emergence of the "welfare state" (which is usually translated in Russia as the "socially responsible state") is attributed not only to capitalism's own internal contradictions, but also to the emergence and progressive development of socialism.[29] The East, on the other hand, continues to try to learn from the West the dynamism of its economy, which was evident in Vladimir Lenin's attempts to introduce the New Economic Policy, as well as in Gorbachev's Perestroika. The constant exchange and circulation of various technological developments is another dimension of mutual borrowing.

Cultural adaptation is the second component of inter-societal learning, and it includes the mobilization of domestic social mechanisms for incorporating the borrowed technological and institutional features. The ultimate purpose of cultural adaptation is to make the borrowed feature one of the domestic society's own by integrating it into the society's most fundamental structures, such as values and beliefs. Unless this is accomplished, Social Democrats argue, the newly borrowed technology or institution is not going to function effectively and may instead stimulate the processes of social disintegration. In Eduard Batalov's words,

> If we hypothesize that the Soviet Union witnessed the emergence of some powerful political forces with the agenda of reproducing the Western system of socio-economic relations on Soviet ground, then such development would most likely lead not to rapid solutions of the country's problems, but to the sharp rise of social, political, and economic instability, with the possible outcome of a neo-totalitarian dictatorship. As a result, the country would be thrown even farther behind its current level of development.[30]

This argument must be distinguished from that of cultural relativism, which places emphasis on domestic structures and tends to view every aspect of social development as meaningful only in a domestic context and as almost exclusively domestically determined.[31] Social Democrats, in their turn, view domestic and external influences as equally significant, albeit not easily compatible, in a society's development. They argue for learning from domestic experience, as well as from that of other societies, and for a constant effort to synthesize the two sources in attempting to deal with new problems.

Some might argue that this worldview of mutually advantageous learning is too good to be true and has little to do with the reality of competition for power and resources in the modern world. Fukuyama's view, they could continue, is simply more realistic, as it represents how the West has been progressively gaining control over the world's resources through the expansion of Western values and institutions. This is a misleading picture, Social Democrats respond, and the world we live in signifies the end of the industrial stage of human civilization as we know it, and not the "end of history" or the triumph of liberalism.[32] To continue living in the world of power politics and to abide by its laws means only to further exacerbate all its problems—nuclear arms races, poverty, and ecological disasters—which have already put human civilization on the edge of self-destruction. It means to continue living in denial, while the challenge is to move beyond the power politics of the modern world toward the stage of intercultural negotiations and search for common solutions to human problems.[33] In this increasingly interdependent and yet persistently dynamic and pluralist world, it would be irrelevant to live by some overarching ideology of liberalism or any other "ism" in order to solve human problems. Indeed, under such conditions, as Yuri Zamoshkin argued in his response to Fukuyama, "the belief that an ideology can bring 'the final rational form of society' and, therefore, the end to the history of humanity's intellectual searches is extremely dangerous."[34]

These three ethical propositions—the moral authority of global humanity, the East's and West's equally creative contributions to the world, and the need for their mutually advantageous learning—help to interpret the reaction of Social Democrats to Fukuyama's vision. They constituted the core of Gorbachev's vision and played a vital role of meta-theoretical beliefs, or assumptions, through which many other issues—foreign policy, economic reform, the socialist theory of formation—could be debated and, ultimately, solved.[35] Gorbachev and his supporters tirelessly advanced these propositions in intellectual and political discussions with their more pro-Western and nationalist opponents.

2.2. WESTERNIZERS

As with the Social Democrats, Westernizers or pro-Western Liberals were not a cohesive school of thought. Some Westernizers were originally supportive of Gorbachev's reform in a hope that it would soon develop into a fully liberal project and abandon its initially socialist features. Others became more pro-Western as a result of disappointment with Gorbachev's slow and gradual movement toward reform.[36] As the debate on New Thinking progressed, more and more people became impatient with Gorbachev's socialist design and demanded more radical solutions.[37] By the time Fukuyama's article appeared, the core of Westernizers' propositions was clear, as was its difference from that of the Social Democrats.

First, this school unequivocally viewed the West as the ultimate moral authority and the model to follow. Academic institutions, especially the Institute of the World Economy and International Relations and the Institute of the U.S.A. and Canada were particularly active in advancing the view.[38] The leading researcher at the Institute of the World Economy, El'giz Pozdnyakov, expressed the typical attitude in his series of articles.[39] Along with many other Westernizers, he rejected the theory of formations and advanced a vision unmistakably akin to that of Fukuyama. In his critique of the notion of formation, Pozdnyakov identifies two ways of making the argument about the priority of common human values. One is the familiar Social Democratic way, with the emphasis on various local contributions to the global world, but this was not the tack preferred by Pozdnyakov.[40] Instead, he proposes to view common human values as those "that are based on the criteria of the Western civilization, with its Liberal-democratic values and the level of scientific-technological development."[41] He writes,

> The West today is not merely a geographic concept, nor even the concept of capitalism. This is the expression of the highest

existing level of economic, scientific-technological, and democratic development, without reaching which no society can be
called modern. That is why Japan is the West, as are Singapore
and South Korea; and this is why we are still not the West.[42]

By advocating along with Fukuyama a dualistic, "the more versus the
less advanced societies" vision of the world, Pozdnyakov demonstrates
a limited understanding of dialectics.[43] Ironically, in his critique of the
linear character of the Marxist theory of formations, he quickly became
the advocate of the no less linear Western modernization theory.

This pro-Western approach and the lack of dialectical thinking led
Westernizers to essential agreement with Fukuyama on how one
should view non-Western societies and their contributions to the
world. With the nineteenth-century thinker Petr Chaadayev, Russian
Westernizers continued to believe that "we [Russians] are placed somewhat outside of the times" and, therefore, hardly have a coherent cultural tradition to utilize in order to contribute to the world history.[44]
It is hardly surprising then that many pro-Western Liberals, in reaction
to Fukuyama's writing and independently of him, reached essentially
the same pessimistic conclusions about their country's ability to modernize without Westernizing.[45] According to this school of thought,
Russia is a yet-to-become Western society, and the Russian and Soviet
way of development should be viewed as a failed attempt to catch up
with the West, not as an attempt to express its own approach to world
development.

This dualistic logic—"the modernized versus the modernizing
societies"—led Westernizers to share the other part of Fukuyama's
reasoning. According to this reasoning, since the alternative way of
development is no longer available, the non-Western part of the world
should adjust its thinking and practices to become like the West. In
Fukuyama's spirit, Russian Westernizers offered little if any discussion
of alternative means of dealing with the dilemmas of modernity. In
their view, the dilemma before former Soviet Russia is either modern-
ization-Westernization, or autarchy and backwardness. In Pozdnyakov's
words, "we either continue to practice archaic isolation and thereby
hopelessly fall behind civilization [which was earlier defined as based on
Western criteria] while preserving our own unique socialism, or we
enter the universal world civilization and admit that the experience of
the local socialism failed."[46]

2.3. NATIONAL COMMUNISTS AND EXPANSIONISTS

Another alternative to Gorbachev's Social Democratic vision emerged from the conservative side of the political spectrum. National Communists and Expansionists are those who do not want to part with the core principles of Soviet society. Intellectually, they are divided along many lines.[47] However, the two schools were united in their hatred of Gorbachev. They attacked Gorbachev for what they perceived as unwarranted policies of Westernization that could only lead to Russia's social and political disintegration. While Liberals faulted Gorbachev for not being sufficiently Western, nationalists blamed the leader of Perestroika for going too far and being too pro-Western. It should not be surprising then that National Communists and Expansionists vigorously attacked Fukuyama's propositions.

To nationalist-minded National Communists and Expansionists, moral authority lies unquestionably with Russia and the non-Western world. This school agreed with the "end of history" author that modernity was essentially a Western phenomenon. However, it adopted Fukuyama's logic to go in an entirely different direction and argued that Russia should stay away from Western modernity and preserve its own historical tradition and cultural identity. Following the philosophy of the nineteenth-century Slavophiles, some nationalists viewed Russia as a holder of traditional values such as firm religious beliefs and faith in one God, an empire, and political authoritarianism as well as a predominantly agrarian economy. Within such an empire, they were willing to allow for a diversity of various social and political forms, so long as such forms did not question the cohesiveness of the empire, which was viewed as the principle of preserving social integrity and cultural identity.[48] Others viewed Russia as a technologically advanced and multi-religious society, but one that nonetheless had a powerful civil religion or ideology serving to cement social integrity.[49] Both of these images emphasized the domestic, rather than international, imperatives of Russia's development and left little or no room for Russian engagement with Western ideas.

National Communists and Expansionists viewed the West as an alternative or inferior moral community. They typically portrayed the West as having no moral values and no unifying social idea. It was merely a collection of atomized individuals united by rational aspiration to become rich at the expense of the rest of the world. It was through a critique of the power of rational individualism that these schools evaluated Fukuyama's thesis. To them, the "end of history" was a product of the ideology of Rationalism, yet another attempt to exploit the world economically and corrupt it morally. It was this ideology of Rationalism, as expressed in the institutions of market economy and political democracy that was responsible for secessionism, Nazism, and consumerism (everything that Russian nationalists condemn). To National Communists, the rationalist ideology was bad news for Russia, because it corrupted its culture and provoked a totalitarian reaction.[50] In the words of the prominent National Communist intellectual Sergei Kurginyan, Fukuyama's argument meant to contribute to the spread of the ideology of common human values in the Soviet Union but, in reality, it created room for the emergence of fascism.[51]

What to do? How to preserve what many National Communists define as Russia's organic integrity? And what should be the practical alternative to the "end of history" scenario? Here the key word for National Communists and Expansionists was "resistance." Unlike Social Democrats, National Communist and Expansionist schools saw no point in learning from a society that seeks to undermine their cultural integrity and take advantage of their natural resources. Instead, they proposed strategies of conservatism (Nationalism) and conservative revolution (Expansionism). The former assumes power accumulation through economic and technological development, and abstention from global military conflicts, while the latter suggests immediate and widespread expansion to fill the geopolitical vacuum.[52]

As the time of Perestroika was elapsing, National Communist and Expansionist visions remained relatively marginalized in the Russian discourse. On the other hand, Gorbachev's reforms were failing to live up to rising expectations. The Social Democratic vision began to lose its original attractiveness and the hegemonic position it occupied in national discourse since 1986. The relative position of Westernizers, therefore, improved considerably. As Russians continued to have little faith in the power of isolationist or Expansionist ideas, the vacuum was to be filled with the ideas of pro-Western Liberals.

3. THE POST-SOVIET RECEPTION

The departure of Gorbachev as president in late 1991 and the end of the Soviet Union marked the beginning of a new era and, with it, a new national discourse. For several years, Russia was to become a laboratory for a pro-Western Liberal experiment. It seemed that Fukuyama's vision was becoming the country's everyday reality. However, as the proposed vision of Westernization failed to bring any visible improvements in people's living standards, the society became increasingly disillusioned and skeptical. The Soviet collapse critically added to this changing attitude; many Russians felt that the "talk shop" and the absence of material accomplishments were now exacerbated by the significant losses of territory and world status. The pro-Western Liberal rhetoric was lauded on the surface, but the society had already begun to withdraw its support for it.[53]

Elites, too, were growing increasingly disappointed with attempted postcommunist reform. Westernizers continued to defend the liberal path for Russia, but they faced growing intellectual resistance, without yet fully understanding its sources.[54] National Communists, with their ideas of rebuilding the Soviet empire and military power, were ready to fill the ideological void left by the failure of reform and began to gain influence outside their traditional circles.[55] But the most important and truly symbolic development was the emergence and rapid growth of a new school of thought soon to be dubbed "Statism." The Liberal's vision of the country's identity was about to be replaced by the rediscovered geopolitical identity of national interests.[56]

Originally emerging as a new form of nationalism that was influenced by ideas from both the Globalist and Nationalist schools, Statism quickly obtained an independent intellectual and political status. The newly emerged school advocated the notion of Russia as a strong state or *Derzhava*.[57] Many self-proclaimed Statists were in fact former Liberals who remained attracted to the idea that Russia should strive to build a market economy and political democracy. However, they no longer agreed that Russia was becoming a part of the West and argued that the country must have its own interests to defend. From National Communists and Expansionists, Statists borrowed a conflictual vision of the world, in which power-seeking states seek to defend their geopolitical interests and areas of influence. Without implying an extreme confrontation with the West (often at the core in the writings of National Communists and Expansionists), Statists incorporated much National Communist terminology, such as "national idea," "great power," "Eurasia," "geopolitics," into their own vocabulary.[58]

Many prominent Liberals and Social Democrats became suscep-tible to the rhetoric and agenda of Statists, which served as another powerful indicator of the coming change in Russia's national discourse. Even Kozyrev, Russia's outspokenly liberal foreign minister, began to frame his speeches in terms of national interests, rather than as merely modernizing and becoming a part of the West.[59] Social Democrats, too, had to succumb to the new social demand to clarify what kind of Russia was to follow the end of the USSR, and they engaged in debates on national interests.[60] Geopolitics was quickly becoming the name of the discourse, and both Liberals and Social Democrats could have hardly participated in the public discourse without shaping what they had to say in geopolitical categories.[61]

It was in this context of Russia's rediscovery of its national inter-ests that Fukuyama's new article "The Ambiguity of National In-terest" appeared. It was published in *Nezavisimaya gazeta*, the lead-ing periodical of rising Statism.[62] In this article, Fukuyama argued against the notion of objective and geographically defined national interests, and he insisted that a country's modernization, rather than geo-political considerations, should serve as the primary foreign policy goal. He selected examples of post-Ottoman Turkey and post-war Japan and Germany to illustrate the priority of modernization over maintaining power and geopolitical spheres of interest. These exam-ples served to imply the model for Russia to follow. For example, Fukuyama presented Turkey under Kemal Ataturk as if it put mod-ernization above the interests of millions of Turkic people living in Iran, the Caucasus, and Soviet Central Asia, and he explicitly recom-mended that Russia do the same vis-à-vis ethnic Russians outside Russia's new borders. This, in his view, was the path to modernization and a "normal" nation-state.

The argument was supportive of Russia's Liberal foreign minister Andrei Kozyrev's policies and openly critical of some leading Statists, including the Russian ambassador in the United States Vladimir Lukin and presidential advisor Sergei Stankevich.[63] Fukuyama, therefore, became a direct participant in Russia's domestic debates, and he par-ticipated on the side of Russian liberal Westernizers at a time when Russia was going through the process of rediscovering its differences from the West.

Analytically, Fukuyama's argument was closely tied to the "end of history" thesis. It was based on the familiar assumptions about the superiority of Western institutions and the path of development. It had little faith in social creativity outside of the West and, yet again, explicitly recommended that the Other should strive to become the Self. To Russia, this logic meant that the country had only one choice: to follow in lockstep with the West.[64] Predictably, such assumptions and recommendations received a highly critical reaction from across the Russian intellectual spectrum.

3.1. LIBERALS

Even during the course of a changing nationalist discourse, some Russian Liberals supported the thrust of Fukuyama's new article. Having now to frame their views in categories of national interests, they continued to advocate their essentially pro-Western vision. With Fukuyama, they argued against geographically defined national interests and defended Russia's pro-Western foreign policy, which was consistent with the Western liberal view of the post–cold war world order. In agreement with Fukuyama, the Russian Westernizers also proclaimed economic and political modernization as the country's only true national interest.[65]

At the same time, Westernized Liberal elites in Russia demonstrated disarray and an inability to offer an adequate response to the challenge presented by Soviet disintegration. Like Fukuyama, they had little new to say and, at the time, were hesitant to address vital questions of Russia's historical and political role.[66] Criticism of the West was abounding, and Fukuyama seemed to do Liberals a disservice by openly embracing their arguments. As a result, Russia's Westernized Liberals often came across as defensive and shying away from important intellectual and political debates. In the meantime, the discourse was increasingly shaped by the old (National Communists and Expansionist) and new (Statist) nationalists.[67] Even more symptomatically, many Liberals began to change their original views and gravitate toward either Statism or National Communism.[68] Even Andrei Kozyrev began to emphasize things other than his previously favored "strategic partnership" with the West.

3.2. STATISTS

After the Soviet collapse, it was Statism, armed with nationalist ideas, that was able to shape the domestic debate about Russia's national interests. Challenging the argument formulated by Fukuyama in his two articles and embraced by Russian Westernizers became an important part of the Statist agenda. Statists' objections to Fukuyama's argument can be summarized along four dimensions: the content of Russia's national interests; the main factors responsible for their definition; the image of the newly emerging international system; and Russia's appropriate foreign policy strategy.

The first dimension concerned Statists' definition of national interests. Here Statists agreed with Fukuyama and domestic Liberals about the importance of building a market economy and political democracy, but they disagreed that this should be set above all other national priorities. To this school of thought, establishing market democracy was important, but should be subordinated to another, truly first priority goal: building a strong state. In the Statist perspective, a market economy made sense when it provided a state with vitality and ensured survival, but it was not the most important component of national interest. For example, for Sergei Stankevich the most important parts of national interest had to do with the country's geographic location, history, culture, ethnic composition, and political tradition. These components remained relatively stable throughout the entire national history and, therefore, "many of a country's national interests leave, in fact, almost no room for real debate."[69]

It should thus be clear why Statists believed that Russia, while working toward building new economic and political institutions and aspiring to a good relationship with the West, was also entitled to advance its own "legitimate" interests, especially in Russia's immediate periphery (which Statists commonly refer to as the *Near Abroad*, treating it as not quite falling under the foreign policy agenda). Characteristically, Stankevich rejected Fukuyama's interpretation of Turkish and German development as if these countries only followed modernization's imperatives. Instead, he argued, both countries remained highly sensitive to the fate of their people outside the countries' territories, and so should Russia.[70] For Statists, to be sensitive to ethnic Russians in the former Soviet region was crucial from the point of view of providing stability and continuity in the region; it was viewed as being perfectly compatible with the objective of modernization and had nothing to do with temptations to preserve the imperial power.[71]

Statists' image of the emerging international system was also fundamentally different from that of Fukuyama. In a move similar to that of some Western realists,[72] Russian Statists began to argue the virtues of multipolarity. Their logic was simple: the power dictates its rules, and under the conditions of a unipolar world Russia would have no independent voice in international politics.[73] Not surprisingly, Statists interpreted Fukuyama's true intentions as merely favoring the establishment of a U.S.–dominant unipolar world, which was not necessarily going to be "liberal" or "democratic" regardless of its prophets' promises.[74]

Finally, if Russia's interests were found in maintaining its traditional spheres of influence in the former Soviet area and in developing a multipolar system of international relations, its strategy should be what Statists referred to as "multi-vector foreign policy" or a foreign policy that counterbalanced relations with the West with non-Western countries. Because the unipolar world was not necessarily going to be liberal or democratic,[75] Statists recommended that Russia not succumb to Fukuyama and other unipolarity prophets but develop a counterbalance against them for its own sake.[76]

3.3. NATIONAL COMMUNISTS AND EXPANSIONISTS

National Communists and Expansionists actively participated in Russia's debate on national interests and provided their own critique of Fukuyama's argument. With Statists, they advanced the notion of objectively and geographically defined national interests,[77] but they carried this line politically further by insisting that Russian interests, almost by definition, are anti-Western. Unlike Statists, these two schools had no regard for market economy and political democracy, and their view of Russia's domestic institutions was diametrically opposed to the view Western institutions had of them. For example, their concept of a strong state included a state-controlled economy and an authoritarian regime of government. Responding to Fukuyama's points about the emergence of the post-historical cosmopolitan man and writing in the newspaper *Den'*, one prominent Expansionist argued along these lines of cultural relativism:

> There is no such thing as cosmopolitan "common human" values. It is merely a form of geopolitical ideology behind an aggressive Western culture (an Anglo-Saxon one, to be more precise) that pretends to be universal, but in reality wants to rule

the world. . . . Looking at the geopolitical development of the last two centuries, one can clearly trace the fundamental rivalry of the two continents, America and Eurasia. These two are the opposite geopolitical and geocultural poles.[78]

This makes it clear that, in addition to rejecting Fukuyama's concept of national interests, National Communists and Expansionists were extremely critical of his image of the international system and the proposed role for Russia within it. Like the Statists, they held the view that the system of liberal democracy advanced by Fukuyama was merely unipolarity in making. But where Statists formulated their view in carefully chosen words, the old Nationalists shot from the hip: "If the new manifesto [Fukuyama's article] has already emerged, it is not too long before the alien military planes will appear in the Russian sky."[79] Russia then must respond to the threat and try to avert a military confrontation by building a bi- or multipolar system. It must preserve control over Eurasia, National Communists and Expansionists argued, to balance what they viewed as aggressive intentions of the West, and the United States in particular.[80] In the words of the conservative periodical *Nash Sovremennik*, "The historical task before Russia and all other nations of the world is not to allow the twenty-first century to become the worldwide American century and a totalitarian New World Order of the United States and the world financial conspiracy to result in the end of history."[81]

3.4. SOCIAL DEMOCRATS

Social Democrats likewise rejected Fukuyama's interpretation of national interest in general and of Russia's national interest in particular, and they delivered their own critique of it. They agreed with Fukuyama and the Liberals that national interest was socially constructed rather than defined by objective factors such as a country's geographic location or ethnic composition, but disagreed with his interpretation of the process of social construction.[82] Specifically, Social Democrats advanced two ways of challenging the idea that the West serves as the model for Russia. First, they insisted that in constructing Russia's national interests, the country's relations with the whole world, not the West alone, were of key significance.[83] Second, even when Russia's interests were constructed in the process of interaction with the West, the outcome was not likely to be Russia's passive absorption of Western values and institutions. The interactions with a different culture were to serve to situate Russia internationally by borrowing some features from outside and mobilizing others domestically. As a result, Russia was likely to find its national interest defined in neither Western nor essentialist terms. For example, Alexandr Galkin and Yuri Krasin, experts at the Gorbachev Foundation, proposed the following definition of national interest:

> National interests include interests and needs of a particular socio-cultural community, satisfaction and defense of which is a necessary precondition for this community's existence and identification as a subject of history. National interests reflect the need for a national community to occupy the place in the world society that most adequately corresponds with its cultural and historical traditions and allows for implementation of its potential resources to the fullest extent.[84]

Following their earlier line of critique, Social Democrats advanced a vision of the emerging international system and Russia's role in it that is distinct from either the pro-Western Fukuyama vision or that of new and old domestic nationalists. According to Social Democrats, the world in making was the ascendance of global civil society, which, in Yuri Krasin's words, gradually created the "relevant infrastructure for establishment of a new democratic world order, which would function on the basis of network, rather than hierarchy-based principles of relations."[85] Social Democrats recommended that Russia participate fully in this process of building a more democratic world order by learning along the way, but they condemned any attempts to shape the world in accordance with a particular culture's standards. They had some harsh words saved for the proponents of the worldwide hegemony of the West and United States, in particular. For example, Boris Kapustin exclaimed in his *Sovremennost' kak predmet politicheskoi teoriyi* that, with Fukuyama, Western liberalism had been seriously degraded because its triumph became associated with the absence of alternatives, the very same freedom of choice which lies at the heart of liberal philosophy.[86] Others joined Statists and other nationalists in condemning, to use Gorbachev's words, the temptation to "play geopolitical games," particularly those existing in the West.[87]

Social Democrats' voices, however, were not always heard in a discourse that was increasingly shaped by Statists. As a particular synthesis of liberal and nationalist principles, Statist political philosophy maintains its dominant position among Russia's elites and in society. The disintegration of the USSR and the subsequent failure of Yeltsin's economic reforms marginalized Social Democrats and Liberals who are still in the process of recovering from their losses. These destabilizing domestic trends were accompanied by alarming external developments, such as the decision of NATO to expand by incorporating some former members of the Soviet bloc and the intervention of the West in Yugoslavia. These external developments further exacerbated the feelings of wounded national pride and pushed Russia toward embracing a nationalist discourse. While extreme nationalists remained relatively isolated, President Vladimir Putin skillfully exploited the society's national feelings and borrowed significantly from the foreign policy discourse of Statism.[88] This often translates into a cautious and pragmatic foreign policy. Thus, Putin supported the United States' post–September 11 intervention in Afghanistan but opposed the war with Iraq.

4. Lessons from Fukuyama's Engagement with Russia

4.1. Russia's Discursive Reception

To summarize the preceding analysis, Russia rejected Fukuyama's ideas twice, before and after the Soviet disintegration and, over time, that criticism has become stronger. Table 4.1. sums up the Russian reaction. At the late-Soviet stage, Liberals advanced arguments that were similar to that of Fukuyama, and some strata of the society were quite receptive to their arguments. However, Social Democrats, National Communists, and Expansionists rejected the "end of history" thesis and perceived it as limiting freedom in the world. After the Soviet disintegration, Fukuyama's ideas had even less ability to influence Russian discourse positively. Liberals were rapidly losing their support in the national discourse, and nationalism in its Statist form was gaining societywide influence. This influence was further solidified in the debate on national interest, during which Statists rejected Fukuyama's renewed argument as an attack on legitimate Russian interests in

TABLE 4.1.   Russia's Perception of Fukuyama's Thesis

	Fukuyama: the "end of history" or global triumph of Western-style economic and political freedom

Russia's Late-Soviet Reception	*Russia's Post-Soviet Reception*
Social Democrats: rejected, perceived as a limitation of freedom and social creativity in the world	*Social/National Democrats:* rejected, perceived as attack on Russia's attempts to re-define its interests after the cold war
Pro-Western Liberals: generally accepted	*Pro-Western Liberals:* generally accepted
National Communists/ Expansionists: rejected, perceived as an attempt to advance the West-centered world	*Statists/National Communists/Expansionists:* rejected, perceived as attack on Russia's legitimate national interests and spheres of geopolitical influence

the post–cold war era. By providing their own rationales, the Social Democratic, National Communist, and Expansionist schools supported the Statist stance.

Because of its ethnocentrism, Fukuyama's thesis could not be well received by Russia, a society with a distinct tradition and an image of its own. At first, the "end of history" idea was taken seriously and discussed in depth. However, because the idea did not offer any way of utilizing Russia's historical experience it could not be welcomed and soon produced estrangement. It was only a matter of time before the sheer arrogance of the argument strengthened Russia's nationalist and anti-Western forces.

Before the Soviet collapse, Russia was relatively open to the impact of external ideas, particularly those from the West. Although it differed from the West in its historical experience, Russia's present concerns seemed fundamentally similar to those of the West, or so it seemed to

Gorbachev when he initiated openness and New Thinking in order to emphasize the commonness of human problems and the need for their common solutions. At the time, Gorbachev and the Liberals dominated the public discourse, and the society was generally receptive to their ideas and hopeful for their successful practical implementation. This was the time to engage Russia and try to bring it into international society.

After the Soviet disintegration, the situation drastically changed in at least two important respects. First, Russia shrank considerably in geographic size and, therefore, found itself in an entirely different geopolitical situation. Second, by late 1992, the domestic economic situation was much worse, as the failure of Western-style shock therapy reform put most of the population on the verge of poverty. As a result of these two dramatic changes, Russia's present concerns departed significantly from those of the West. Russia's present preoccupation with loss of international prestige, poverty, crime, and corruption illustrates the shift in status from a country that, under Gorbachev, saw itself catching up with the world of industrialized nations to that of a more peripheral developing country.

This change led to a much more pessimistic outlook that further complicated engagement with the Westernized ethnocentric idea. So great was the disappointment with Fukuyama's idea that scholars or politicians rarely referred to it as even being worthy of serious discussion.[89] This was the time when Statism arose as the dominant political philosophy and a particular synthesis of liberal and nationalist principles. Statism increasingly shaped the political discourse and the setting of the policy agenda, whereas Social Democratic and Liberal voices were quieted considerably. At that time, perhaps even less ethnocentric ideas would have stood little chance of being taken seriously.

4.2. RUSSIA'S INSTITUTIONAL DEVELOPMENTS

If the ten years that have passed since Fukuyama's first article is sufficient time for testing his theoretical expectations, Russian modernization does not necessarily entail Westernization. In the economic realm, Russia has built not a free market model of capitalism, but rather what scholars call oligarchy.[90] Under oligarchical capitalism, the economy was largely controlled by and divided among former high-ranking party and state officials and their associates. The so-called oligarchs, or a group of extremely wealthy individuals, played the role of the new, post-Soviet nomenklatura; they influenced many key decisions of the state and successfully blocked the development of small and medium business in the country. The state only began to win some control back under President Putin.[91]

In the area of political and legal institutions, Russia developed a super-presidential system with few effective checks and balances. Under the 1993 Constitution, the president has enormous power, even greater than that of the last Russian czar. The president can dissolve the parliament and rule by decree. He can veto bills and appoint judges to the Constitutional Court. His power is sufficient for shaping the political process in the regions and controlling mass media. Some scholars referred to the system as populist, or delegative democracy, a concept developed by Guillermo O'Donnell for characterizing a situation in which elected officials have no respect for democratic institutions other than elections. In fact, the very essence of elected officials' political activity was to prevent a strongly integrated opposition from emerging.[92] Utilizing this system, Putin tightened his grip over the legislature, party building, regions, and electronic media. Given his enormous power resources and close relations with at least some of the oligarchs, he has disproportionate advantages should he run for reelection. In 1996, when Yeltsin's popularity rating was low, it was these power resources that kept him in the presidency. Again, this political system hardly qualifies as Fukuyama's image of liberal democracy.

Fukuyama's expectations were also faulty in the area of Russia's security institutions. NATO's decision to expand to the East and, especially, its 1999 military intervention in Yugoslavia affected Russia's core perceptions of the West.[93] Ten years after the Soviet break-up, Russia perceived the West as a potential threat, rather than as a friend or a strategic partner. For example, in early 2001, according to the respectable polling agency "Public Opinion," 53 percent of the Russian public viewed the United States as an "unfriendly" state.[94] Consistently, throughout 2001, about 50 percent of Russians agreed with the statement "in today's world, the United States plays a negative, rather than positive, role."[95] In 2003—in response to American military intervention in Iraq—almost 90 percent felt that the United States violated international law.[96] The Russian elite, instead of following Fukuyama's and others' recommendation to leave geopolitical considerations aside, jealously guarded what it perceived as the country's legitimate interests and vowed to compete with the West for power and resources in Eurasia.

Fukuyama's engagement with Russia and its national discourse can only be evaluated as a moral failure. Obviously, the author of the "End of History" cannot be held solely responsible for the rise of anti-Western feelings in Russia; the overall picture was far more complex. Yet Fukuyama's share of the responsibility is undeniable. His ethno-centric argument has only strengthened Russian nationalists, the very same forces it sought to defeat, and undermined the position of those sympathetic with the West. Fukuyama contributed to Russia's growing isolation because, at the time when Russia was desperately searching for self-definition, his vision gave no consideration to the country's past experience and present concerns. In fact, the advice Fukuyama had for Russia denied it the very legitimacy of a search for its own post–cold war identity. The author of the "End of History" bears respon-sibility for the fact that his argument was widely exploited by radically anti-Western forces in Russia as being the voice of the West. Fuku-yama's overall contribution to and direct participation in Russia's debates were anything but an assistance in the country's painful process of self-definition.

CHAPTER 5

CLASH OF CIVILIZATIONS?

The Reception of Samuel Huntington's Project

1. HUNTINGTON'S THESIS

1.1. THE SOCIAL AND INTELLECTUAL CONTEXT

As was the case with Fukuyama's "end of history" thesis, Huntington's vision reflected the social and political stereotypes of its time and society. It, too, was not considerate of non-Western concerns and promoted exclusively defined Western values. This made it even more difficult to engage Russia. By the time Huntington's project appeared Russia had experienced its first serious difficulties of post-Soviet reform and had its own set of concerns. This discrepancy between Western and Russian contexts laid the foundation for the negative perception of Huntington's vision.

The Western context in the early 1990s differed from that which stimulated the emergence of Fukuyama-like triumphalist ideas. The spread of new ethnic conflicts in Europe and the former Soviet Union, the perceived threat from Iraq after a successful intervention in the Persian Gulf, and the continuous environmental and demographic pressures in Asia and Africa were increasingly viewed by prominent intellectuals as signs of the Western inability to secure peace and stability throughout the world.[1] For example, in early 1994 veteran diplomat George Kennan suggested that "what we see is a highly unsettled and unstable world—a world full of squabbles, conflicts and violent encounters," which "presents a challenge for which we are poorly prepared." The solution, argued Kennan, is to be selective, rather than global, in America's international engagements and for the country to exert its most useful influence beyond its borders "primarily by example, never by precept."[2] Robert D. Kaplan, writing in the influential *Atlantic Monthly*, went even further and described the post–cold war world order as leading to criminal anarchy.[3]

Many perceived the rise of various ethnic and religious identities as especially worrisome. In 1992, Benjamin R. Barber summarized these feelings by arguing that the "world real actors" were "cultures, not countries; parts, not wholes; sects, not religions; rebellious factions and dissenting minorities" that were "at war with the traditional nation-state."[4] Ted Gurr's influential study *Minorities at Risk* identified tensions between states and ethnic groups and mapped the potential future conflicts.[5] With the growing awareness of new dangers came fear and suspicion of the non-Western world. It was within this context that Huntington's vision emerged.

Huntington was in a good position to formulate the vision of clashing civilizations as the future world order. Since his now classic *Political Order in Changing Societies,* he had concentrated on maintaining stability in modernizing Third World societies and argued against the simultaneous spread of liberal economic and political institutions in non-Western worlds.[6] Skeptical of mainstream modernization theory, he was highly critical of Fukuyama's "end of history" thesis.[7] Huntington's skeptical attitude resonated with the growing fear of global instability shared by many in Washington. No less significantly, Huntington was not a newcomer to the policy world. His lengthy career spanned not only elite universities, but influential political foundations, such as the Council on Foreign Relations. In addition to teaching and research, he was a government advisor, serving as coordinator of security planning for the National Security Council from 1977 to 1978.[8] While formulating his new idea, Huntington served as the director of the Olin Institute, a leading conservative institute on security affairs at Harvard University, and had an interest in keeping American and other Western militaries strong. The views he expressed were his own, yet were at the same time similar to those supporting the work of such an institute.[9] With the Soviet threat gone, Huntington was keenly aware of the conservative demand to map global geopolitical space around a new threat.[10]

The Russian context changed as well. Whereas the United States was preoccupied with the search for global order and stability, Russia was trying to solve its regional and domestic problems. Its domestic context had changed dramatically from the one in which Perestroika and the early post-Soviet reforms were designed. The prevailing mood of the mid-1990s was that of gradually increasing criticism of the West and its role in Russian reform and foreign policy. A number of events, including the Soviet collapse, the failure of shock therapy, and the prospect of NATO expansion toward Russia's borders, caused a shift in the mindset of the Russian people. Fairly united under Gorbachev, by the mid-1990s the society was lacking consensus over crucial policy issues. Although some social groups maintained a generally optimistic outlook, a general shift from hopeful to more pessimistic, suspicious, and even cynical attitudes toward domestic reforms and the outside world was impossible to deny. The fact that social support for liberal reforms had substantially decreased was convincingly demonstrated by the December 1993 and 1995 parliamentary elections, in which nationalist and communist forces won a majority of the votes. Intellectually, Russia moved from discussing how to join the "world civilization" to debates about its geopolitical identity and national interests.[11]

1.2. THE CONTENT OF THE THESIS

Unlike Fukuyama, Huntington was convinced that the West as a civilization was unique, not universal. With some modifications, his picture of the world was a familiar realist one that gave no acknowledgment to growing global interdependence but continued to view world development in cyclical, not progressive terms. His definition of civilizations, their motives of behavior, and external environment confirms this conclusion.

In Huntington's view, civilizations were meaningful entities, with distinctive borders between them.[12] They were cultural entities that, with the end of the cold war, were coming to replace nation-states and were differentiated from each other by history, language, tradition, and most importantly, religion.[13] In addition to the West, Huntington identified seven other civilizations—Confucian, Japanese, Islamic, Hindu,

Slavic-Orthodox, Latin American, and possibly African—each with its own set of cultural values.

Civilizations strive to protect their values and beliefs. Western values were widely known to include Western Christianity, rule of law, social pluralism, representative government, and individualism.[14] Along with Fukuyama, Huntington was firmly committed to the values of the West, but he defined them as local, rather than universal, and saw little use in trying to spread Western values outside their originating civilization. Huntington saw no reason to believe that the rest of the world would adopt Western values. On the contrary, he felt that these values were in danger, and that the West must strive for power to effectively protect itself.

Despite some blending and overlapping, civilizations essentially operated in an anarchical environment. Huntington expected that differences in power and struggles for military, economic, and institutional resources would continue to be a major driving force in world politics.[15] Since there was essentially nothing to prevent or mitigate the drive for power and domination, the West should therefore have no illusions about the world's growing interdependence. One characteristic example was the way Huntington treated international institutions' status and authority vis-à-vis the status and authority of civilizations. Through international economic institutions, he asserted, the "West promotes its economic interests and imposes on other nations the economic policies it thinks appropriate."[16] Through international security institutions, the West dominates politically.

Having based his idea on crude realist assumptions, Huntington quite logically arrived at his thesis about the clash of civilizations. The clash, according to him, occurred at the macro and micro levels. The macro level referred to the international level of the struggle between civilizations, while the micro level implied threats to states' internal stability if the fault lines between civilizations happened to cut across their territories.[17]

Since civilizations were fundamentally irreconcilable and were ready to stand up for their values, their clash represented a threat to international stability: "Violent conflicts between groups in different civilizations are the most likely and most dangerous source of escalation that could lead to global wars," warned Huntington.[18] This is especially the case since non-Western civilizations increasingly had the "desire, the will and the resources to shape the world in non-Western ways."[19] In his first article, Huntington specifically identified civilizational or cultural conflicts between Western Christianity, on the one hand, and Orthodox Christianity and Islam in Europe, on the other; worldwide conflicts occurring between Western and Islamic civilizations; between Orthodox and Muslim people in Europe and Eurasia; between Muslim and Hindu in Asia; between China and America; and between Japan and the United States.

At the domestic level, continued Huntington, the clash of civilizations may take the form of state dismemberment. He discussed the three most likely candidates ("torn countries")—Turkey, Mexico, and Russia—for such a scenario in the future because in his view those three demonstrated particularly high degrees of cultural heterogeneity. Turkey was divided between a Western and a Middle Eastern Muslim identity, Mexico between the identity of a Latin American and a North American country; and Russia between European and Eurasian orientations. Of the three, Russia was seen to be in the most dangerous position because it lacked all the necessary requirements for a successful redefinition of its civilizational identity: its political and economic elite was undecided about joining the West, it was not clear whether the public was ready for such redefinition, and the West did not seem eager to embrace Russia.[20]

In the world of cultural clashes, argued Huntington, coercing other civilizations to follow the West, as Fukuyama's thesis implicitly suggested, was a recipe for disaster. The West should take a defensive and not an expansionist posture, and be prepared to protect its values. Huntington believed that this policy could be accomplished through the greater integration of Western civilization, developing a better understanding of other civilizations and their motives, and establishing an alliance with Russia for preventing the rise of Chinese and Islamic civilizations.

Because of increasing civilization-consciousness, the West would do well to develop its greater economic and security integration, particularly between its European and North American components. Other ways of accomplishing greater integration were to limit the expansion of the military strength of Confucian and Islamic states and support those groups that were more sympathetic to Western values and interests.[21]

At the same time, the West should develop a more sophisticated understanding of other civilizations.[22] It should become more sensitive to the basic religious and philosophical assumptions underlying other civilizations and the ways in which the people of those civilizations conceive their interests. Non-Western civilizations would continue to acquire wealth, technology, and weapons, and hence the West would increasingly have to accommodate these civilizations.

Being particularly worried about the rise of Chinese and Islamic civilizations, Huntington recommended containment of the threat from the Confucian-Islamic states by promoting and maintaining cooperative relations with Russia. His book developed the point by stating that a "Russia working closely with the West would provide additional counterbalance to the Confucian-Islamic connection on global issues" and that the West should accept "Russia as the core state of Orthodoxy and a major regional power with legitimate interests in the security of its southern borders."[23]

2. RUSSIA'S RECEPTION OF HUNTINGTON'S PROJECT

Both Globalist and Nationalist voices appeared to be critical of Huntington's thesis, but their criticisms were based on fundamentally different visions of Russia's post–cold war identity and shaded in very different political tones. While Globalists attacked Huntington (and the West, to the extent that it is represented in Huntington's writing) for seeking new enemies instead of allowing for a genuine pluralism of civilizations, Nationalists were worried about Russia losing its political autonomy to the West and the West (as represented by Huntington) trying to subject Russia to its domination by exploiting its internal weaknesses.[24]

With the Soviet disintegration and changes in the country's domestic context, Russia's Globalists and Nationalists began to change as well. Globalists became less pro-Western and more sensitive to Russia's indigenous tradition. They were now framing their arguments about global interdependence in more culture-sensitive terms. Nationalists invented some new arguments in order to defend the path of Russia's autarchic development and the rebuilding of Russian influence in post-Soviet Eurasia.

2.1. GLOBALISTS, OLD AND NEW

As a result of the country's disillusionment with its economic and political reforms, the old view of Westernizers—still influential in some policy circles—became increasingly marginalized in Russian discourse. The old school, associated with politicians like Yegor Gaidar and Andrei Kozyrev, perceived the West as the only viable and progressive civilization in the world. In Fukuyama's spirit, the school argued that the main threats to Russia's "true" identity came from its economic and political backwardness, and that the country must incorporate Western institutions and join the coalition of "Western civilized nations." The old Globalists have not been active in taking on the intellectual challenge presented by Huntington's thesis.

The new and more nationally oriented Globalists shared a community-based view of the world, but disagreed with their pro-Western counterparts over universally acceptable rules. They argued that basic human rights were not the product of Western civilization alone and rejected a view of the world as divided between a "progressive" civilization and other, yet-to-become civilized nations. Instead, they viewed Russia as an independent civilization and a part of international society learning how to live in an increasingly interdependent, yet diverse world. For this school, the Russian challenge is not to copy the Western pattern but to find an appropriate culture-sensitive path to a world economic and security system.[25]

The new Globalists appreciated Huntington's interest in the cultural aspects of world politics and gave him credit for raising the issue of civilizations and their interactions within and across states.[26] Yet most of them were dissatisfied with the way Huntington defined civilizations and interpreted their interactions. Igor Pantin, the editor of *Polis* (Political Studies) expressed the dominant mode of Globalists' dissatisfaction.[27] Pantin called for a conceptual rethinking of the "clash of civilizations" thesis which would go beyond Huntington's paradigm, rather than merely criticizing him on his own ground or within his own theoretical assumptions.[28]

Huntington, Globalists argued, was never consistent in defining what he meant by civilizations,[29] but he consistently overlooked the fundamental processes of globalization cutting across nations and civilizations and analyzed civilizations as local phenomena separated from each other, with their own hardly reconcilable interests in the world. Yet world politics was characterized not only by the trend toward units' separateness and differences, but also by the trend toward units' constant interactions and integration. Globalists insisted that civilizations viewed from this perspective were not separated from each other, and one could make a strong argument in favor of an emerging world civilization, with shared norms and values across nations and local civilizations. Most Russian Globalists pointed to the fact that among civilizations interaction took place in the context of material globalization that formed the preconditions for the emerging global civilization. For example, Anatoli Utkin wrote, in response to Huntington's cultural argument,

> The evaluation of the contemporary system of international relations cannot be adequate if one considers only one side. . . . One needs to have, at least, two sides, the vertical and the horizontal. Vertically, one has to emphasize the nature of technological and economic development; and horizontally, one must take into account the social and historical experience valued by a society. The former depends on the extent of a society's participation in the world technological revolution, and the latter on the degree of this society's commitment to a historically formed style of living.[30]

Globalists also pointed to the existence of the global problems of environment, overpopulation, and economic development.[31] At this point, their argument was in part normative: the existing global problems would require, in their view, a solution based on global Reason, common to all humankind.[32] Viewed this way, local civilizations were far from being the only important players in world politics. Nor were they exclusively placed in an anarchical environment where the sole goal was power maximization and only capabilities mattered.

Being highly critical of Huntington's conflictual image of the world, Globalists were also (and unsurprisingly) critical of the substance of Huntington's argument. The image of world politics as an arena of civilizational clashes was, in their view, a flawed one. It reflected Western ethnocentrism and a fear that order in world affairs after the end of the cold war would not be possible. As Alexei Shestopal puts it, both Fukuyama's and Huntington's works, despite their differences, could be viewed as indicators of the same phenomenon of the "decrease in the level of historicity."[33] These works were representative of a Western style of historicity that was relatively limited in its scope and magnitude of time and was not capable of being applicable to non-Western worlds or civilizations. The end of the cold war signified the end of this kind of historicity[34] and taught, among other things, that acceptance of cultural pluralism should become the *modus operandi* of world politics. Not only were Huntington's analysis and prediction of future cultural conflicts along civilizational lines mistaken, they were also dangerous in and of themselves. In the words of one scholar,

> Huntington's scenarios of the future can only lead to one accomplishment, and that is to a world catastrophe. The worldwide struggle, the struggle along the "fault lines of civilizations" . . . does not make any sense. For a long time, inhabitants of the globe have been well aware . . . that a dignified future can only be accomplished by the way of reasonable and joint peoples' efforts.[35]

Globalists believed that Russia should demonstrate the other, more interactive way of thinking about civilizations in world politics, one that emphasizes the openness of various civilizations to change and restores the "spirit of genuinely worldwide history."[36] This was the road taken by Max Scheler, Jacques Maritain, Pierre Tielhard de Chardin, Sergei and Yevgeni Trubetskoi, Lev Karsavin, Pitirim Sorokin, Jawaharlal Nehru, Sun Yat-sen, Albert Schweitzer, and Nikolai Rerikh, and avoided by both Fukuyama and Huntington. It was not conflict, but cooperation, mutual influences, and mutual enrichments of religions, cultures, and nations that were of the primary concern.[37]

This argument was extended into Russia's domestic scene. Rather than viewing Russia as a "torn country," Globalists emphasized the advantages of multicultural, multiethnic, and multi-religious communities.[38] Such communities contained a wide variety of ideas and alternative options, and were particularly susceptible to social creativity.[39]

Huntington's recommendation to pursue the greater integration of the West through the tightening of immigration policies and international economic and security alliances was taken by Russia's Globalists as a call for greater Western isolation from the worldwide transformation of economic and security architectures. Instead, the West should demonstrate its willingness to solve economic (poverty), security, and ecological problems through cooperative arrangements. It was hard to imagine, Globalists argued, that in this "tight," interdependent world Western countries could provide themselves with security and prosperity without serious consideration given to the problems of non-Western countries.

In addition, Western societies faced a number of serious problems, such as those related to "ecology, the superficial cult of consumption, and the increasing oversimplification of everyday life due to the power of the mass culture."[40] World progress thus became highly dependent on "co-development" and mutual security.[41]

It should thus be clear that Huntington's advice to minimize Western interference in the affairs of other civilizations, while not being addressed directly, was not likely to be supported by most Globalists. One can speculate that the Globalist view of a world requiring world-wide cooperation and collaboration would likely voice concern about brutal violations of human rights in other civilizations.[42]

Finally, while favoring Huntington's proposal to conclude a strategic alliance between Russia and the West—after all, this was what Gorbachev and Kozyrev tried to accomplish for years (although with no particular success)—most Globalists did not see such an alliance as defending Western values against a potential threat from alien Muslim or Chinese civilizations.[43] Rather than seeing the Russo-Western alliance as one *against* "the other," they proposed to treat it as one *for* accomplishing mutually acceptable security and economic goals. Globalists were also open to the development of various political and economic arrangements with Russia's southern and eastern neighbors, although not at the expense of Russia's relations with the West.[44] In the words of senior foreign affairs official Alexei Podtserob,

> In contrast to many other European countries, Russia relates to and even absorbs part of the Islamic east and, for that reason, it is capable of playing an important role in developing mutual understanding between European and Muslim civilizations (which, of course, does not imply our country's "turning its back" to the West). Because of its geographic location, as well as its historical development, Russia seems destined to serve as a bridge between various cultural areas—West-European, Islamic, Indian, and Far Eastern—which should further enrich Russia's civilization and provide additional impulses for its development.[45]

The "bridge" notion resulted from Russia's historical concern with stability of its borders and is widely popular among the country's geopolitical thinkers. It became especially prominent in political philosophy of Eurasianism, a Russian emigree movement that emerged during the

1920s and argued for the historical and cultural unity of a diverse Euro-Asian population.[46] In application to Huntington's argument, playing the role of a bridge means working together with representatives of other cultures, rather than viewing their values in conflicting terms. To Russia's Globalist thinkers, Huntington's fears that the values of Islamic or other civilizations were "incommensurable" with Western values of democracy and market economy were not justified. In today's world, no civilization, despite culturally specific characteristics, could escape being involved in global processes of economic and political modernization. Even Islam, perhaps the most rigid religion of all, slowly yielded itself to the imperatives of modernization, and the appearance of Islamic fundamentalism could also be viewed as an attempt by the Islamic civilization to adjust to, rather than escape from, modernity.[47]

2.2. NATIONALISTS

However paradoxical it may sound, on the level of assumptions and definitions, Russian Nationalist-minded intellectuals were more or less in agreement with Huntington and his security doctrine.[48] They also shared a significant part of Huntington's argument about the clash of civilizations,[49] although they vehemently rejected most of his practical implications. Nationalist schools objected that, in practical terms, the argument sought to deprive Russia of its own voice in world affairs by making it dependent on the West. The disagreement between Nationalists and Huntington can be viewed as a difference of opinion within the same paradigm.

Russian Nationalists could be divided into two camps, defensive and aggressive.[50] Both accepted that Russia's political security was the strongest motivation in the unfavorable international environment of the post–cold war era, but they had opposing views about the most effective way of achieving it. The aggressive Nationalist posture was advocated by National Communists and Eurasianists, who were prepared to carry out some offensive military actions and who defended expansion of Russia's territory toward the former Soviet borders or even beyond it. Defensive nationalism, as advocated by Statists, was more status quo oriented and relied on means other than offensive action for defending Russia's national interests.

While Nationalist voices were not always in agreement with the way Huntington defined civilizations, they did share his skepticism regarding the possibility of forming a universal civilization. Like Huntington, they emphasized the paramount significance of local civilizations in world politics: "On the whole, it is impossible to disagree with [Huntington] that critics of the civilizations paradigm did not manage to come up with anything better for explaining what is going on in the world," wrote Statist Sergei Samuilov.[51]

Not only did Nationalists share Huntington's view that local civilizations were the key units in world politics, they also agreed with his views on the goals of civilizations, their environment, and their way of interacting with each other. To them, civilizations fought for "prestige and resources" (Tsymburski),[52] "economic, cultural, and political identity" (Karagodin),[53] or "economic capabilities" (Samuilov),[54] and they did so in an environment that was dramatically different from the one depicted by Globalists. Instead of the trends of globalization and interdependence emphasized by Globalists, Nationalists made clear their view that arguments about global coordination and the formation of a universal civilization were premature at best and had a little to do with reality.[55]

In sharing Huntington's basic assumptions, Russian Nationalists were generally supportive of his argument. This was particularly true when applying the "clash of civilizations" thesis to world politics. The thesis was typically supported with some additional examples.[56] At the same time, because not all Nationalists shared Huntington's definition of local civilizations some of them identified an inconsistency in his argument and demonstrated that Huntington's actual goal was to counterpose the West to all non-Western civilizations, rather than to warn about the clash of various civilizations among each other. In other words, Huntington's major concern was the "West against the rest,"[57] and this was the reason he overlooked a number of important potential inter-civilization conflicts, for example, between Russia and China, or within China itself (the problem of Tibet), or between India and Pakistan, but instead postulated an informal Muslim-Chinese bloc.[58] Huntington, while raising an important problem, could thus be seen as ideologically biased and inconsistent in delivering his own argument. To this camp of Huntington's critics, the "clash of civilizations" thesis did represent the substance of world politics, but not in the way Huntington depicted it.

The application of the "clash" thesis to the analysis of domestic, intra-state politics was also supported by Nationalist theorists only in its general form and in application to some countries other than Russia.[59] When it came to the analysis of Russia's future, however, Nationalists presented a drastically different picture. For most of them, Russia was not a "torn" country, divided between East and West, as Huntington viewed it. Rather, Russia was Eurasia, an example of a local civilization, with a special geopolitical role as a bridge between Europe and Asia. As Samuilov argued,

> One cannot agree with Huntington that Russia is a Slav-Orthodox civilization. Historically the Slav-Orthodox component was very significant for Russia's civilization, but cannot be considered equal to it. The formation of the Moscow Rus' was based upon the Eurasianist alternative, which took the upper hand in historical polemics with the pro-Western one, associated with the Great Lithuanian Princedom. Since the time of the Moscow Rus', Russia has been built as a multi-ethnic, mainly Slav-Turkish-Ugro-Finn state and later as a multi-religious (Orthodoxy, Islam, Buddhism, Catholicism, Lutheranism, Judaism, etc.) one.[60]

Thus, Russia, unlike the West, managed to combine Orthodox Christian Europe and the Turkish-Muslim East for a common good. It was this Eurasian way that Nationalists view as a natural for Russia, and therefore what awaited Russia in the near future was ethnocultural diversity and collaboration within a unified civilization, not a clash.[61]

Unlike Globalists, Nationalist intellectuals sought to respond to Huntington's policy recommendations within the same conflict paradigm.[62] In response to Huntington's call for greater integration of the West to counter the coming dangers, they argued in favor of the greater integration of Russia's civilization and its sphere of influence, the former Soviet region.[63] They were generally supportive of Huntington's claim that the West should minimize its interference with the affairs of other civilizations, because that way Russia's civilization would face less resistance on the path to its greater integration. Finally, they vehemently opposed the idea of a Russo-Western alliance for the purpose of counterbalancing any perceived threat from Islamic or Chinese civilizations. Statist Vadim Tsymburski summarized the objections of the Russia's Nationalist-minded intellectual community:

> The alliance between Russia and the West against the "Muslim-Confucian bloc" might be an extremely dangerous one. . . . The

Chinese and Islamic cards have been played against us for too long a time, and we cannot allow the West to direct the aggressive energy of other non-Western civilizations against the so-called "Russo-Orthodox civilization."[64]

National Communists and Eurasianists, while generally sharing the line of critique advanced by Nationalists of Statist orientation, took it a step further. In response to Huntington, they advanced a highly essentialist vision of Russia as an anti-Western Eurasian imperial power that was tightly integrated, dominant in the former Soviet regions, and eventually rising as a major counterpole to American hegemony. Whereas Statists were defensive and pragmatic in their nationalism and, in some areas, open to cooperation with the West, National Communists and Eurasianists were open in their anti-Western animosity and wanted to have practically no relations with what they referred to as the Atlanticist geopolitical bloc.[65] By accepting Huntington's categories and diagnosis, aggressive Nationalists openly announced that the essence of Russia's geopolitical strategy was, in words of Eurasianist Alexei Mitrofanov, a former member of the State Duma and the Chairman of the Duma's Committee on Geopolitics, to transform Eurasia into a unified continental bloc.[66] They believed that Eurasia was the last pillar of world stability, and Russia must contribute to the maintenance of geopolitical equilibrium by counterbalancing Western and other civilizations.[67]

Russia's Globalists and Nationalists were thus critical of Huntington's image of world politics, but in a different way. Globalists were highly critical of Huntington's assumptions as well as the content and practical prescriptions of his thesis. Nationalists, too, were highly critical of the thesis' practical implications, but found themselves in general agreement regarding the substance and the main assumption of the "clash of civilizations."

3. RUSSIAN ALTERNATIVES TO HUNTINGTON

3.1. GLOBALISTS

Globalists' disagreement with Huntington's security-seeking program was not limited to simply another vision of Russia's interests in the post–cold war world. Globalists contested the very picture of the world as a place where fundamentally different civilizations clash. To compensate for the weaknesses of Huntington's paradigm, a different paradigm of world politics was pursued, one that was relevant for both analysis and practice. According to the alternative paradigm, the post–cold war world represented a place where different civilizations not only coexisted peacefully, but where they would engage in a constructive dialogue, a mutually productive effort to make this world a better place to live.[68] For Russian Globalists it was, therefore, precisely epistemological questions that were at the heart of the debate in Huntington's security program: "It is clear as never before, they argued, that it is an epistemological standpoint that defines the system of our views and the analysis of future of our country and of the world as a whole."[69]

The core assumption of the Globalist argument was that the pluralism of civilizations was not an obstacle to efforts to stabilize international order; on the contrary, it was only such diversity that could provide the world with a necessary equilibrium. And even if and when institutions of the market economy and political democracy eventually became accepted throughout the world, this still would not mean unification and homogeneity—cultural factors would never allow this to happen. The approach was a dialectical one, because the reverse should also be true: all attempts to impose worldwide unification in the name of stability and democracy were likely to collapse and, against expectations, to provoke conflicts and instability.[70] The "pluralist paradigm,"[71] therefore, was imperative for maintaining world order.

In order to sustain the pluralist order, Globalists proposed the strengthening of the United Nations as a prototype for future world government, with the General Assembly as parliament, the Security Council as executive body, and the Secretary General as president of the world state. For example, former Gorbachev advisor Georgi Shakhnazarov argued that such a structure was necessary in order to address urgent global problems, such as growing militarism, depletion of world resources, overpopulation, and environmental degradation, and to mitigate the selfish impulses of local civilizations. In his view, the Huntington-proposed restructuring of the Security Council in accordance with the civilizational representation would mean throwing away all the positive potential of the United Nations and returning to the times of isolation and the rule of crude force in world politics. Instead, he proposed a piecemeal development of the United Nations by gradually incorporating in the Security Council those states that have acquired indisputable world influence, including Germany, Japan, and possibly even India, Brazil, and other states.[72]

The "pluralist paradigm" was counterposed to the monist one, associated with the Hegelian-Marxian tradition of viewing history as a gradual linear process, a product of "historical people" or "superior classes":[73]

> [As compared with the monist paradigm,] the pluralist paradigm approaches history with more trust and less control. It respects the right of history for experiments that were not pre-designed by the plans of the "world spirit" or of the "demon of progress," presumably possessing absolute knowledge and power.[74]

This paradigm, Globalists argue, was far from alien to Russian culture and could be traced back to Alexandr Pushkin and Fyodor Dostoyevski, both of whom associated Russia with what Dostoyevski labeled the "responsiveness to the whole world" (*vsemirnaya otzyvchivost'*) as well as to Russian religious philosophy.[75]

This way of seeing the outside world led Russian Globalists to conclude that the optimal strategy for Russia is to seek adjustment to, rather than isolation from, the external world. Since the pluralism of civilizations was becoming the *modus operandi* of the post–cold war world, Russia should not exaggerate the danger of losing its cultural specificity. The fact of the matter was that this specificity could only be maintained by successful modernization and adaptation to an open, post-industrial global society. As Russian Globalist ex-foreign minister Kozyrev put it in a slightly different context, "It is only through the policy of openness to the outside world that Russia's unique historic role can be fully revealed and implemented."[76]

Eurasia, too, was viewed by Globalists as an arena for the pursuit of cooperation in a multicultural region. The region was not doomed to be a battlefield for conflict between different civilizations, but instead must become a place where various cultures live side by side and practice a mutually fertile dialogue and cooperative economic and security arrangements. Eurasia served and should continue to serve as a cultural entity capable of bridging and pacifying European and Asian civilizations, as well as maintaining a delicate equilibrium among a wide variety of ethnic groups.[77]

In order to preserve such a special role for Eurasia, Globalists argued that Russia ought to encourage its openness to various influences from the West, the East, and the South, rather than building the region as autarchic and Russia-dominant. For example, in his *Eurasian Strategy for Russia,* Sergei Rogov proposed that Russia focus on building the "communicational bridge" that would link Eurasia's southern, western, and eastern peripheries through the development of ground, air, and electronic transportation routes crossing Russia's and the ex-Soviet states' territory. The economic rationale of such a design was, in Rogov's view, to shorten the length of communication networks that link Europe and East Asia, which would be mutually beneficial for all the participants involved.[78] At the same time, Eurasia would be preserved as an open and yet economically and politically stable region.[79] Similar cooperative economic and security arrangements were proposed in Russia's bilateral relations with other Eurasian countries (China, Iran, and India), as well as with countries to the west.[80]

3.2. NATIONALISTS

In their turn, Russian Nationalists argue that it was regional isolation or regionalization, not globalization or transnationalization that represented the dominant trend of the post–cold war era.[81] Nationalist writers analyzed civilizations in a way that was methodologically more similar to Huntington's "Clash of Civilizations" than it was to Russian Globalists. Consciously or not, they reproduced all of Huntington's main assumptions about civilizations' status, goals, environment, and ways of interacting. For this reason, I suggest that the Nationalist alternative to Huntington's thesis be viewed as an alternative within, rather than beyond Huntington's paradigm. This is ironic, because Huntington was perceived by Russian Nationalists with a greater degree of animosity than by his Globalist critics.[82]

Unlike Globalists, Russian Nationalist analysts relied heavily on geopolitical theories, specifically Russia's theories of Eurasianism and Arnold Toynbee's analysis of civilizations. The former was helpful in justifying a sense of meaningfulness and uniqueness of Russia's culture as Eurasian rather than European in its character, along with the task of resisting Western influences.[83] Toynbee's analysis was used to demonstrate that Russia was a separate, full-fledged civilization[84] and, even more importantly, to explain the dynamic relationships between civilizations and barbarism, or the "external proletariat" as it was labeled by Toynbee. In the minds of some Nationalist theorists, it was this external proletariat that represented a threat to the West and to Russia, not other civilizations as Huntington argued.[85]

Russia therefore could not afford to hold naïve illusions of integration in the world economy. Instead, Nationalists recommended that it pursue a strategy of integration and moderate isolation from the world[86] in order to maintain the independence of its own civilization by protecting itself from the pressures of the external proletariat (mainly from the Third World), and by avoiding an involvement in contemporary conflicts of civilizations caused by alliances with the West. Russia was temporarily weak, and it was in the Western interest to get it involved in military confrontations with the Muslim world or China in order to redirect the flows of the external proletariat away from the West or to complete a world re-division and form a new world order at the expense of Russia.[87] Instead of allying with the West, Russia should pursue a strategy of inner concentration and of the restoration of its traditional geopolitical space within the territory of the former Soviet Union.

An example of such a strategy was offered in the writings of Vadim Tsymburski, a prominent Statist who developed his ideas in polemics with Huntington's thesis. Like Russian Globalists, Tsymburski proposed a project of rebuilding Eurasia through the development of transportation networks linking Russia to the West, on the one hand, and to Asia, on the other. Unlike Globalists, however, his primary concern was to rebuild Russia's power and influence in the region by reducing rather than increasing its dependency on transportation routes. To accomplish this, Tsymburski proposed that Russia build three such routes, not just one, by purposefully linking itself to China, on the one hand, and to Iran, on the other. Such a geoeconomic triangle would provide Russia with the required space for political maneuvering and, incidentally, would create the conditions for developing a Russia-China-Iran connection in order to protect the region from any potential interference by "fourth" countries.[88]

National Communists and Eurasianists proposed a more extreme response to Huntington's and other Western geopolitical theories, the essence of which was in the territorial integration of the western, eastern, and southern parts of Eurasia and pitting them against the United States. In Europe, it was proposed that Russia urgently integrate those areas (first and foremost, Belarus and Serbia) that were ready to be a part of "Greater Eurasia," work on involving others (Ukraine, Moldova, and some Central European states) in its sphere of influence, and cooperate with those states where there was the potential of increasing differences with the United States.

Ever since the Soviet disintegration, some Nationalist geopoliticians have argued for turning the Europe "from Atlantic Ocean to the Ural Mountains" (once advocated by General De Gaulle) into the Europe "from the Atlantic Ocean to Vladivostok." According to this view, in order for the world to be stabilized Europe must be liberated from American hegemony and united with Russia.[89] Germany and France were often seen as states with the potential to play a critical role in liberating the western part of the European continent from U.S. influence. For example, Alexei Mitrofanov argued that Germany, as an economic powerhouse in Europe, was crucial to Russia; Germany was also deprived of nuclear capabilities and might be interested in establishing a security alliance with Russia for the sake of reducing U.S. influence in Eurasia.[90] Alexandr Dugin defended a proposed Russian alliance with Germany and France, justifying it as a grouping of "land-based powers" against "sea-based powers," such as the United States and Great Britain.[91]

National Communists and Eurasianists also recommended that Russia find reliable partners in the east and the south. In the words of Russian communist leader Gennadi Zyuganov, "It is among the eastern nations that Soviet Russia has found its allies to confront the pressures and blackmail from the West."[92] The Russo-Chinese partnership was sometimes attributed a particular significance both in terms of their physical capabilities and as an alternative locus for anti-American sentiments.[93] Russia's relations with neighboring Muslim countries were likewise viewed in the light of potential resistance to U.S. influences. Iran, for example, was interested in reducing U.S. economic influence in the region while advancing its own. In addition, Muslim values were viewed as being similar to those of Russia, particularly when it comes to the roles of the state, family, and society. The fact that the West has been traditionally suspicious of the Muslim world should, in the Nationalists' minds, drive Islamic neighbors of Russia into an anti-American geopolitical alliance.[94] Finally, an important role was sometimes attributed to India—a Russia-India axis was meant to secure the so-called "vertical" dimension of Eurasia in addition to building the "horizontal" Russia-Siberia-China axis.[95] In sum, Russia must combine tactics of balance and expansion to build a strategic alliance against the U.S. threat and maintain a multipolar world.

4. LESSONS FROM HUNTINGTON'S ENGAGEMENT WITH RUSSIA

4.1. RUSSIA'S DISCURSIVE RECEPTION

Huntington's "clash of civilizations" vision met a highly critical reaction from the Russian intellectual audience. The debate with Huntington and between Russian Globalists and Nationalists took place after the Soviet break-up and in the context of Russia's self-definition as a new Eurasian power. Both Globalists and Nationalists perceived Huntington's vision as destabilizing for both Eurasia and the world. Globalists argued that the project was undermining the genuine pluralism or diversity of civilizations and building an unnecessary image of enemies out of the potentially cooperative Chinese and Muslim cultures. Nationalists, with both defensive and aggressive postures, perceived the "clash of civilizations" thesis as exploitative of Russia's internal weakness and potentially undermining its political autonomy. In their view, Russia must turn to Asian and Muslim cultures for security purposes, rather than relying exclusively on the West. (These perceptions are summarized in table 5.1.)

Russia's perception of Huntington's thesis was cultural, rather than merely political. As was the case with Fukuyama, the author of the "Clash of Civilizations" failed to appreciate Russia's distinct historical tradition and present concerns. Driven by an ethnocentric desire to explain the complexity of the entire post–cold war world through some centuries-old religious divisions, Huntington demonstrated minimal sensitivity toward Russia's Eurasian identity. For years, Russia's intellectuals and politicians of both Globalist and Nationalist orientation had been articulating the point that their country, by the virtue of its borderland location, was destined to serve as a bridge between Europe and Asia. The "bridge" notion resulted from Russia's historical concern with the stability of its borders and has always lain at the heart of the country's geopolitical thinking.

The same concerns about security and borders, albeit in the new post-Soviet geopolitical situation, give Eurasianism a new life in today's

TABLE 5.1.   Russia's Perception of Huntington's Thesis

Huntington: the "clash of civilizations" that in Eurasia can be prevented by Russia's alliance with the West against China and the Muslim world

Russia's Globalists	*Russia's Nationalists*
Huntington's vision: rejected, perceived as a limitation to dialogue and cooperation among civilizations that may lead to destabilization in Eurasia	*Huntington's vision:* rejected, perceived as an attempt to split Eurasia and to further weaken Russia by pushing it into a war against China and the Muslim world
The alternative vision: intercivilizational cooperation, "pluralism," and the "unity in diversity"	*The alternative vision:* Isolation of local civilizations, with potential conflict among them
The recommended policies: The West should encourage the integration of other civilizations into the world community	*The recommended policies:* Russia should pursue the greater integration of its own civilization
Russia should cooperate with the West, but not for the purpose of balancing against other civilizations	Russia should balance against all other civilizations for the purpose of maintaining its autonomy in world affairs

Russia. Many contemporary Russian thinkers, while differing in some key respects, view Russia as the Heartland, or the state responsible for organizing the post-Soviet disorder. Some Russian intellectuals propose transnational economic projects to secure peace in the region. Others put their faith into a Eurasian collective security system that would involve China, Europe, India, Iran, Russia, and the United States as key participants. Still others emphasize development of

Russia's bilateral relations with its key regional neighbors, such as China and Iran.[96] But all agree that Russia cannot merely isolate itself in the manner of the United States, which is separated from Europe and Asia by thousands of miles of ocean. Russia is destined to live with the religious, ethnic, and linguistic differences of the region. Nationalists and Globalists viewed such a location as a threat or as an opportunity, respectively, but both were keenly aware of Russia's Eurasian cultural distinctness.

Huntington also failed to appreciate sufficiently Russia's post-1991 political and cultural concerns. Ever since Sergei Stankevich, then President Yeltsin's advisor, formulated Russia's Eurasian "mission"[97] by borrowing the theme from hard-line Nationalists, Russia's mainstream discourse has moved to reflection on appropriate ways of "organizing" Eurasia economically and politically, as well as on the country's cultural identification vis-à-vis its immediate European and Asian neighbors. The debate in Russia is not whether to isolate itself from Eurasia by aligning with the West, but how to efficiently develop relations with major southern neighbors, including the Central Asian republics, China, and Iran.

4.2. Russia's Institutional Development

Russia's institutional development, like its discourse, did not confirm Huntington's expectations. For Russia, the "clash of civilizations" thesis implied two things. First, as the core state of Orthodox civilization, Russia was expected to face a major threat from the Confucian-Islamic states, which were to seriously compromise its national security.[98] Second, being culturally split between European and Eurasian orientations domestically, Russia was not likely to preserve its national cohesion and would be expected to disintegrate. Contrary to these expectations, however, Russia has not moved closer to the scenario of cultural conflicts either with its neighbors or within its own territory. Despite the absence of a formal alliance with the West, Russia's relations with its southern and eastern neighbors has remained stable and, in a number of areas, grown stronger. In addition, with the exception of Chechnya, Russia is not facing serious challenges to its territorial integrity.

Regionally, Russia has moved toward consolidation of its Eurasian identity. In 1995, the replacement of pro-Western foreign minister Kozyrev with a more nationalist-minded Primakov began the era of

Russia's rapprochement with the East. President Putin has been actively building upon Primakov's accomplishments. In addition to traveling to Europe, Putin visited some key Eurasian states. In the wake of an Asia-Pacific economic summit, he announced, "Russia has always been aware of its Eurasian identity" and now "should decisively turn to the Asia-Pacific region."[99] Selecting some expert proposals,[100] he also outlined how Russia's unique intermediate location between Asia, Europe, and the United States might contribute to the economic development and political stability of the region. The international agreements he has signed point to the changed quality of Russia's relations in the region.[101]

Domestically, Russia's development also does not fit Huntington's vision, despite the great challenge presented by the country's ethnic diversity.[102] Rather than giving ethnic Russians "a leading role" as some have proposed,[103] Russia's leaders have been consistently promoting what some political commentators interpreted as "hybrid, an eclectic mixture of values," while others viewed it as a Eurasian vision of multicultural federalism.[104] Most important in this respect was Presidential Decree No. 909 issued in June 1996 to approve the concept of a state nationalities policy for the Russian Federation and stating the goal of a multiethnic Russia to ensure "the cultural self-preservation and further development of national traditions and cooperation of Slavic, Turkic, Caucasian, Finno-Ugric, Mongolian and other peoples of Russia within the framework of Eurasian national-cultural space."[105] The decree came close to Spain's model of offering autonomy to all interested constituent units by encouraging them to enter into power-sharing agreements with the center, rather than pursuing a path of complete independence. By March 1999, about fifty of Russia's eighty-nine constituent units had successfully negotiated various degrees of privileged status, with "work in progress" on a dozen or more.

The Eurasian multicultural federalism was not without problems. Some scholars argued that the asymmetrical federalism's unequal and inconsistent agreements would lead to the enrichment of some exploitative local elites at the expense of Russia's people and even to the danger of political secessionism.[106] It is in response to these dangers that Putin later moved to regularize federal policies and strengthen central control. In May 2000, he issued an important decree that divided Russia into seven federal districts, each with a plenipotentiary representative appointed directly by the president. Putin also wanted to obtain the power to dismiss executive, legislative, and local government officials throughout the Federation. This centralization drive, while responding to serious problems, can only be successful if conducted within a coherent legal framework.[107] Developing legal arrangements through power-sharing agreements with the center, rather than following the more traditional imperial pattern of centralization, seems the only reasonable way to address the problem. As one expert wrote,

> In the present period of social flux, in which identities are especially fluid, a federation needs to be flexible enough to devolve powers to smaller, autonomous national groupings. It could well be that working towards such a democratic federalism . . . may provide the best counterweight to the perils of both Russian and minority nationalism.[108]

When the cultural rights of autonomous regions are clearly articulated and differentiated, the model of Russia's multicultural federalism might begin to function more successfully.[109] A solution can come not from fearing multicultural federalism, as Huntington does, or trying to suppress local aspirations of a culturally and geographically diverse territory, but rather from legally consistent efforts to accommodate such aspirations.

Chechnya has been a notorious example of a violent deviation from the model of multicultural federalism. Huntington has used this case to argue yet again in favor of Russia's abandonment of its project of multicultural federalism. In his words,

> The age of multicivilizational empires is over, and Russia will be able to maintain its rule over Chechnya only at unsustainable costs. The next leader of Russia would do well to emulate Mustafa Kemal Ataturk's realism about the lost Turkish empire and espouse a Russian-only Russia rather than pursue the obsolete dream of a multiethnic, multicivilizational empire.[110]

Yet the case of Chechnya's conflict with Russia represents an exception, rather than a rule. It is not easily generalized and can hardly be explained satisfactorily by civilizational differences across Orthodox Christianity and Islam. A key reason for Chechnya's fight for independence from Russia, one overlooked by Huntington, is the republic's historical, rather than religious, dimension. For more than one hundred years, Chechens have been resisting assaults from Russian and Soviet rulers, and the fight against the "northern neighbor" became an important aspect of their identity. Other Muslim republics such as Dagestan, Ossetia, Tatarstan, and Bashkortostan were incorporated into the empire earlier and did not go through a similar experience. As a result, these republics do not separate themselves psychologically from Russia to the extent that Chechnya does. For example, the president of the Republic of Northern Ossetia, Alexandr Dzasokhov, responding to the statements of some European officials about the Caucasus region, spoke against the "obvious attempts to drive a wedge between the two Russias, the Orthodox and the Muslim" and emphasized the "Eurasian essence" of Russia.[111]

Despite Huntington's efforts to appear neutral and establish distance between his argument and political practice, he did in fact participate in a political and discursive process in a very direct manner. The fact that the West constantly figured either as a friend, as a cold and indifferent observer, or as a foe in Russia's intellectual and political debates suggests that Huntington was fundamentally wrong about defining civilizations in mutually exclusive terms. If anything, the analysis of Russia's foreign policy debates teaches us that civilizations are mutual learners quite capable of constructive interaction and cooperation rather than war-prone, mutually threatening entities. Russia's political identity is far from fixed, and there is hardly anything inherently predetermined about how Russia will see itself and will act in world politics. What type of identity Russia will eventually choose is still an open question, and the "clash of civilizations" argument did participate in shaping Russia's choice. If, for example, global trends toward peace and cooperation prevail, Russia is more likely to follow a path of accommodation and cooperation and to be influenced by the Globalist ideals of collective security. However, if surrounded by conflictual ideas à la the "clash of civilizations" thesis, Russia may become more susceptible to the rhetoric of the extreme Nationalists and eventually adopt either an expansionist or isolationist foreign policy. The ideas that are less influential today may become more influential tomorrow; what is marginal today may become a dominant mode of thinking in the future.[112]

Like Fukuyama, Huntington bears responsibility for how his ideas are perceived in the world. To many Russian intellectuals, Huntington, along with other leading U.S. scholars and foreign policy experts, represented *the* West (or a significant part of it), thereby offering the Russian audience the answers about the future of world politics that it sought to acquire. Fortunately or unfortunately, Huntington did indeed take sides and so made some policy outcomes more likely than others. In particular, Huntington's argument strengthened the discourse of Russia's Nationalists by offering them a simplistic and seemingly plausible picture of future world conflicts, one that resonated well with their essentially pessimistic view of world politics. The bitter irony is that, contrary to his own efforts, Huntington's contribution to making the West stronger and more secure boiled down to strengthening those who were frequently hostile and assertive in conceiving Russia's relations with the democratic West.[113] As one Russian Globalist put it, "Huntington's notion of Russia as the core state of Orthodoxy . . . may be more easily manipulated by the states and groups pursuing extremist policies, which would ultimately set Russia on a collision course with both the West and Islam."[114]

More generally, our analysis bolsters the conclusion that, in an increasingly globalized world, as scholars we ought to be particularly aware of the moral contexts in which our theories are placed and of the moral implications these theories have for the human world we study. From this perspective, Huntington's thesis contributed to trends toward further isolationism and hostility, rather than to promoting pluralism and mutual understanding in international relations. Formulated in the realist spirit, the thesis was all too often resented by scholars in the West and beyond. Along with other realist approaches, it was justifiably perceived as primarily Western and parochial in its orientations, displaying a lack of empathetic understanding of other cultures, and looking at the world primarily from the vantage point of the West.[115] It was thus unable to forward a truly global international scholarship, a scholarship concerned with the moral choices confronting contemporary international relations.

THE WORLD ORDER
AFTER SEPTEMBER 11

1. RUSSIA AND AMERICAN WORLD ORDER PROJECTS

Ideas of world order can make important contributions to how local cultures and civilizations perceive each other. By impacting upon domestic societies, ideas can serve as both facilitators and impediments to world peace and prosperity. In order to be successfully incorporated, an idea must be filtered through the channels of a local culture's leadership, political elite, and larger society. However, since ideas are never socially neutral and are generated out of a specific culture, they are often perceived differently and even negatively in different social contexts. Such negative perceptions can be especially severe when both ideas and the local society are structured in ethnocentric or culturally exclusive ways.

Fukuyama's "end of history" thesis implied that the rest of the world must modernize in the manner of Western societies. However, "the rest of the world" did not necessarily perceive the idea as liberating or beneficial. Russia is a case in point.

Russia wrestled with Fukuyama's ideas twice, both before and after the Soviet disintegration. Before the disintegration, the thesis was perceived as either suppressing alternative modes of modernization (Social Democrats) or imposing on Russia an imperialist ideology that is morally corrupt and politically dangerous (National Communists and

Eurasianists). Only early Russian Liberals advanced arguments that were quite similar to those of Fukuyama. After the Soviet collapse, the Liberals found themselves in a hegemonic position and tried to pursue policies that were loosely consistent with the "end of history" worldview. However, the Liberal discourse was challenged by the rising school of Statism, which perceived Fukuyama's project as an attack on Russia's legitimate national interests. Liberals could not command sufficient social support, and the debate on Russian national interests further solidified the influence of Statists and marginalized Social Democrats, on the one hand, and extreme Nationalists, on the other. The rise of Statism also prepared the ground for the eventual replacement of Russia's pro-Liberal foreign minister Andrei Kozyrev with leading Statist Yevgeni Primakov.

In a similar manner, Russia negatively perceived and eventually rejected Huntington's "clash of civilizations" project. Like Fukuyama, Huntington conceived Western values in exclusive and essentialist terms. Huntington hoped to convince Russians that, in light of a perceived threat from the Confucian-Islamic states, they would be better off joining an alliance with the West. Huntington's project backfired.

Both Globalists and Nationalists attacked Huntington's project as destabilizing Eurasia and the world. Globalists perceived the project as undermining the genuine pluralism or diversity of civilizations and unnecessarily creating an image of enemies. Nationalists perceived the thesis as exploitative of Russia's internal weakness as well as potentially undermining of its political autonomy. In their view, Russia must turn to Asian and Muslim cultures for security purposes, rather than relying exclusively on the West. (These perceptions are summarized in table 6.1.)

Why did Russia perceive negatively and eventually reject Fukuyama's and Huntington's projects? Further, why did these two American ideas contribute to the discourse of isolation and hostility in Russia? Both the "end of history" and the "clash of civilizations" shared assumptions of the West's superiority and were framed in culturally exclusive terms. Despite some notable differences, Fukuyama and Huntington were both blind to Russia's distinct historical tradition and present-day concerns. Fukuyama failed to seriously consider that every country—and certainly one that is as large and old as Russia—would modernize in its own way, in accordance with its own social memory and at a socially appropriate pace. Similarly, Huntington

TABLE 6.I.   Western Visions of Future World Order and Russian
Perceptions of Them

Western Visions of Future World Order	Globalist and Nationalist Perceptions in Russia
Fukuyama: the "end of history" or global triumph of Western-style economic and political freedom	*Globalists:* Fukuyama argument is a limitation of freedom and social creativity
	Nationalists: Fukuyama argument is a justification of a global West-centered dictatorship
Huntington: the "clash of civilizations" that in Eurasia can be prevented by Russia's alliance with the West against China and the Muslim world	*Globalists:* Huntington thesis is a limitation on dialogue and cooperation among civilizations that may lead to destabilization in Eurasia
	Nationalists: Huntington thesis is an attempt to split Eurasia and to further weaken Russia by pushing it into a war against China and the Muslim world

"forgot" about Russia's distinct Eurasian identity and geographic location. The two scholars failed to appreciate the fact that Russia's interests are found both in Europe *and* Asia, and that the country is fated
to live side by side and get along with the religious, ethnic, and linguistic diversity of the region. The Russian intellectual and political
community carefully discussed both American ideas, but because of
these ideas' ethnocentric nature, they were bound to be perceived as
unsuitable and thus rejected in the Russian cultural context.

2. RUSSIA AND THE WORLD ORDER AFTER SEPTEMBER 11

President Vladimir Putin's decision to support the United States in the post–September 11 struggle against terrorism led to an important change in the Russian discourse. Although Putin began his term as a Nationalist of Statist orientation, building on Primakov's philosophy of multi-polarity, he became increasingly viewed as a Globalist and even a pro-American Liberal. In reality, however, the post-September Putin is neither a pro-Western Liberal, nor a Statist-Primakovite. The new international political circumstances pushed the president to adopt the new foreign policy philosophy of Pragmatism. Pragmatism is a synthesis of ideas that goes beyond the old-style Statism and Westernism, and is tailored to respond to new international realities. As a result of his political move, Putin was conditionally supported by Globalists, but increasingly criticized by Statists, National Communists, and Eurasianists. In general, the Russian foreign policy elites remind the president that an unqualified support for the United States has the potential to damage Russia's relations with Europe, China, and the Muslim countries. The Russian intellectuals and politicians worry that U.S. policies may undermine, rather than strengthen, peace and stability in a multicultural world.

2.1. PUTIN'S POLICY AND THE CHANGE OF THE RUSSIAN DISCOURSE

Immediately after September 11, President Putin offered the United States broad support for anti-terrorist operations in Afghanistan. The measures included intelligence sharing, opening Russian airspace to relief missions, taking part in search-and-rescue operations, rallying Central Asian countries to the American cause, and arming anti-Taliban forces inside Afghanistan.[1] At the same time, Putin emphasized the significance of the United Nations in defeating terrorism worldwide, maintaining that he would not commit Russian troops to operations inside Afghanistan because the Russian Constitution proscribed such operations and the United Nations had yet to authorize them.[2]

Putin's actions reflected a new conceptualization of the world political scene and Russia's national interests. In the earlier period of his presidency, he indicated that he was wary of U.S. policies and intentions, and he acted in ways consistent with Primakov's Statist philosophy of multipolarity. In several speeches, Putin outlined a vision of Russia as a country with a unique intermediate location between Europe and Asia. He argued that Russia should now "decisively turn to the Asia-Pacific region," and he also signed some key agreements with both European and Asian countries.[3] However, immediately after September 11, and despite the risks involved,[4] Putin became far more active in promoting Russia's relationships with the United States and Europe, and more passive on the Eastern or Asian orientation. His support for the concept of multipolarity became more muted; instead, the emphasis was on pragmatism and self-concentration in foreign policy.[5]

The newly adopted philosophy of Pragmatism (while awaiting further development) had two clear components. The first was a continuation of Primakov's vision and reflected Russia's readiness to defend its own interests in the power- and competition-driven world.[6] The second aspect was a departure from the early Statist philosophy in its emphasis of the economic, rather than security, dimension of world politics, and so had a more liberal appeal. The new foreign policy philosophy was therefore a synthesis of Statist and Liberal principles. It assumed that in today's world, geoeconomics gained an upper hand over geopolitics, and thus Russia must defend its national interests primarily by economic means and not overstretch itself politically.[7]

Putin's Pragmatism was an attempt to defend Russia's interests in the new environment and solve two key tasks. The first task was to improve the state of the Russian economy by capitalizing on domestic oil reserves and the Russian ability to increase exports to the West (provided that the West would invest more actively in the Russian petroleum industry). The second was to preserve the space to maneuver required for defending Russia's political interests in world politics. Without antagonizing the West and the United States, Russia planned to continue to deal with Chechnya, Iran, and Iraq as it saw fit. Given the West's need to have Russia as an ally,[8] Russia's president sought to strengthen what he saw as his country's national interests. This policy was culturally sustainable so long as Putin was trying to synthesize across Russia's political spectrum and incorporate both moderate nationalist visions and those of Russia as a country of a long-suppressed Western identity.

Although Putin is not a Westernizer per se,[9] as a result of his actions, Russia may eventually develop closer relations with the West. The West, as Russia's external significant Other, has an important role to play and may encourage or discourage Russia to pursue cooperative actions. The West may encourage Russia to develop liberal policies and institutions or, by its own hegemonic actions, it may contribute to Russia's return to its traditional authoritarian worldview. It is important, however, that the West develop a better appreciation of Russia's cultural distinctness and foreign policy concerns. Russia is unlikely to adopt pro-Western, let alone pro-American, policies when such policies contradict its cultural expectations. Such policies have a potential for undermining Russia's fragile religious, ethnic, and historical Euro-Asian balance. For instance, Putin's criticism of the United States–led military intervention in Iraq reflected, in part, the Kremlin's desire to avoid a split in Russian's own Muslim community.[10] It is also critical that Western nations act in concert to avoid serious disagreement, such as over the war in Iraq, and send Russia a unified, rather than conflicting, message of peace, democracy, and cultural sensitivity.[11]

2.2. GLOBALISTS: REENGAGING THE WEST

The Russian Globalists were generally supportive of the Putin's post–September 11 policy shift. However, the views of Westernizers and National Democrats continued to differ. The difference was visible in the two schools' evaluation of Russia's policy response, as well as in their perceptions of the causes and consequences of the September 11 attacks.

Liberals and the old Globalists were supportive of Putin's decision to side with the United States after September 11, and they argued that the alliance of Russia with the West should go beyond solving some tactical purposes and forge the development of common identity and cultural values. A leader of the liberal Yabloko Party, Grigori Yavlinski, in an article entitled "A temporary friendship or an eternal alliance?" insisted that Putin's choice must be viewed as a "choice in favor of a long-term unity[12] with Western or European civilization, of which Russia is an organic part."[13] Without such a long-term strategic partnership with the West, Russia would be doomed to remain in what Yavlinski referred to as an "oligarchic capitalism" and a political system with limited human rights and freedom of expression.[14] An ideologist of another liberal party, the Union of Right-Wing Forces, Alexei Kara-Murza went even further. He contrasted the Western "civilization" with a cultural "barbarianism," and proposed that Russia make a decisive "choice" between "barbarians" and "civilized nations."[15]

Not unlike some Western conservatives and liberals, this group viewed the events of September 11 as a clash of "civilization" and "barbarians," who have yet to learn the "universal" rules of "civilization."[16] In a similar way, President George W. Bush and his Defense Secretary Donald Rumsfeld viewed the problem of terrorism in terms of pure evil against the "fabulous" America and "freedom-loving people" throughout the world (to use Bush's own expressions).[17] Thomas Friedman, writing in the *New York Times,* specified the evil as not just Osama bin Laden, but "angry people" from "failing states in the Muslim and third world." For Friedman, the real war was between those with a modern and progressive outlook and those with a medieval one.[18] Russian Liberals, too, tended to define the complex problem through the lenses of the oversimplified "good guy versus bad guy" dichotomy. They insisted that Russia must either join the "civilized" West or become a leader of those "poor" and "marginalized."[19]

The attitude of Globalists of National Democratic orientation was more complex and cautious. Because National Democrats viewed the world as culturally pluralist, rather than West-centered, they were more inclined to search for solutions to terrorism by developing a global intercultural dialogue. While this group, with supporters in the broader political center, was supportive of Putin's decision and sympathetic toward the West, they cautioned that among the causes of the spread of terrorism was the unilateral use of power by the United States and the chosen narrowly pro-American model of globalization. The quest for future policy choices for Russia, as leader of Russia's Democratic Socialist Movement Alexandr Buzgalin put it, "needs to be pursued in the context of looking at alternatives to the current model of globalization."[20]

The National Democratic group did not view the West as a culturally essentialist entity shaped by the American liberal capitalist outlook, as did the Russian Liberals. Instead, National Democrats perceived the West as an arena of competition between liberal capitalist and social democratic values, often represented by the American and European models, respectively. Accordingly, the choice for Russia was broader than merely "joining the West versus remaining marginalized." As the group was less inclined to view America and Europe as culturally similar, some National Democrats recommended that Putin explicitly side with Europe. For instance, Valeri Fedorov urged Russia's president to choose in favor of the "social-democratic" Europe of Tony Blair and Gerhard Schroeder, and not the American "neo-conservatism" of George W. Bush. The former, argued Fedorov, had a broad domestic appeal and would improve Russia's international standing, whereas the latter had the potential to isolate Russia from Europe and turn it into a raw material appendage of the American economy.[21] Other National Democrats also cautioned against Russia's pro-American choice, which they feared would strengthen (and not weaken, as Yavlinski has argued) Russian non-democratic tendencies.[22] Many other scholars in Russia and elsewhere have called for the formation of a broad coalition of countries and cultures, including China and India, to respond to the global terrorist threat.[23]

In several respects, the views of this school of thought corresponded with those of President Putin. First, Putin downplayed military intervention as a long-term solution to the problem of terrorism. He did not commit Russian troops to the effort, and instead emphasized the relevance of international law and the United Nations.[24] He was also careful to not cast his actions in a pro-American or an anti-Islamic light and, immediately after the terrorist attack, warned against framing the policy response as a "war of civilizations."[25] This is important given the tendency of some of the Russia's Liberals to move closer to Fukuyama-Huntingtonian language in characterizing the terrorist attack as a clash of the Western "civilization" with a cultural "barbarianism." National Democrats themselves outlined the role of international/intercultural dialogue, in particular within the framework of the United Nations.[26] Second, and somewhat consistent with the National Democrats' philosophy, Putin seemed to have differentiated between Europe and America, and indicated his interest in developing strategic relationships with European countries. In his April 2002 state of the nation address, Putin strongly emphasized Russia's European priority.[27] In 2003, Putin joined France and Germany in criticizing U.S. military intervention in Iraq without approval of the United Nations.

2.3. NATIONALISTS: DEFENDING RUSSIA'S INDEPENDENCE FROM THE WEST

Despite Putin's decision to support the West after September 11, the Russian majority remained wary of Western intentions. The country's traumatic postcommunist experience and the failure of Gorbachev's and Yeltsin's attempts to develop a strategic partnership with the West made the Russian political class, military, media, and general public skeptical of new efforts at rapprochement. At least three major issues drew public attention. First, many politicians and military officers pointed to the unilateral U.S. decision to develop a national missile defense system and abandon the ABM treaty, which they continued to view as a cornerstone of strategic stability. Second, there was the issue of NATO's expansion, often perceived as an essentially anti-Russian process that continued to follow the old maxim "Keep America in, Germany down, and Russia out."[28] In addition, there was a concern over U.S. military interventionism and American and NATO troops' presence in the Central Asian states that are in immediate geographic proximity to Russia.[29]

Because all these issues were in the spotlight of attention, few factions in the Russian Duma initially supported Putin's decision.[30] Russia's Muslim leaders preferred not to issue any formal statement of support for Putin and reacted critically to the American military campaign in Afghanistan.[31] Of special importance was a series of published "open letters" signed by retired generals, including one of Yeltsin's former defense ministers, accusing Putin of "selling out" the country and "betraying" the nation's vital interests.[32] Federal Border Guard Service head Konstantin Totski issued a typical statement maintaining that if U.S. forces remain in Central Asia after the counter-terrorist operation in Afghanistan, "we are unlikely to remain friends."[33] Even the mainstream media described what they perceived as a sense of Russian "encirclement" by the U.S. and NATO troops. For example, *Rossiyskaya gazeta*, the newspaper of the Russian government, rang the alarm: "One way or another Russia, like the entire former USSR, remains encircled by a dense ring of military and intelligence-gathering installations belonging to the North Atlantic alliance."[34] In the end, the Russian general public, too, showed signs of increased concern over American actions in the world. According to data from the Russian Center for the Study of Public Opinion, 63 percent of all Russians felt that the terrorist attack on the United States was a form of "retribution for American foreign policy,"[35] and 64 percent of respondents perceived Washington's military activities in Afghanistan as dangerous for Russia.[36]

It was in this context that Nationalists of various stripes offered their advice to Putin. The range of this advice varied from developing a tactical and pragmatic cooperation against the "common enemy" of terrorism to an outright rejection of any association with the West.

Statists who were former supporters of Primakov's foreign policy course aimed to preserve Russia's independence and great power status in world politics. This school continued to view preservation of such status and the development of a multipolar world as Russia's main national priority. Accordingly, Statists emphasized the "harmful" aspects of American military hegemony and political unilateralism as one of the reasons for the attacks of September 11.[37] A broad coalition of great powers, including Russia, China, and India, was something that most Statists favored as the most appropriate response to the threat of global terrorism.[38] Thus, Vadim Tsymburski argued that Russia must preserve control over the area of its geopolitical responsibility, specifically in Central Asia and Caucasus, by developing cultural and political alliances with China, India, and Iran.[39] He complained, however, that Putin's policy had left little hope for accomplishing this task by deciding to "fight the alien war" and "surrendering" Central Asia and Georgia to Americans.[40]

Sergei Kortunov, another influential Statist,[41] insisted:

> Under the slogan of the struggle with terrorism, the United States achieved an important geopolitical victory, especially in Central Asia and Caucasus—regions that Russia viewed in the area of its vital interests. . . . As the result of the antiterrorist operation, Russia has lost important mechanisms of international influence related to the CIS Collective Security treaty and the "Shanghai Six"—these mechanisms have never been mobilized and are now falling apart.[42]

Unlike Tsymburski, Kortunov saw benefits of cooperation with the United States in some areas,[43] including Central Asia, but he insisted on the tactical, rather than strategic, nature of the cooperation. Strategically, Russia's pro-American and, more broadly, pro-Western choice had the effect of worsening the country's relations with the Muslim and Asian regions and irreparably damaging its moral, economic, and political standing.[44]

National Communists and Eurasianists went even further than Statists in condemning the decision of Putin and the response of the West to the events of September 11. Although this group also placed blame for the tragedy on Western shoulders, its representatives conceptualized the role of the West differently. The problem, in the minds of the Communist/Eurasianist group, was not merely the American strategy and hegemonic ambitions; such strategy and ambitions themselves should be viewed as inevitable products of the Western culture. For this group, the politics of the West were inseparable from its culture and economics. For Alexandr Panarin, the tragedy of September 11 had cultural foundations and "reflected the spiritual program of modern history and the West (first of all, the United States)."[45] For Alexandr Dugin, Gennadi Zyuganov, and Leonid Ivashev, the forces responsible for September 11 were of a transnational economic and military nature, and had little to do with developments in the Third World.[46]

For this group, September 11 was nothing less than a part of an epic struggle for liberation from the unipolar/unicultural Western world, a world in which Russia had a duty to side overtly with anti-Western, and especially anti-American forces. Much like President Bush, the National Communists and Eurasianists viewed the post–September 11 world in terms of struggle between "good" and "evil," except they found themselves on the other side of the barricade. Panarin summarized the views of the school:

> We are at war. This war cannot disappear and will be repeated tomorrow, because the spiritual situation of the time remains the same. The new language of the West is a language of war. . . . Therefore, by providing military bases for attacks on Afghanistan, Russia in fact attacked its own cultural identity and its own people, who had no desire to be "democratized" otherwise, without an American intervention.[47]

To win in this "war," National Communists and Eurasianists recommended building a coalition of anti-American cultures and civilizations. Among these cultures and civilizations, some saw an alliance of Russia and Muslim countries as having the strongest potential of successfully resisting Western modernity and hegemonic policies.[48] In the words of National Communist leader Zyuganov, the important point was not to get involved in a war against the Islamic world on the American side.[49] Others visualized a multicultural coalition of an anti-American nature naming Iran as an influential coalition member, but also adding China and even, potentially, Germany.[50]

These Russian foreign policy perceptions are summarized in table 6.2.

TABLE 6.2. Russia's Perceptions of September 11

	Liberals	National Democrats	Nationalists
Causes of September 11	Non-West: "barbarism"	Both West and non-West	West: unilateralism and modernity
The necessary response	Spread Western values	Develop intercultural dialogue	Avert Western hegemony
Implications for Russia	Side with the West	Support the U.N.; integrate with Europe	Balance against the West

3. WHAT FUKUYAMA AND HUNTINGTON HAVE LEARNED FROM SEPTEMBER 11

The authors of the "end of history" and the "clash of civilizations" have reacted differently to the terrorist attack of September 11. Whereas Fukuyama has insisted on the applicability of his theory to the post–September 11 world, Huntington has modified considerably his original views. However, both scholars have continued to downplay any connection of the attack with Western exclusionary practices. This is not surprising: acknowledging such a connection would also entail admitting at least partial responsibility for provoking such violence. Responding to the feelings of the mainstream political class, the two American scholars preferred to place most of the blame for the attack on the Muslim world. While not being surprising, this is disappointing, as the two American ideas continue to provide nationalists in Russia and the Muslim world with an argument of anti-American/anti-Western nature.

Fukuyama's intellectual response to the terrorist attack on the United States was a relatively straightforward extension of his "end of history" thesis. What some other scholars perceived as a pivotal point defining the emergence of principally new international relations,[51] Fukuyama regarded as a stage in the same old process that was set by the West's "universal" logic of development. In his view,

> Despite the events since September 11, modernity as represented by the United States and other developed democracies will re-

main the dominant force in world politics, and the institutions embodying the West's underlying principles of freedom and equality will continue to spread around the world. The September 11 attacks represent a desperate backlash against the modern world, which appears to be a speeding freight train to those unwilling to get onboard.[52]

Those "unwilling to get onboard" were representatives of the Muslim world, more specifically "Islamo-fascists" driven by the "radically intolerant and antimodern doctrine," such as Saudi Arabian Wahhabism.[53] For Fukuyama, that Islamo-fascism came from the Muslim world was no accident, as Islam is the world culture that has some "very basic problems with modernity," and most Muslim societies could not establish democracy or see an economic breakthrough as Korea and Singapore had done.[54]

Fukuyama thus framed the post–September 11 world as one of confrontation between Western liberal democracy and "Islamo-fascism," where liberal democracy continued to thrive and "hold all the cards" mainly because it could master modern science, technology, and economic prosperity. Such was the long-run scenario. To survive in the short run, however, he recommended not relying on his own favorite "inner historical logic," but rather applying all power available to the West and fighting with all determination for the "values that make modern democracies possible." "Conversely," Fukuyama warned, "if the military conflict drags on ineffectively, Islamo-fascism will pick up support."[55]

September 11 only reinforced Fukuyama's belief in the West's continued technological, military, and cultural superiority. Intellectually, however, he was on the defensive and proved unable to offer anything but a crude logic of force to address the growing world terrorist threat. Various observers noticed the defensive posture of Fukuyama's new argument: instead of admitting the potential for serious conflict in the world, he continued to foresee a Western hegemony of values and lifestyle.[56] By repeating many of Samuel Huntington's lines on the world's cultural conflicts, in fact sounding almost like the author of "clash of civilizations," Fukuyama felt obliged to rhetorically refute Huntington's theory.[57] Despite all the new conflictual developments since the end of the cold war and the worldwide rise of anti-Americanism,[58] he saw nothing exclusionary about Western modernity practices. In a typical ethnocentric manner, he continued to insist on the "universal applicability" of Western institutions and a "long term convergence across cultural boundaries."[59] Fukuyama thus persisted in denying the West's and his own responsibility for how the West was perceived in the outside world, and instead blamed Muslim countries for the rise of terrorism. He continued to believe that there was not much the West could or should change about its policies and promoted a unilateral military response to the September 11 attacks.

On September 20, 2001, Fukuyama signed an "Open Letter to the President" together with William Kristol, Jeane Kirkpatrick, Richard Perle, Martin Peretz, Norman Podhoretz, Charles Krauthammer, and others. The letter urged Bush to "capture or kill Osama bin Laden," and warned that failure to invade Iraq and topple Saddam Hussein would "constitute an early and perhaps decisive surrender in the war on international terrorism." This should be done "even if evidence does not link Iraq directly to the attack."[60]

Samuel Huntington's reaction to September 11 was more complicated and marked a serious departure from his original "clash of civilizations" thesis. Rather than validating his earlier argument about an Islamic threat to the West as many expected,[61] Huntington advanced the thesis of "Muslim wars." This time, he argued that "Muslim wars," which include "wars of terrorism, guerrilla wars, civil wars and interstate conflicts," have "replaced the cold war as the principle form of international conflict."[62] This was a major revision of his original theory, as he shifted the emphasis from his once main "West vs. Islam" cleavage to one within the world of Islam itself. Self-correcting the "clash of civilizations" thesis, Huntington explained:

> These instances of Muslim violence could congeal into one major clash of civilizations between Islam and the West or between Islam and the Rest. That, however, is not inevitable, and it is more likely that violence involving Muslims will remain dispersed, varied and frequent.[63]

The violence among Muslims, he went on to argue, had to do with four factors: the resurgence of Islamic consciousness in response to modernization, Western imperialist policies, various divisions within the Muslim world, and high birthrates in the region.[64]

Why did Huntington, unlike Fukuyama, choose not to insist on his original argument, where the main conflict lines in post–cold war world politics would be of a culture-religious nature? One could view this as a fear of the self-fulfilling potential of his own "prophecy." That Huntington's theory had such potential has been one of the principal arguments of this study, and many scholars have argued similar points.[65] Ironically, even Francis Fukuyama added to this chorus of criticism by assessing Huntington's thesis as having a "mischievous impact on the way people around the world thought about these things."[66] After September 11, Huntington's theory received a new currency. Both conservative and progressive commentators pointed to the theory's fit with reality. Robert Kaplan, in the *Atlantic Monthly,* praised Huntington for being unafraid to "look the world in the eye."[67] The British *Economist* complimented the scholar for his "cruel and sweeping, but nonetheless acute" observations about Islam.[68] On the left, Benjamin Barber, a University of Maryland political scientist and author of *Jihad vs. McWorld,* called bin Laden "the primary publicist for Huntington's theory."[69]

Could one deduce, then, that Huntington's modification of his original theory was a sign that he has finally come to understand this theory's dangerous implications? This would be a premature conclusion. Despite the obvious connection of his theory to the reality of September 11, Huntington has remained defensive about it and has never explicitly acknowledged that his latest writings were in fact "exploding the foundations of the edifice he had so carefully constructed," as one scholar put it.[70] To save face, Huntington insisted that he was merely misunderstood.[71] Even more importantly, he continued to blame Islamic "civilization" for conflict in the world. Although he attributed a share of responsibility for September 11 to Western foreign policies and his criticism of the Muslim culture became more sophisticated, Huntington continued to view the key origins of the world's problems as emanating from this region. Perhaps a more reasonable explanation of his intellectual turn might be that he merely followed the new policy line, according to which America was at war with terrorism worldwide, rather than with the world of Islam.

The two American scholars turned out to display some important similarities after all. September 11 has led to an even larger convergence in their already ethnocentric arguments. Although their policy recommendations continued to differ,[72] both Fukuyama and Huntington traced the violence to the Muslim world. Both denied their contribution to the West's exclusionary practices and, therefore, their share of responsibility for the increase of violence in the world. To the extent that these scholars represent the West, Russian or Muslim or any other cultural nationalists in the non-Western world would then continue to have a compelling argument that dialogue with such a West is impossible and that the use of force is the only effective option remaining.

4. LESSONS FOR WORLD ORDER SCHOLARS

The fact that international ideas can travel across the world and shape various local discourses suggests the existence of a global political and intellectual society. This further implies the need for both explanatory and normative studies of global society.

We must be fully aware, however, that, in contrast to what Fukuyama thinks, the global world is not a product of the West or of Western technology alone; it develops and strengthens as local cultures participate in devising some basic common rules of world politics. Globality is a process, in which bottom-up processes and influences are just as valuable as those of a top-down nature. The purpose of this project is to encourage scholars to study cultural perceptions in world politics and acquire knowledge about the cultural progress and obstacles on the way to a truly global society. The project invites further empirical investigations of how various local cultures perceive global ideas, as well as behavioral phenomena, and how domestic societies can reach a consensus on the most appropriate rules of global behavior.

The existence of global society is found not only in the global movement of ideas and their effects on local discourses, but also in these ideas and their authors' responsiveness to the reactions they generate. As George H. Mead once formulated, "the question whether we belong to a larger community is answered in terms of whether our own action calls out a response in this wider community, and whether its response is reflected back into our own conduct."[73] This raises an important question of a normative nature: to what extent are intellectuals producing world order projects morally responsible for the global effects of their ideas, and what are the implications for IR theory? Throughout the book, I have argued that Fukuyama's and Huntington's engagements with Russia and its national discourse can be evaluated only as a moral failure. Their overall contributions to and direct participation in Russia's debates was anything but helpful to the country's painful process of self-definition.

Clearly, these American scholars do not bear the full burden of responsibility for Russia's negative perceptions; several domestic and international developments contributed to Russia's reception of their ideas. Undoubtedly, Russia's Nationalists are themselves guilty of demonizing the West and presenting Russia as a culturally essentialist, anti-Western civilization. Russia's hard-line intellectuals bear direct responsibility for feeding Westophobia to the domestic public and generating feelings of Russophobia in the outside world. Yet, to the extent that the "end of history" and "clash of civilizations" theses were involved in Russia's domestic intellectual developments, their authors are responsible for the rise of Russian discourses of isolation and anti-Western hostility. These ideas were widely exploited by radically anti-Western forces in Russia as *the* voices of the West. As far as circumstances allowed, the "end of history" and "clash of civilizations" projects actively participated in Russia's national debates and, contrary to Fukuyama's and Huntington's apparent intentions, strengthened the voices of local nationalism and undermined those of liberalism.[74]

The central moral lesson of Fukuyama's and Huntington's engagements with Russia is that an intellectual is responsible for how his or her ideas are perceived outside the idea's immediate cultural context. Because we continue to live in a multicultural world, a certain degree of negative perception is inevitable, but it is in our power to reduce it. Intellectual ethnocentrism is, by definition, bound to produce negative reactions across cultures, but it is we who design and think through our projects, and it is our responsibility to minimize the potential harm and maximize the potential good.

Taking ethnocentrism seriously is vital for knowledge cumulation and theory building. Without facing this dilemma, we cannot confidently do research in international studies because we do not know if and how far we can extend our knowledge outside its social context. To study and make progress in the field of cultural perception, we must begin by recognizing the emergence of global society and the existence of a delicate dialectical balance between cultural plurality and diversity, on the one hand, and the increased commonness of humanity, on the other. Furthermore, we ought to produce our knowledge with an awareness of the possible reactions of the outside world. Specifically, we ought to be able to answer the following three questions: Who is the Other that might critically react to our scholarship? How different is the Other's historical experience? And how distinct or specific are the Other's present concerns? Answering these implies the need to move beyond realist and cosmopolitan discourses and take more seriously the development of various communitarian projects in International Relations.

For Western scholars, this study suggests the need to be aware of other moral contexts and possible reactions to locally generated world order projects. We must fully realize that, in non-Western contexts, Western ethnocentric projects will inevitably strengthen the discourse of cultural nationalism and weaken that of cultural liberalism. This means that a truly global international scholarship capable of improving trust and respect among different cultures and civilizations can proceed only on the premise of plurality and diversity in global society.

For Russian and other non-Western scholars, the argument about moral responsibility entails the need to move beyond cultural nationalism. In an increasingly global world, isolationism is no answer to global dilemmas. The non-Western world ought to aim for a strategy of culturally sensitive adaptation in, rather than isolation from, the world. The mission of non-Western intellectuals is then to explain to the often insensitive and ethnocentric West that they want integration into the world, but not merely any integration and not just at any cost. To use the language of Edward Said, the mission of the intellectual is to "write back" to the imperial center and enter into the discourse of the West with the view "to mix with it, transform it, to make it acknowledge marginalized or suppressed or forgotten histories."[75]

With these considerations in mind, let us conclude by summarizing some moral guidelines for culturally sensitive scholarship in both Western and non-Western societies. In order to remedy the problems articulated above, let us propose five criteria that might guide scholars of world order through the debris of their disciplinary, methodological, cultural, political, and other prejudices.[76] Table 6.3 summarizes those criteria.

To reduce various ethnocentric prejudices, world order scholarship should be multi-disciplinary, rather than develop within the limitations of one discipline, whether it is political science, history, sociology, or economics. International Relations is, in principle, an appropriate ground for developing multi-disciplinary world order research, but it

TABLE 6.3.   World Order Scholarship: Ethnocentrism
                versus Cultural Sensitivity

Ethnocentrism	*Cultural Sensitivity*
Disciplinary hegemony	Multi-disciplinarity
Epistemological hegemony	Dialectics and multiple epistemologies
Cultural parochialism	Cross-culturalism
Political dogmatism	Political diversity
Locally oriented political recommendations	Globally oriented political recommendations

must rid itself of its serious West-centric bias and open up to the variety of approaches taken outside the West.[77]

World order scholarship must also overcome the epistemological hegemony of positivism and adopt instead multiple methodological approaches. In addition to being often exclusively pro-Western in the nature of the produced knowledge, positivism tends to be "ethically dead," and therefore blocks development of normative studies of world order.[78]

Cultural parochialism is yet another typical amnesia in our research. This amnesia is perhaps the most serious impediment on the path to a truly global world order scholarship. Exposure to a demand to work together with scholars from different cultures would quickly, and positively, affect our disciplinary, methodological, and political biases, and provide a powerful impetus to think differently and think globally. Serious world order research must be reflective of various localities, and no one can provide a richer account of those localities than their own residents.[79]

Finally, world order scholars could and should move beyond typically dogmatic and status quo oriented accounts of world order. Normally, authors of such accounts also have a particular cultural community in mind and develop their policy recommendations exclusively for this community and without further contemplation of the outside world. A non-ethnocentric world order scholarship need not be apolitical, but it must make a serious effort to overcome political biases by incorporating diverse participants. Then and only then will our global political recommendations carry weight and make an important impact.

If we adopt similar guidelines and criteria in our research, we can contribute to overcoming the heavy legacy of particularism and violence in the world. Scholars has never really lived in the Ivory Tower, and, with such criteria, we can help in building a truly diverse, pluralistic, and multidimensional world. In this model of pluralism, which William E. Connoly has called "network pluralism," the majority center will exist in a less circular shape, and it will further devolve into multiple lines of connection across numerous dimensions of difference.[80] Such is the nature of the world that, outside some commonly agreed practices, cultural differences across the globe will always persist. However, these differences need not be destructive and conflict generating; instead, they can and should stimulate dialogue, learning, and creativity.

NOTES

CHAPTER 1 INTRODUCTION: WHOSE WORLD ORDER?

1. This study's main emphasis is on ideas relevant for understanding the global regularity of social life, specifically as generated by scholars of international relations. For various overviews of the substance and role of ideas in international affairs see Alker, Biersteker, and Inoguchi, "From Imperial Power Balancing to People's Wars"; Goldstein and Keohane, *Ideas and Foreign Policy;* Yee, "The Causal Effects of Ideas on Policies"; Ruggie, "What Makes the World Hang Together"; Milliken, "The Study of Discourse in IR"; Walt, "Fads, Fevers, and Firestorms"; Hall, *The Political Power of Economic Ideas;* Woods, "Economic Ideas and International Relations."

2. For overviews see "International Relations Theory and the New World Order"; Bobrow, "Prospects for International Relations."

3. Furedi, "The Enthronement of Low Expectations"; Alker, Amin, Biersteker, and Inoguchi, "How Should We Theorize Contemporary Macro-Encounters"; Rajaee, *Globalization on Trial.*

4. This was Robert Cooper's characterization (as cited in Nicholas Wroe, "History's Pallbearer," *The Guardian*, May 10, 2002).

5. Brzezinski, *The Grand Failure.*

6. Ibid., 1. At about the same time, another influential article appeared in the January 1990 issue of *Daedalus*. Similar to Brzezinski's book, the anonymous author "Z" questioned the success of Gorbachev's Perestroika by emphasizing the Soviet system's principal inability to achieve structural reform ("To the Stalin Mausoleum"). Widely discussed in both the West and

the USSR, the article was later attributed to Martin Malia, a history professor at the University of California at Berkeley.

7. Plattner, "The Democratic Moment." Plattner later became co-editor of the *Journal of Democracy*. Also see Marc C. Plattner, "Democracy Outwits the Pessimists," *Wall Street Journal*, October 12, 1988.

8. Krauthammer, "The Unipolar Moment."

9. For good overviews, see Steger, "Of Means and Ends" and Isaac, "The Meanings of 1989." Later, as Manfred B. Steger noted, "such promising 'civil society talk' has been largely co-opted by influential neoliberal voices" that deemphasized the radical potential of civil society and highlighted the "role of liberal democracy in furthering the ends of free enterprise" (Steger, *op. cit.*, 125). For a different perspective emphasizing geoeconomic changes and a world increasingly dominated by Europe and Japan, see *Millennium* by Jacques Attali, an influential thinker and advisor to French president François Mitterand.

10. Garton Ash, *The Magic Lantern*, 154.

11. Fukuyama's views on the Soviet Union and Russia are summarized in his article "The Modernizing Imperative." See also his "Capitalism and Democracy."

12. Specifically, Fukuyama sought to refute Paul Kennedy's celebrated book *The Rise and Fall of Great Powers*, first published in 1988. The book predicted the relative decline of the two superpowers and set the stage for discussion in mainstream American periodicals on the nature of the post–cold war order (Alker, Amin, Biersteker, and Inoguchi, "How Should We Theorize Contemporary Macro-Encounters," 2).

13. Fukuyama, "The End of History?" 4.

14. Barber, "Jihad vs. McWorld."

15. Ibid.

16. Ibid.

17. Kaplan, "The Coming Anarchy."

18. Ibid. Zbigniew Brzezinski produced a new book, in which he too drew the reader's attention to what he described as a "situation of intensifying global instability" (Brzezinski, *Out of Control*, xiii).

19. Huntington, "The Clash of Civilizations?" 23–25.

20. Huntington, "The West: Unique, Not Universal."

21. See, for example, Kapustin, *Sovremennost' kak predmet politicheskoi teoriyi*, 103.

22. Gadzhiyev, *Geopolitika*, 366–367; Panarin, "Amerikanski global'nyi vyzov."

23. In words of Joan Urban and Valerii Solovei, Huntington's renowned article "had become a powerful weapon in the hands of Russian nationalists of all political stripes, for it enables them to claim that even a world-class

Harvard professor held that Russia represented a special civilization and that conflicts among civilizations were all but inevitable" (*Russia's Communists at the Crossroads*, 98).

24. For example, the Russian public perceived the growth of U.S. military power as a great threat to Russia's security. Some scholars reported that from 1993 to 1999, the number of respondents with such perceptions increased from 46 to 76 percent (Zimmerman, *The Russian People and Foreign Policy*, 225). Others demonstrated a less significant, but still considerable (about 50 percent or more) amount of hostility in perceptions of the West and of the United States, in particular (*Amerika: vzglyad iz Rossiyi*, 137, 215). For more recent Russian perceptions, see this study's concluding chapter.

25. Russia faces a great multicultural challenge, with some 140 ethnic groups and only five of its twenty-one ethnic republics having a clear majority in the titular nation (Chechnya, Chuvashiya, Ingushetiya, Tuva, and North Ossetiya) (G. Smith, *Post-Soviet States*, 133, 143).

26. Huntington has used the case of Chechnya to argue yet again in favor of Russia's "consolidations" of its culture and abandonment of its project of multicultural federalism ("A Local Front of a Global War," *New York Times*, December 16, 1999). Several Russian politicians and intellectuals objected to such interpretation. Chapter 5 returns to this point.

27. These large states, of course, are highly significant. The Western model often draws criticism from other Asian countries as well. For example, a high-ranking official of the Japanese Ministry of Finance, Eisuke Sakakibra, argued that it was Progressivism, or the belief in only one ideal end and path for all human beings, that was defeated with the demise of Soviet socialism, not socialism per se. Neoclassical capitalism, too, has proved an illusion in the face of the challenges of environmental pollution and sustainable growth. Fukuyama traced not the "end of history," but the end of one particular history (C. Brown, "History Ends, Worlds Collide," 51–52). For a more nationalist critique, see the piece by a leading Singaporean foreign policy official and intellectual Mahbubani, "The Dangers of Decadence."

28. Many Chinese share Henry Kissinger's, and not Huntington's, vision of a post–cold war world order as a multipolar one stabilized through a balance of power (Hughes, "Globalization and Nationalism," 115–116). This criticism of Huntington is rooted in China's officially pronounced Five Principles of Peaceful Coexistence, which have been continuously re-emphasized by Deng Xiaoping and other Chinese officials since 1988 (Deng, "Conception of National Interests," 51–52).

29. Deng, "Conception of National Interests," 56.

30. Hughes, "Globalization and Nationalism," 117.

31. On various ways to classify Iranian political and intellectual discourse, see Hassan, "Islamic Revivalism and Its Impact"; Amin, *Nationalism and*

Internationalism; Leander, "Bertrand Badie: Cultural Diversity Changing International Relations?"; Salla, "Political Islam and the West"; Hashmi, "Islamic Ethics in International Society"; Tibi, "Post-Bipolar Order in Crisis." These are the primary sources of my own analysis.

32. At least at this stage, Khatami does not view Islam as a threat to modernization and does not attempt to completely eliminate it from public life. Iranian scholars have long advocated a synthesis between rational modern values and traditional Islamic ones (Boroujerdi, "Iranian Islam and the Faustian Bargain"; Hashmi, "Islamic Ethics in International Society"). For an argument in favor of convergence of, rather than confrontation between, political Islam and Western liberal democratic norms, see Salla, "Political Islam and the West."

33. Khatami, "Empathy and Compassion."

34. Marc Lynch argued that Khatami's call for a dialogue succeeded in reframing intercivilizational relations and creating an international public sphere in which communicative action has produced new conditions for the relations between the West and Islam ("The Dialogue of Civilizations and International Public Sphere").

35. For a good overview of anthropological and sociological literature on ethnocentrism, see especially Van der Dennen, "Ethnocentrism and Ingroup/Out-group Differentiation," 1. For the earlier theoretical and experimental treatment of the ethnocentric syndrome in ethnography and psychology, see LeVine, "Socialization, Social Structure, and Intersocietal Images"; LeVine and Campbell, *Ethnocentrism;* Brewer and Campbell, *Ethnocentrism and Intergroup Attitudes.*

36. Harding, *Is Science Multicultural?* 12.

37. Huntington, "The Clash of Civilizations?"; "The West: Unique, Not Universal."

38. In the words of Wang Huning, for example, Western pressure on "political ideologies, lifestyles, and values" is but a Western attempt to reinforce its hegemony over the rest of the world, and is in particular meant to "discipline" a rising China (as cited in Deng, "Conception of National Interests," 51–52).

39. For more details, see Tibi, "Post-Bipolar Order in Crisis," 844–849.

40. "From Civilizational Clash." Many Muslim scholars advanced a similar dialectical vision of world order and a similar critique of the "end of history" and "clash of civilizations" ideas. For a comprehensive analysis that builds on both Islamic and Western literature, see Rajaee, *Globalization on Trial.*

41. As similar as they might be to Huntington's line of thinking, Russian hard-line Eurasianists emerged before the "clash of civilization" thesis. For more details see A. Tsygankov, "Hard-line Eurasianism" and "Mastering Space in Eurasia."

42. Brzezinski, *The Grand Chessboard;* Clover, "Dreams of the Eurasian Heartland."

43. Breton and Breton, "Nationalism Revisited." See Breton et al., *Nationalism and Rationality,* for various rational choice accounts of nationalism.

44. Sogrin, "Zapadnyi liberalizm i rossiyskiye reformy," 32.

45. Adda Bozeman's essay ("The International Order in a Multicultural World") is a renowned example of such a perspective. In studies of nationalism, one recent influential neo-cultural statement is that of Brubaker (*Nationalism Reframed*).

46. In Western media and policy circles, these two visions remain popular as intellectual justifications for the West's policies.

47. Culturally exclusive ideas are not new in Western intellectual development and fit within a long tradition of writings by Georg Hegel, Oswald Spengler, Alexandre Kojève, Arthur Koestler, Daniel Bell, and other Western authors.

48. Huntington treats Russia as the core state of Orthodox-Slavic civilization.

49. Fukuyama, "The End of History?" 3. As Perry Anderson notes about Fukuyama's argument, "Without this global turning-point [the Soviet failure], the other parts of his story—restoration of democracy in Latin America, export growth in East Asia, breakdown of apartheid in South Africa—would remain scattered episodes" (*A Zone of Engagement,* 351).

50. The closest approximation of such analysis is represented by Alker, Biersteker, and Inoguchi, "From Imperial Power Balancing to People's Wars." See also Wight, *International Theory.* For recent attempts to apply the schools of thought approach to the analysis of post-Soviet foreign policy discourse, see Light, "Foreign Policy Thinking"; Shlapentokh, " 'Old,' 'New' and 'Post' Liberal Attitudes towards the West"; Sergounin, "Russian Post-Communist Foreign Policy Thinking"; A. Tsygankov, "From Liberal Internationalism to Revolutionary Expansionism," "Hard-line Eurasianism," "Final Triumph of the Pax Americana?" and "Mastering Space in Eurasia."

51. In Hedley Bull's memorable formulation, such analysis is "philosophical in character." "Confronted by controversy . . . we may identify the assumptions that are made in each camp, probe them, juxtapose them, relate them to circumstances, but we cannot expect to settle the controversy except provisionally, on the basis of assumptions of our own that are themselves open to debate" ("Martin Wight and the Theory of International Relations," xxi).

52. It is worth noting that in Russia, and particularly in Moscow, it is difficult to separate meaningfully the notion of "academic circles" from the notion of "policy community." The situation in which university professors consult with political parties, preside over various foreign policy councils, act as advisors to the president and State Duma deputies, and teach adjunct

courses in various educational institutions is still much more typical in Russia than in the United States, with its relatively well-defined division of labor between the "Ivory Tower" and the "inside the Beltway" communities.

53. A poll taken in April by the All-Russian Center for Public Opinion Studies (VTsIOM) found that only 2 percent approved of the U.S. military action, while 83 percent were opposed. This was a matter of anti-American, not pro-Iraqi feeling. Only 45 percent sympathized with the Iraqis, whereas 46 percent were undecided and a mere 5 percent supportive of the Americans (Nikolai Petrov, "The War in Iraq and the Myth of Putin," *Russia and Eurasia Review* 2, 8 [April 15, 2003], www.jamestown.org).

54. Lilia Shevtsova, "Iraq's Impact on Russia," *Moscow Times,* April 20, 2003; Aleksei Arbatov, "Irakskiye uroki," *Moscow News,* June 18–24, 2003.

55. For example, at a conference marking the anniversary of the Nazi invasion of the Soviet Union, a former defense minister General Igor' Rodionov told an audience that "Russian now is an occupied country." In obvious reference to the United States, he went on to say that "our geopolitical enemy has achieved what Hitler wanted to do [and] neither our nuclear forces and tank armadas nor the KGB could save us." Communist lawmaker Viktor Ilyukhin issued similar dark warnings of alleged U.S. hostile intentions. "Russia may suffer another tragedy," he said. "American pressure is now focused on Russia" ("Ex-defense minister accuses US of seeking to dominate Russia," Associated Press, June 19, 2003, as cited by *CDI Russia Weekly,* no. 262, June 2003).

56. Nikolai Zlobin, "Mesto v istoriyi ili reyting," *Izvestiya,* April 10, 2003.

57. The survey was conducted over July–October 2002 among 38,000 respondents of forty-four nations. It found that "despite an initial outpouring of public sympathy for America following the September 11, 2001 terrorist attacks . . . images of the U.S. have been tarnished in all types of nations: among longtime NATO allies, in developing countries, in Eastern Europe, and most dramatically, in Muslim societies" (*What the World Thinks in 2002* [Washington, D.C.: The Pew Research Center for the People and the Press, December 4, 2002, available at www.people-press.org).

CHAPTER 2 WORLD ORDER:
IDEAS, PERCEPTION, AND RESPONSIBILITY

1. Bull, *The Anarchical Society,* 20–22.

2. For rich overviews of recent visions of global politics, see "International Relations Theory and the New World Order"; Bobrow, "Prospects for International Relations"; and Kaufman, "Approaches to Global Politics in the Twenty-first Century."

3. Wendt, "Constructing International Politics," 74.

4. See especially Ruggie, "International Regimes, Transactions, and Change"; Walker, *Culture, Ideology, and World Order;* Onuf, *The World of Our Making;* Wendt, *Social Theory of International Politics.*

5. Waltz, *Theory of International Politics.*

6. Ruggie, "Continuity and Transformation in the World Polity." Following Karl Polanyi's lead, Ruggie developed a similar analysis of international economic order arguing that it, too, should be viewed as a product of a social context and state-society relations, rather than merely of interstate hegemony ("International Regimes, Transactions, and Change"; "At Home Abroad, Abroad at Home").

7. Ashley, "The Geopolitics of Geopolitical Space."

8. Falk, *The End of World Order;* Der-Derian and Shapiro, *International/ Intertextual Relations;* Walker, *Inside/Outside;* Lapid and Kratochwil, *The Return of Culture and Identity in IR Theory;* Linklater, *The Transformation of Political Community;* O Tuathail and Dalby, *Rethinking Geopolitics.*

9. Ruggie, "Continuity and Transformation in the World Polity."

10. My thinking on the issue has been especially influenced by the work of Hayward Alker and his collaborators (Alker, "Dialectical Foundations of Global Disparities" and "Dialectical Thinking about World Order"; Alker, Biersteker, and Inoguchi, "From Imperial Power Balancing to People's Wars"; Alker, Amin, Biersteker, and Inoguchi, "How Should We Theorize Contemporary Macro-Encounters"; see also "Twelve World Order Debates Which Have Made Our Days").

11. For analyses of various responses to the idea of a West-centered economic and security order across the globe see, for example, Falk, "False Universalism and the Geopolitics of Exclusion"; Hughes, "Globalization and Nationalism"; Salla, "Political Islam and the West"; Wiatr, "Central Europe in the World Order"; Tsygankov, "Discovering National Interests after the 'End of History'."

12. Alker, Amin, Biersteker, and Inoguchi, "How Should We Theorize Contemporary Macro-Encounters," 19.

13. Identity is a relational phenomenon, and therefore the Self simply cannot exist without the Other existing too. The Other initiates the process of the Self's socialization and transfers a relevant knowledge and its meaning to the Self, thereby imbuing him with the decisive influence. For various overviews of the relations between Self and Other in international relations, see Bloom, *Personal Identity, National Identity and International Relations;* Neumann, "Self and Other in International Relations"; Weller, "Collective Identities in World Society."

14. Alker, Amin, Biersteker, and Inoguchi, "How Should We Theorize Contemporary Macro-Encounters," 29.

15. For elaboration see, Meyer et al., "World Society and the Nation-State."

16. Beginning at least with Hans Morgenthau, scholars have studied extensively power capabilities and polarity in international politics. A world order–relevant classic statement remains that of Waltz (*Theory of International Politics*). For more sophisticated treatments of polarity, see, for example, Buzan, Jones, and Little, *The Logic of Anarchy* and Ikenberry, *After Victory.*

17. In political science, one commonly used example of an ethnocentric idea is that of economic and political modernization as it has been articulated in the West in its unilinear and progressively pro-Western form. For critiques of this conservative form of ethnocentrism, see especially Wiarda, "The Ethnocentrism of the Social Science" and Oren, "Is Culture Independent of National Security?" For a critique of radical forms of ethnocentrism, see Mohanty, "Under Western Eyes." For analysis of political, as well as geographical, linguistic, and methodological forms of ethnocentrism, see Biersteker, "Eroding Boundaries, Contested Terrain." For various analyses of IR as a discipline that is ethnocentric and reflects American/Western civilizational biases, see Hoffmann, "An American Social Science: International Relations"; Alker and Biersteker, "The Dialectics of World Order"; Holsti, *The Dividing Discipline;* Inayatullah and Blaney, "Knowing Encounters"; Waever, "The Sociology of a Not So International Discipline"; Crawford and Jarvis, *International Relations—Still an American Social Science?*

18. Of course, the ethnocentrism may be just as widespread in non-Western Russian, Chinese, Iranian, and other intellectual contexts, although the issue still awaits thorough research.

19. See especially the discussion among the participants of the project on international regimes (Krasner, *International Regimes*).

20. See, for example, John Ruggie's critique of globalization as "disembedded" and non-sustainable (*Winning the Peace,* 156). The debate was sparked anew after the failure of the WTO meeting in Seattle.

21. For a summary of the debate, see Brown, Lynn-Jones, and Miller, *Debating the Democratic Peace.* For a critique of the democratic peace claim as ahistorical and reflecting distinctly American values, see Oren, "The Subjectivity of the 'Democratic' Peace." For a postcommunist application, see MacFarlane, "Democratization, Nationalism, and Regional Security in the Southern Caucasus."

22. For example, Robert Vitalis ("The Graceful and Generous Liberal Gesture") argued that humanitarianism and humanitarian norms, as these are studied in mainstream U.S. constructivism, reflect the hidden global norm of white supremacy.

23. A. Tsygankov, "The Final Triumph of the Pax Americana?"; Naim, "Why the World Loves to Hate America."

24. Fukuyama, "The End of History?" 3. For a similar work in Western literature, see Friedman, *The Lexus and the Olive Tree*. For a radical, rather than conservative, vision of the triumph of Westernized modernity, see Wallerstein, *Geopolitics and Geoculture*.

25. For example, like some of the radical Marxists in the past, some of the Russian contemporary Eurasianists cherish the ambition of reshaping the world in accordance with their standards of what is "right" politically and culturally. With some Western globalists of a radical orientation, Russian Eurasianists view westernized modernity as regression and enslavement, but their vision is curiously similar to that of Fukuyama and also portrays modernity as homogeneous and identity-insensitive. Chapters four and five return to the Russian Eurasianists.

26. For approaches that bear some political and analytical similarity to that of Huntington, see Brzezinski, *Out of Control;* Kaplan, "The Coming Anarchy."

27. Bull and Watson, *The Expansion of International Society*, 2.

28. Ibid., 6. A more progressive version of this approach is that of the Western global society school, which argues for the emergence of new structures and institutions of governance at the supranational and transnational levels. (See, for example, Held, *Democracy and Global Order;* Linklater, *The Transformation of Political Community*.) The global civil society school recognizes the pluralism of local cultures and identities, and proposes that this plurality of identities flourish, not disappear, during the globalization era. At the same time, calls of this school's supporters for radical global democratization transcending the currently existing system of nation-states (Held, "The Changing Contours of Political Community," 283) place the school in the class of "expansion and learning," rather than of "dialogue and learning" (see table 2.2). Held's procedural universalism can hardly be neutral and may eventually encourage new divisions between exclusively defined Self and Other. For more "bottom up" perspectives, see Alker, Amin, Biersteker, and Inoguchi, "How Should We Theorize Contemporary Macro-Encounters?"; Cox, "Civilizations: Encounters and Transformations"; Dallmayr, "Globalization from Below."

29. "Culture, as we have argued, follows power" (*The Clash of Civilizations,* 310). Alker, Amin, Biersteker, and Inoguchi drew my attention to this point in their "Twelve World Order Debates," 9.

30. Cox, "Civilizations: Encounters and Transformations," 10–11.

31. Ibid., 13. For a similar account of civilizations, see Alker, "If Not Huntington's 'Civilizations,' Then Whose?"

32. Ibid., 26. See also, Cox, *Approaches to World Order.*

33. For the purpose of this project, such brief illustrations of the four visions should suffice, and I do so using examples of the United States, China, Russia, and Iran. For a more comprehensive presentation of world leaders' views on global order, see, for example, Lepor, *After the Cold War.*

34. As cited in Alker, Amin, Biersteker, and Inoguchi, "How Should We Theorize Contemporary Macro-Encounters?" 18.

35. In its clearest form, the strategy was articulated in the speech made at the 2002 Graduation Exercise of the United States Military Academy, West Point. Bush pointed to the enemies that "are totalitarians, holding a creed of power with no place for human dignity" and argued the necessity to "call evil by its name" and to confront it (George W. Bush, "West Point Commencement Speech," in *America and the World* [New York: Foreign Affairs, Council on Foreign Relations Book, 2002], 368).

36. Hughes, "Globalization and Nationalism," 104–105.

37. Ibid., 107.

38. For example, in his *On My Country and the World*, Gorbachev devoted a key portion to the October revolution's global significance.

39. This is the subtitle of Gorbachev's book *Perestroika.*

40. Gorbachev, *Perestroika,* 152.

41. Khatami, "Empathy and Compassion."

42. Ibid.

43. This point is easy to demonstrate by surveying IR textbooks. In the United States, for example, culture and national perceptions are rarely given textbook space and almost always are overshadowed by analyses of power, economics, and legal aspects of international relations. The only exception in the field seems to have been *The Logic of International Relations* by Walter S. Jones, in which the logic of perceptions was analyzed as equal in importance to the logic of power and the logic of international trade and exchange.

44. I build here on work of Robert Jervis who, writing about individual perceptions, pointed to an actor's previously existing experiences and beliefs about the domestic system, the impact of international history, and more immediate concerns ("evoked sets") (Jervis, "Hypotheses on Misperception," 479–483; Jervis, *Perception and Misperception in International Politics*).

45. Inayatullah and Blaney, "Toward an Ethnological IPE," 320.

46. These three can be relatively independent, as leadership, political elite, and larger society move, adapt to changes, and react to external ideas with various speeds and intensities. When these three are in agreement, one can speak of a cultural consensus. Somewhat similar lists of social levels were compiled by other scholars researching communicative, psychological, and sociological aspects of cross-cultural perceptions. For example, Everett M. Rogers, in his work on diffusion of innovation, identified formal and informal social

structures, norms, and opinion leadership as components of a system responding to the spread of innovative ideas (*Diffusion of Innovations,* 24–28). Cortell and Davis described how international norms can be accepted on the domestic level and pointed to the impact of national political rhetoric, the material interests of domestic actors, domestic political institutions, and socializing forces ("Understanding the Domestic Impact of International Norms").

47. The closest approximation of such analysis is represented by Alker, Biersteker, and Inoguchi, "From Imperial Power Balancing to People's Wars."

48. This debate is typically referred to as being between realists and idealists. These two attitudes are "ideal types" and serve an analytical purpose, rather than perfectly reflect reality or the identity of these attitudes' representatives. If necessary this dual typology can be further complicated. For example, in his *International Theory,* Martin Wight delineated three, rather than two, theoretical views on international relations: those who emphasized international anarchy and control (the realists), those who concentrated on international interactions as a civilizing force in world politics (the rationalists), and those who focused on various transformations of the international system (the revolutionists).

49. The description is that of Grzegorz Kolodko, as cited in Bunce, "The Political Economy of Postsocialism," 769. The literature on cross-national reception of Western economic ideas is large. For overviews, see Hall, *The Political Power of Economic Ideas*; Woods, "Economic Ideas and International Relations."

50. The postcommunist record of economic outcomes has also been mixed. For elaboration, see Bunce, "The Political Economy of Postsocialism"; A. Tsygankov, "The Culture of Economic Security."

51. Historical practices are referred to here as various facts, events, and experiences nations go through during their development.

52. As cited in Bull and Watson, *The Expansion of International Society.*

53. Some scholars have made a strong case against the acceptance of external ideas and cross-cultural learning. For example, in her well-known essay, Adda Bozeman challenged a "world culture" approach by emphasizing the absence of a common language, a common religion, a common pool of memories, and shared ways of thinking in the world. If this is so, then Hedley Bull's and Adam Watson's idea of international society was hardly more that an expression of Western culture, one likely to be rejected outside the West. Writing at the end of the cold war, Bozeman warned of the coming of a world that would have no commonly perceived rules and political order and would function, "as it did before the nineteenth century" (Bozeman, "The International Order in a Multicultural World," 406). Bertrand Badie, a French scholar, pursued a similar line of argument in most

of his writings (Leander, "Bertrand Badie: Cultural Diversity Changing International Relations?").

54. In addition to *subjective* qualities of ideas and local societies, perception and eventual incorporation of an idea may be a function of the *material* support behind it. Backed by considerable physical (economic or military) resources, an idea has a better chance to overcome the resistance of a local culture. For example, Germany and Japan after the Second World War were not highly receptive of the liberal capitalist idea as introduced by the United States. However, confronted with a need to restore their economies and the America-designed Marshall Plan, both societies eventually incorporated and modified, rather than rejected, the initially American idea.

55. These principles were first enunciated in the 1950s and have been continuously re-emphasized by Deng Xiaoping and other Chinese officials since 1988. As the late Deng stated, "National sovereignty and national security should be the top priority . . . national rights are more important than human rights" (Deng "Conception of National Interests," 51).

56. Iranian scholars have long advocated a synthesis between rational modern values and traditional Islamic ones (Boroujerdi, "Iranian Islam and the Faustian Bargain"; Hashmi, "Islamic Ethics in International Society").

57. One example of a Khatami-supportive organization is the Organization for Defending Victims of Violence (ODVV), based in Teheran and active in the field of human rights and humanitarian activities. In its internet statement, the organization embraced Khatami's call for dialogue among civilizations and expressed a strong criticism of Fukuyama and Huntington's visions, condemning them as "a means of propaganda for violence" ("From Civilizational Clash"). For a comprehensive critique of these two visions and the advancement of a dialectical vision of world order by Muslim scholars, see Rajaee, *Globalization on Trial*; Tibi, "Post-Bipolar Order in Crisis."

58. Hashmi, "Islamic Ethics in International Society," 234.

59. This tradition has been reconstructed in Haan, Bellah, Rabinow, and Sullivan, *Social Science as Moral Inquiry* (see especially the papers by William Sullivan, Robert Bellah, and Bruce Sievers). In IR, the tradition of "practical reasoning" may be traced to critical theory and social constructivism although it has been implicitly present throughout all the debates (Alker, "The Return of Practical Reason to International Theory" and "Aristotelian Political Methodologies" in his *Rediscoveries and Reformulations*).

60. This definition is generally consistent with that of moral obligation in sociology and refers to the importance of peoples' being aware of and following the existing set of moral rules by which they ought to live in a society (for a good discussion of moral obligation, see Wolfe, *Whose Keeper?* chaps. 1, 8).

61. For an extended discussion of Weber's individualist bias, see Warner, *An Ethic of Responsibility in International Relations*, chap. 1. For a

critique of the individualist ethic of responsibility in international political theory, see Linklater, *Men and Citizens in the Theory of International Relations*.

62. Jonas, *The Imperative of Responsibility*.

63. Vernadski, *Nauchnaya mysl' kak planetarnoye yavleniye*.

64. Mikhail Gorbachev's concept of the crisis of human civilization was but one attempt to reappraise ethically the late–twentieth-century world (see his *The Search for a New Beginning*).

65. See especially works by Alasdair MacIntyre (*After Virtue* and *Whose Justice? Whose Rationality?*), Michael Walzer (*Just and Unjust Wars*), and Charles Taylor (*Sources of the Self, The Ethics of Authenticity,* and with others, *Multiculturalism and "The Politics of Recognition"*). For various applications of these communitarian insights in IR, see especially Warner, *An Ethic of Responsibility;* Walker, *Inside/Outside;* Campbell and Shapiro, *Moral Spaces;* Mapel and Nardin, *International Society*. For various overviews of relationships between communitarianism and IR, see Rengger, "A City Which Sustains All Things"; C. Brown, "International Political Theory and the Idea of World Community"; Morrice, "The Liberal-Communitarian Debate"; Ruiz, "Culture, Politics, and the Sense of the Ethical."

66. Here, more traditionally oriented theorists like MacIntyre appealed to premodern morality (*After Virtue*), whereas more postmodernist thinkers argued for a need to radically reinterpret the notion of ethics and morality (see Taylor et al., *Multiculturalism and "The Politics of Recognition,"* and Gilligan, *In a Different Voice*).

67. See *Vekhi*.

68. In 1974, Aleksandr Solzhenitsyn continued this tradition of self-reflection and self-critique by publishing the *samizdat* (underground publishing) collective volume *Iz-pod glyb*. Solzhenitsyn charged that the intelligensia had essentially lost its sense of social responsibility and turned itself into a loyal servant of the Soviet regime (187–221). The Russian tradition of intellectual repentance and responsibility is alive and well. See Siniyavski for an example of liberal self-reflections ("Intelligentsiya i vlast'") and Panarin (*Rossiya v tsyklakh mirovoi istoriyi*, especially chap. 6), for a more conservative perspective.

69. That theory is a form of action has been acknowledged by several influential schools of thought. The sociology of knowledge tradition studied the social conditions of emergence, development, and decline of political ideas and argued that such ideas only function meaningfully in and respond to particular social circumstances (see especially Mannheim, *Ideology and Utopia;* Berger and Luckmann, *The Social Construction of Reality;* and Harding, *Is Science Multicultural?*). Aristotelian practical reasoning viewed the theorist as ethically involved with, rather than neutral toward, social

developments (Haan, Bellah, Rabinow, and Sullivan, *Social Science as Moral Inquiry*), and the Frankfurt school more forcefully placed theory in the center of social and political transformation (see, for example, Habermas, *Theory and Practice*).

70. Communitarianism in IR is not a homogeneous movement and represents a spectrum of ideas and theories. For example, the above discussed projects of Cox ("Civilizations") and Linklater (*The Transformation of Political Community*) differ in the extent of emphasis on local and global sources of moral authority.

71. Hayward Alker and his collaborators proposed to apply the term "cultural-neorealists" for characterizing IR writers such as Francis Fukuyama, Samuel P. Huntington, Paul Kennedy, Robert D. Kaplan, and Joseph Nye (Alker, Amin, Biersteker and Inoguchi, "How Should We Theorize Contemporary Macro-Encounters?" 14).

72. For example, some realists emphasize the role of ethnicities, states, and civilizations in the emerging post–cold war order and study these local cultures' politicized claims to larger recognition and status in the anarchical international system (Posen, "The Security Dilemma and Ethnic Conflict"; Huntington, *The Clash of Civilizations*). Others theorize world order as a "culture of anarchy" and one that is created by and for states themselves through their interaction (Wendt, "Anarchy is What States Make of It"; *Social Theory of International Politics*). The culture's nature, historical development, and social roots are left unexplored. (For a similar critique, see Lapid and Kratochwil, *The Return of Culture and Identity*, especially contributions by Naeem Inayatullah and David L. Blaney, and Sujata Chakrabarti Pasic). Defined in such a way, culture can hardly have genuinely independent effects on state actions and is therefore not a serious departure from the traditional realist image of world politics.

73. Huntington is especially explicit in dichotomizing the "West against the rest" and perceiving the rise of alternative cultural communities as a threatening development (Huntington, "The Clash of Civilizations?"; "The West: Unique, Not Universal").

74. For example, some radical cosmopolitan writers favoring the classical Marxist tradition emphasize the power of Western capitalism and industrial technology in reshaping the world order and subsuming the diversity of local cultures. Ernst Gellner and Benedict Anderson linked nationalism to industrial modernization and print technology (Gellner, *Nations and Nationalism;* B. Anderson, *Imagined Communities*), and Antony Giddens added the role of information and military technology (*Nation-State and Violence*). Other, more conservative scholars such as Michael Doyle and Francis Fukuyama argue for the progressive spread of Westernized market

democracy throughout the world (Doyle, "Liberalism and World Politics"; Fukuyama, "The End of History?").

75. I am grateful to an anonymous reviewer for suggesting this productive distinction.

76. This is the "cultural pluralism" tradition pioneered by Giambattista Vico in Italy and Johann Herder in Germany, which was traced by Isaiah Berlin (as referred to in Tivnan, *The Moral Imagination*, 252).

77. As cited in Tivnan, *The Moral Imagination*, 259; M. J. Smith, "Moral Reasoning," 47.

CHAPTER 3 RUSSIA: THE FOREIGN POLICY COMMUNITY AND SCHOOLS OF THOUGHT

1. Alker, Biersteker, and Inoguchi represent the closest approximation of such analysis, "From Imperial Power Balancing to People's Wars." See also Wight, *International Theory*. For recent attempts to apply the schools of thought approach to the analysis of post-Soviet foreign policy discourse see Light, "Foreign Policy Thinking"; Shlapentokh, "'Old,' 'New' and 'Post' Liberal Attitudes towards the West"; Sergounin, "Russian post-Communist Foreign Policy Thinking"; A. Tsygankov, "From Liberal Internationalism to Revolutionary Expansionism," "Hard-line Eurasianism," "Final Triumph of the Pax Americana?" and "Mastering Space in Eurasia."

2. This dialectical and interactive aspect of Russia's discourse will be demonstrated in the following chapters on Russia's engagements with Fukuyama and Huntington. The purpose of this chapter is less ambitious— to identify the existing voices and to trace their impact on the discourse as a whole.

3. On diffusion of ideas see Odell, *U.S. International Monetary Policy;* Hall, *The Political Power of Economic Ideas;* Haas, "Introduction: Epistemic Communities"; Goldstein and Keohane, *Ideas and Foreign Policy;* Risse-Kappen, "Ideas Do Not Float Freely"; Yee, "The Causal Effects of Ideas."

4. This is not to diminish the role of Russia's indigenous thought, but simply to suggest that this thought has existed and been developing in the process of constant dialogue with Western ideas. On Russia's engagement with various Western ideas, see A. Lynch, *The Soviet Study of International Relations;* Vucinich, *Darwin in Russian Thought* and *Einstein and Soviet Ideology;* Light, *Marxism and Soviet International Relations;* Neumann, *Russia and the Idea of Europe;* Tolz, *Russia: Inventing the Nation.*

5. See, for example, a book by its prominent spokesman Paul Miliukov, *Russia and Its Crisis.*

6. Neumann, *Russia and the Idea of Europe,* 70, 213.

7. For good overviews of the Russian Westernizer-Slavophile debates, see Neumann, *Russia and the Idea of Europe* and Tolz, *Russia: Inventing the Nation*. For a selection of Russian original writings of Westernizers and Slavophiles, see Kohn, *The Mind of Modern Russia*.

8. Donaldson and Nogee, *The Foreign Policy of Russia*, 69.

9. For analyses of this era, see especially Arbatov, *Zatyuanuvsheyesya vyzdorovleniye*, chaps. 2–3, 5 and English, *Russia and the Idea of the West*, chaps. 2–3.

10. Zimmerman, *Soviet Perspectives on International Relations;* A. Lynch, *The Soviet Study of International Relations;* Shenfield, *The Nuclear Predicament;* Herman, "Identity, Norms, and National Security."

11. Dunlop, *Faces of Contemporary Russian Nationalism*, 15.

12. For important Western studies of Russian nationalism, see Dunlop, *Faces of Contemporary Russian Nationalism,* and *The New Russian Nationalism;* Agurski, *The Third Rome;* Brudny, *Reinventing Russia.*

13. Within Russian nationalism, the so-called National Bolsheviks, to use Mikhail Agurski and John Dunlop's term, were advocating a synthesis of the Bolshevik regime and Russia's indigenous tradition (Agurski, *The Third Rome;* Dunlop, *Faces of Contemporary Russian Nationalism,* 254–265).

14. On these influences, see Gorbachev, *On My Country and the World,* 176; English, *Russia and the Idea of the West;* and Evangelista, *Unarmed Forces.*

15. One such prominent American theory was developed by Joseph S. Nye and Robert O. Keohane in *Transnational Relations and World Politics.* Gorbachev and his team, including Alexander Yakovlev, had been influenced by the interdependence ideas before they came to power. For instance, Gorbachev was exposed to similar thinking through Georgi Shakhnazarov, his future advisor. Shakhnazarov first met Gorbachev in the early 1980s, and they had an extended conversation about world order and Shakhnazarov's unorthodox view was expressed in his book *Gryaduschi miroporyadok* (Moskva: Progress, 1972), which Gorbachev had read. (More details are provided in the more recent book by Shakhnazarov, *S vozhdyami i bez nikh* (Moskva: Vagrius, 2000, 277–282). Yakovlev was familiar with transnationalism's ideas from his academic experience as the previous director of the prominent Institute of the World Economy and International Relations. His future advisor Nikolai Kosolapov was at the time working in the institute and incorporated Keohane and Nye's ideas into the institute's collective volumes on theories of world order (a personal conversation with Kosolapov, 1995). Interestingly enough, after Gorbachev came to power, Nye was one of the first non-Marxist IR theorists to publish several of his articles in the leading Russia's journal *MEiMO (Mirovaya Ekonomika i Mezhdunarodnyiye Otnosheniya).*

16. Wight, *International Theory,* 7–8.

17. Wight's approach was developed out of Western experience, and applying the approach to Russia's conditions has, of course, its costs. My application should be treated as an analytical exercise for the purpose of classifying Russian foreign policy schools of thought in a way that will communicate across cultures. This process is limited in capturing what is culturally specific or unique to Russia. Nor do I pretend to cover the entire diversity of Russian foreign policy debates; there are certainly more than five intellectual currents. Therefore my identification of these five as most significant is, to a certain extent, a judgment call.

18. Wight, *International Theory*, xiii.

19. See, for example, Mikhail Gorbachev, "Vystupleniye Prezidenta SSSR v parlamente Yaponiyi," *Izvestiya*, April 17, 1991.

20. Andrei Kozyrev, "Preobrazhennaya Rossiya v novom mire," *Izvestiya*, January 2, 1992; "Transformatsiya kafkianskoi metamorfozy," *Nezavisimaya gazeta*, August 20, 1992.

21. *Izbiratel'noye ob'edineniye*, 17; Andrei Kozyrev, "And Now: Partnership with Russia's Democrats," *Washington Post*, October 10, 1993; Yegor Gaidar, "Rossiya XXI veka: Ne mirovoi zhandarm, a forpost demokratiyi v Yevraziyi," *Izvestiya*, May 15, 1995.

22. In my further discussions, I will treat Gorbachev's Social Democratic views and the views of the National Democratic school that emerged after the Soviet collapse and Gorbachev's resignation as analytically similar. I will also refer to them interchangeably when it is appropriate. Although the two schools developed in different—the Soviet and post-Soviet—contexts, they defended a similar core of ideas and responded to the same opposing views of Westernizers, on the one hand, and Nationalists and Expansionists, on the other.

23. For a more detailed analysis, see A. Tsygankov, "From Liberal Internationalism to Revolutionary Expansionism," 251–252.

24. Wight, *International Theory*, 114.

25. Gennadi Zyuganov, the leader of the CPRF, is one of the most prominent spokespeople for this view (see, for example, Zyuganov, *Rossiya i sovremennyi mir* and *Geografiya pobedy*).

26. For a detailed analysis of Statists' views, see Kovalev, "Russian 'Realism'."

27. Statists and Neo-Communists often apply the label of neoconservatism to themselves. For example, Alexandr Panarin often uses the label for self-characterization (see Kara-Murza, Panarin, and Pantin, "Dukhovno-ideologicheskaya situatsiya," 17). See also Sergei Kurginyan, "Tseli i tsennosti," *Den'*, November 24, 1991).

28. Here I refer to the culturally essentialist version of post-Soviet Eurasianism, which remains the most prominent school within the Eurasianist movement. It is worth noting that Eurasianism is far from homogeneous in

its worldviews and policy recommendations and does have its statist and even liberal versions. See my "Hard-line Eurasianism" and "Mastering Space in Eurasia" for more details.

29. Sergei Kurginyan, "Yesli ne imperiya, to nichto," *Zavtra*, January 4, 1995; Panarin, "Yevraziyski proyekt."

30. Dugin, "Konservativnaya revolyutsiya."

31. For example, the notions of geopolitics, Eurasia, and Russia's "heartland" location in Eurasian stability were common in Eurasianist theories of the second half of the 1980s, but now are accepted across Russia's political spectrum (albeit without necessarily accepting their originally radical political implications).

32. This formulation is necessarily general, as it may mean different things for different thinkers. Mikhail Gorbachev, for example, proposed that Russia try to find its place in the world by reorganizing the former Soviet space into a confederation, which ensures "the rights and interests of individual nations, nationalities, and ethnic groups and also preserves all the advantages of the existing larger state structures" (*On My Country and the World*, 235).

33. For elaboration, see Gadzhiyev, *Vvedeniye v geopolitiku.*

34. For a detailed analysis of Russian Westernizers' and other schools' reaction to Western intervention in Kosovo, see A. Tsygankov, "The Final Triumph of the Pax Americana?"

35. Nikolai Zlobin, "Mesto v istoriyi ili reyting," *Izvestiya*, April 10, 2003; Pavel Felgenhauer, "Kremlin Taking Bad Advice," *Moscow Times*, April 24, 2003.

36. One of the key statements here is that of Primakov ("Mezhdunarodniye otnosheniya nakanune XXI veka" and "Rossiya v mirovoi politike").

37. The discussion of alternative strategies relies heavily on my earlier published work ("From Liberal Internationalism to Revolutionary Expansionism" and "Hard-line Eurasianism").

38. A summary of this philosophy is available from several published works (see, for example, Gorbachev, *Perestroika; The Search for a New Beginning*).

39. Characteristically, one prominent liberal collected volume was called *Inogo ne dano* (No alternative is available) edited by Yuri Afanasyev. The next chapter returns to this point and offers a more detailed analysis of the Russian liberal discourse.

40. Kozyrev, *Preobrazheniye*, 48.

41. For a good example of this reformed social democratic perspective, see the writings by Dmitri Furman ("Russki vyzov' i kompleks natsionalnoi nepolnotsennosti," *Nezavisimaya gazeta*, April 14, 1994; "Vneshnepoliticheskiye oriyentiry").

42. For more detailed description and analysis, see Pavel Tsygankov, "Identifikatsiya Yevropy vo vneshnei politike Rossiyi"; Aron, "The Foreign Policy Doctrine."

43. Primakov, "Mezhdunarodniye otnosheniya nakanune XXI veka"; "Rossiya v mirovoi politike."

44. See A. Tsygankov, "Hard-line Eurasianism" for a more detailed analysis of proposed Nationalist and Eurasianist visions and strategies.

45. This certainly applies to the year 2000. Characteristically, Primakov withdrew his candidacy from the 1999 presidential elections and has been quite supportive of Putin's domestic and foreign policies. After September 11, 2001, Putin's foreign policy philosophy evolved toward pragmatically pro-Western views, to which I return in chapter 6.

CHAPTER 4   THE TRIUMPH OF LIBERALISM? DEBATING FRANCIS FUKUYAMA'S "END OF HISTORY" THESIS

1. Mannheim, *Ideology and Utopia,* 267.

2. My analysis relies mainly on Fukuyama's original article "The End of History?" and, to a lesser extent, on his book *The End of History and the Last Man* that developed and somewhat modified the original argument and was published three years later. There are two reasons for this: First, I am primarily interested in the social conditions of the late-1980s that gave the rise to Fukuyama's early article. Second, my other major purpose is to trace the reaction of the Russian policy and intellectual community to Fukuyama's thesis and, in Russia, the thesis never appeared in book form, only as the article.

3. I will treat social context as a policy and, to a lesser extent, an intellectual environment, in which an idea emerges, functions, or circulates.

4. Brzezinski, *Grand Failure.*

5. Marc C. Plattner, "Democracy Outwits the Pessimists," *Wall Street Journal,* October 12, 1988; Charles Krauthammer, "Democracy Has Won," *Washington Post National Weekly Edition,* April 3–9, 1989.

6. Huntington, *The Third Wave,* 27.

7. Pfaff, "Redefining World Power," 48. This vision was finally legitimized on the highest policy level when President George H. W. Bush announced the cold war "victory" of the U.S. in his 1992 State of the Union message.

8. For a recent critique of modernization theory, see Oren, "Is Culture Independent of National Security?"; Badie, *The Imported State;* Blaney and Inayatullah, "Neo-Modernization?"

9. Fukuyama's views on the Soviet Union and Russia, rooted firmly in the tradition of modernization theory, are summarized in his article "The Modernizing Imperative." See also his "Capitalism and Democracy."

10. For later works with a similar ideological spin emphasizing the global spread of political and economic institutions, respectively, see especially Muravchik, *Exporting Democracy* and Friedman, *The Lexus and the Olive Tree.*

11. Gorbachev, *Perestroika;* "Sotsial'nyi progress v sovremennom mire."

12. Gorbachev, *Perestroika,* 152.

13. Fukuyama's article first appeared in Russian in the March issue of *Voprosy filosofiyi* in 1990, about eight months after its original publication in *National Interest.* In May of the same year, the article was also reprinted by another leading academic journal *SShA: Ekonomika, Politika, Ideologiya.*

14. Fukuyama, "The End of History?" 4.

15. Ibid., 3.

16. Furedi, "The Enthronement of Low Expectations," 33; C. Brown, "Histories End, Worlds Collide," 50.

17. Fukuyama, "Reflections on the End of History," 246. Analytically related to this is Fukuyama's argument against the concept of national interests, to which I return in the next section.

18. C. Brown "Histories End, Worlds Collide," 45.

19. Furedi, "The Enthronement of Low Expectations," 34.

20. Ibid.

21. Frank Furedi makes this point forcefully ("The Enthronement of Low Expectations"; *The New Ideology of Imperialism*). In his 1989 article, Fukuyama was not as explicit in recommending Western intervention in defending the values of the West. In his book, however, he moved toward a somewhat less deterministic and more geopolitical vision of the world: "The relationship between democracies and non-democracies, he predicts, will still be characterized by mutual mistrust and fear, and despite a growing degree of economic interdependence, force will continue to be the *ultima ratio* in their mutual relations" (*The End of History and the Last Man,* 279).

22. Gorbachev himself was especially influenced by the ideas of Scandinavian and West European Social Democrats (Herman, "Identity, Norms, and National Security," 288–298).

23. The school included people on the right proposing a relatively modest reform of modern capitalism, as well as leftists who were disgusted with capitalism as a system and, in all fairness, may be better referred to as democratic socialists rather than Social Democrats. The left wing shared with the right a disappointment in the Soviet system, but anticipated a reform project that would be considerably more egalitarian and state-controlled than the one favored by the rightist Social Democrats. Initially, Gorbachev appealed to both groups and, for a time, was able to keep them together. As diverse as they were, leftist and the rightist Social Democrats were able to publicize their ideas together, as demonstrated by the well-known collection of articles *Inogo ne dano* (No alternative is available), edited by Yuri Afanasyev.

Eventually, however, the two wings went their ways. After the Soviet collapse, some leading figures such as Boris Kurashvili rejoined the Communist Party; others such as Dmitri Furman and Vladimir Kuvaldin remained loyal to Gorbachev and went on to work for the newly established Gorbachev Foundation; still others like Alexei Kiva shifted their support to the new regime of Boris Yeltsin. My label of Social Democrats is also not something all of these people might prefer to be called. Some, especially those on the right, might like to be referred to as Liberals. For example, Yuri Zamoshkin, a prominent Soviet expert on the United States and an influential thinker, spent considerable time in his response to Fukuyama trying to win back the notion of Liberalism from him (Zamoshkin, "'Konets istoriyi': ideologizm i realizm," 149–152).

24. Krasin, "Vzaiomodeistviye obschestvennykh sistem," 5; Zamoshkin, "'Konets istoriyi': ideologizm i realizm," 149.

25. "Problemy tselostnogo mira," 5; Diligenski, "'Konets istoriyi' ili smena tsivilizatsi?" 30.

26. Batalov, "Yedinstvo v mnogoobraziyi—printsip zhivogo mira," 18. See similar thoughts in Krasin, "Vzaiomodeistviye obschestvennykh sistem," 6–7.

27. Diligenski, "'Konets istoriyi' ili smena tsivilizatsi?" 30–31, 39–40. In their response to Fukuyama's thesis, Mark Khrustalev and Marina Lebedeva emphasized the fact that Fukuyama overlooks the creative potential of non-Western societies (see "'Konets istoriyi' ili konets ideologiyi"). In his subsequent work on social capital in the global economy and cultural preconditions for economic development (Trust; "The Primacy of Culture"; "Social Capital and the Global Economy"), Fukuyama partially amended his view. However, he remained committed to the old vision of modernization theory, according to which the general path of economic development is the only one; therefore, one can speak of different strategies of building a market economy, but not about differences in the outcome.

28. A more general way of expressing this thought was offered by, among others, the prominent historian Mikhail Gefter, originally a strong supporter of Gorbachev, who wrote that "we cannot begin with how and by which means European humanity emerged. We must not throw away everything that has been created through the suffering of our previous generations" (Gefter, Iz tekh i etikh let, 465; see especially his "Rossiyia and Marks," in the same volume, 37–63)

29. Batalov, "Yedinstvo v mnogoobraziyi," 19. Zamoshkin reminds Fukuyama that, up until the late 1970s, the term "Liberalism" was used precisely in reference to the welfare state ("'Konets istoriyi': ideologizm i realizm," 151).

30. Batalov, "Yedinstvo v mnogoobraziyi," 20.

31. This mode of thinking, so common in anthropological studies, is also akin to that of Russian nationalists. I return to this point later in this section.

32. Diligenski, "'Konets istoriyi' ili smena tsivilizatsi?" 35–36.

33. Krasin, "Vzaiomodeistviye obschestvennykh sistem," 8; Diligenski, "'Konets istoriyi' ili smena tsivilizatsi?" To remedy the major problems of human civilization, Social Democrats propose such measures as going beyond the hedonism and individualism of modern civilization, emphasizing community, creative work, and new relations with nature (Diligenski and Lektorski, "Problemy tselostnogo mira"; Diligenski, "'Konets istoriyi' ili smena tsivilizatsi?" 39–40; Moiseyev, "Universal'nyi evolyutsionizm").

34. Zamoshkin, "'Konets istoriyi': ideologizm i realizm," 154.

35. In the debate on theory of formation, for example, Social Democratic intellectuals argued against the Soviet nationalists' zero-sum vision of the struggle between capitalist and socialist formation, on the one hand, and the Westernizers' proposal of abandoning the theory of formation altogether, on the other. Some Social Democrats favored the reformed version of theory formation proposing that this would widen the room for the formation's dialogue and mutual learning (for examples of such thinking, see presentations by Alayev, Altukhov, and Gudozhnik in "Formatsiyi ili tsivilizatsiyi"; Krasin, "Vzaiomodeistviye obschestvennykh sistem"). Others critiqued the very language of formation theory as unable to express the character of world change. They did not join Liberals in praising the Western origins of modern human civilization (see presentation by Mdnoyantz in "Formatsiyi ili tsivilizatsiyi"; Arab-Ogli, "Yevropeiskaya tsivilizatsiya"), but instead proposed to view civilization as a post-modern phenomenon that allows for the diversity of history-determined paths in human development and requires ethical self-awareness (Kapustin in Zagladin and Kapustin, "Al'ternativy i imperativy v mirovoi politike," 23; Diligenski and Lektorski, "Problemy tselostnogo mira," 33, 37, 42; Diligenski, "'Konets istoriyi' ili smena tsivilizatsi?").

36. Westernizers differed on a number of issues and proposed different strategies of Soviet modernization. For example, the debate between supporters of "authoritarian" and "democratic" paths toward Western politico-economic institutions has articulated such differences (for a detailed analysis of the debate, see Sautman, "The Devil to Pay"). Westernizers agreed, however, that the Soviet Union was on its way to becoming part of Europe, or the West.

37. Leonid Batkin captured the mode when he wrote that, for Liberals, the way to be realistic was to demand the impossible (see his article in Afanasyev, *Inogo ne dano*).

38. During the period from 1987 to 1991, this was well expressed in many articles published by the leading academic journals *Mirovaya Ekonomika i*

Mezhdunarodniye Otnosheniya (The World Economy and International Relations) and *SshA: Ekonomika, Politika, Ideologiya* (The U.S.A.: Economy, Politics, and Ideology). Many of these articles were critically comparing the Soviet experience against the far more favorably presented experiences of Western development.

39. See Pozdnyakov, "Natsional'noye i internatsional'noye vo vneshnei politike"; "Vneshnyaya i vnutrennyaya politika"; and especially "Formatsionnyi i tsivilizatsionnyi podkhody." Pozdnyakov completely and stunningly reversed his views in 1991, a development to which I return later in this chapter.

40. Pozdnyakov, "Formatsionnyi i tsivilizatsionnyi podkhody," 142.

41. Ibid., 143.

42. Ibid. For other very similar views, see Batkin, "Stat' Yevropoi"; Arab-Ogli, "Yevropeiskaya tsivilizatsiya."

43. This pattern of thinking is traceable to Pozdnyakov's other articles as well. His method of dealing with dichotomies and polarities is often to make a choice in favor of one over the other, and not by synthesizing them and arriving at a new quality. At one point, for example, he writes that the "acknowledgment of domestic and external policy as a dialectical couple in reality means the acknowledgment of their mutually exclusive qualities" ("Vneshnyaya i vnutrennyaya politika," 43).

44. Chaadaev, "Apology of a Madman," 304.

45. See, for example, Batkin, "Stat' Yevropoi"; Pozdnyakov, "Formatsionnyi i tsivilizatsionnyi podkhody," 144. For a broader context, review the articles published in Russia's academic and literary journals during 1987–91. In academia, *Mirovaya Ekonomika i Mezhdunarodniye Otnosheniya, SshA: Ekonomika, Politika, Ideologiya,* and *Rabochi Klass i Sovremennyi Mir* acquired the reputation of being most outspokenly Liberal and pro-Western. Outside academia, *Vek XX i Mir, Znamya,* and some others gained a similar reputation.

46. Pozdnyakov, "Formatsionnyi i tsivilizatsionnyi podkhody," 144.

47. National Communist and Expansionist visions are explained in more detail in the previous chapter.

48. For a coherent summary of this nationalist view, see the presentation by Yuri M. Borodai in "Rossiya i Zapad: vzaymodeistviye kul'tur," 21–24. For an extended presentation of the view, see Borodai, "Treti put'," "Totalitarizm."

49. See, for example, Kurginyan et al., *Postperestroika;* Prokhanov and Sultanov, "Izmenit'sya, chtoby vyzhit'," *Den',* March 6, 1991; Dugin, "Konservativnaya revolyutsiya."

50. Some National Communists make a dependency argument by insisting that Russia's adoption of a market economy will inevitably transform it

into a colony of the West, as market economies and the West cannot be separated (Khorev, *Rossiyu pribirayut k rukam,* 49–62).

51. Sergei Kurginyan, "Tseli i tsennosti," *Den',* November 24, 1991.

52. For a more detailed treatment of these strategies, see A. Tsygankov, "Hard-Line Eurasianism."

53. According to one mass opinion poll, public support for the U.S. model of society fell from 32 percent in 1990 to 13 percent in 1992, or by more than two-thirds. A similar trend was observed with regard to Russia's general public feelings about Japanese and German models of society (Sogrin, "Zapadnyi liberalizm i rossiyskiye reformy," 32).

54. Some Liberals, latter-day supporters of Gorbachev's agenda, preferred to put all the blame for all the difficulties with reform on Gorbachev personally and even went so far as to implicate him in plotting to restore the communist system (Leonid Batkin in *Literaturnaya gazeta,* September 1991).

55. Along with some Westernizers, they felt that it was all Gorbachev's fault, except that, in the National Communists' view, Gorbachev was guilty of undermining traditional Soviet power by conspiring with Western interests.

56. The new change in Russia's discourse was completed around late 1995, a time when, quite symbolically, Russia's pro-Western foreign minister Andrei Kozyrev was removed from office and replaced by his prominent critic and the father of Russian Statism, chief of foreign intelligence services Yevgeni Primakov.

57. *Derzhava* can be loosely translated as a holder of power. For a more detailed analysis of Statism, see Rahr, "'Atlanticists' versus 'Eurasians'"; Tolz, "The Burden of Imperial Thinking"; Torbakov, "'Statists' and the Ideology"; Kerr, "The New Eurasianism"; Light, "Foreign Policy Thinking"; Kovalev, "Russian 'Realism'." For the most important statements of Statism's main tenets, see various documents of the *SVOP* (Council for Foreign and Defense Policy), an influential non-governmental organization that was established with the purpose of challenging the Liberal political philosophy associated with deputy prime-minister Yegor Gaidar and foreign minister Andrei Kozyrev, and for proposing specific policy recommendations (see especially, "Strategiya dlya Rossiyi," *Nezavisimaya gazeta,* August 1992; "Strategiya-2," *Nezavisimaya gazeta,* May 27, 1994; "Strategiya-3," *Nezavisimaya gazeta,* September 1998).

58. Alexandr Dugin, a prominent National Communist and Expansionist, was right to complain that Statists adopted the form of his Eurasianist ideas without accepting their radical content and implications (Alexandr Dugin, "Yevraziyski proyekt," *Zavtra,* August 1998). The currently skyrocketing influence of geopolitics in politics and academia (see, for example, Sorokin, *Geopolitika sovremennosti;* Baburin, *Territoriya gosudarstva;* Dugin, *Osnovy geopolitiki;* Zyuganov, *Geografiya pobedy;* Mitrofanov, *Shagi novoi*

geopolitiki; Nartov, *Geopolitika;* Orlova, *Yevraziyskaya tsivilizatsiya*) is also something that was long advocated by Russia's extreme nationalists.

59. See more about this change in Pavel Tsygankov, "Identifikatsiya Yevropy."

60. For Liberal views on national interests, see Kozyrev, *Preobrazheniye.* For a Social Democratic perspective on national interests and geopolitics, see Spasski, "Novoye mishleniye po amerikanski"; Krasin, *Natsional'nyiye interesy* and "O rossiyskikh natsional'nykh interesakh"; Gadzhiyev, *Vvedeniye geopolitiki.*

61. Liberal and Social Democratic interpretations of national interests were, of course, different from that of Statists, a point upon which I elaborate later in this section.

62. Fukuyama, "Neyasnost' natsional'nogo interesa."

63. By the time of the article's appearance, Russia had already gone through some major debates of the issue of ethnic Russians. For example, Stankevich and Kozyrev took markedly different views while presenting at the conference "The Transformed Russia in the New World" organized by Russia's foreign ministry and held in February 1992 ("Preobrazhennaya Rossiya v novom mire"). They further disagreed in public whether Russia should or should not rely on Western institutions, such as the OSCE, in defending ethnic Russians and its broader interests in the former Soviet region (Rahr, "'Atlanticists' versus 'Eurasians'," 20).

64. Many other influential Western observers argued from a similar standpoint that Russia must learn how to be a "good neighbor" and that it cannot be a democracy and an empire at the same time (see, for example, Goble, "Can We Help Russia Become a Good Neighbor?"; Brzezinski, "Premature Partnership").

65. See especially Afanasyev, *God posle Avgusta;* Kozyrev, *Preobrazheniye.*

66. Characteristically, what seemed obvious and necessary to some Liberals was unnecessary and utopian for others. To Liliya Shevtsova, for example, it was clear "that the main task of Russia's leadership is currently to define Russia's new statehood in view of the new geopolitical reality, drawing lessons from the past, making it clear what should be inherited from tsarist Russia or the Soviet Union and what should be dropped altogether," and that "the amorphous . . . nature of Russia's statehood is dangerous not only for the reform process but also for the other states that were set up as a result of the disintegration of the USSR." The others, such as Marina Pavlova-Silvanskaya, advised concentrating on practical issues of everyday life and not bother thinking about Russia's historical past and role, because any attempts to find answers to these abstract questions might lead to further utopian thinking (Tolz, "The Burden of Imperial Thinking," 3).

67. Some Liberals emphasized the widespread effects of economic globalization and formulated a notion of the Pax Economica, or the economy-centric world. In general agreement with Fukuyama's vision, they maintain that Russia has no choice but to participate in the globalization project and they argue in favor of adopting economically, rather than geopolitically, defined national interests (see, for example, Zagorski, "'Monopolyarnost'"; Neklessa, "Postsovremennyi mir" and "Epilog istoriyi"; Proektor, *Noviye izmereniya rossiyskoi politiki bezopasnosti*). On the same basis, they reject the notion of a multipolar world, a position shared by the Statists and National Communists (Leonid Ionin, "Pragmatizm globalnoi ideiyi," *NG-Dipkuryer,* April 6, 2000; Viktor Kremeniuk, "Vernut'sya v lono sovremennoi tsivilizatsiyi," *NG-Dipkuryer,* April 6, 2000; Veniamin Sokolov, "Rossiya pered vyborom. Stoit li nam borot'sya za monopolyarnyi mir?" *NG-Stsenariyi,* May 11, 2001).

68. For example, the head of Russia's parliamentary committee on international affairs and foreign economic relations Evgeni Ambartsumov, the presidential political advisor Sergei Stankevich, and influential political scientist Andranik Migranyan defected to the Statist camp. Others, such as the executive secretary of the parliamentary constitutional commission Oleg Rumiantsev, writer and athlete Yuri Vlasov, and prominent international relations scholar El'giz Pozdnyakov switched to the ranks of National Communists. Western observers are correct to point out the similarity of Pozdniakov and other former "democrats" with some of the points made by National Communists (see, for example, Porter, "Russia and Europe"; Patomäki and Pursiainen, "Western Models and the Russian Idea"), but they often fail to appreciate fully the reasons for these scholars' intellectual and political evolution.

69. Stankevich, "Toward a New 'National Idea'," 24.

70. Ibid., 26–27.

71. Ibid.; Sergei Stankevich, "Derzhava v poiskakh sebya," *Nezavisimaya gazeta,* March 28, 1992; Lukin, "Russia and Its Interests," 108–109; Migranyan, "Rossiya i blizhneye zarubezhiye."

72. See, for example, Layne, "From Preponderance to Offshore Balancing"; Kupchan, "After Pax Americana"; Huntington, "Lonely Superpower."

73. See, for example, Primakov, "Mezhdunarodniye otnosheniya nakanune XXI veka," "Rossiya v mirovoi politike"; Kortunov, "Imperskoye i natsional'noye v rossiiskom soznaniyi."

74. Bogaturov, "Iskusheniye yasnostyu," 174; Beloborodov, "Konets istoriyi."

75. Some Statists were inclined to believe that U.S.-based unipolarity may lead to worldwide chaos or fascism and authoritarianism as a preventive

reaction to the unipolar impulses (Tsymburski in "'Tsivilizatsionnaya model'"; Beloborodov, "Konets istoriyi").

76. Beloborodov, "Konets istoriyi."

77. It should be noted that the National Communist and Expansionist view on national interests was challenged by Russian "white" nationalists. The "white" nationalists emphasized Russia's Slavic roots and proposed that the nation be defined in ethnic terms. The "Red" nationalists, in their turn, rejected ethnicity as the key defining characteristic and proposed to focus on geopolitics of national interests, referring to the Soviet "nation" as a model to follow (see more on various models of Russia's nation-building in Tolz, "Forging the Nation").

78. Dugin's presentation in "Yevraziyskoye soprotivleniye," *Den'*, January 2, 1992. Elsewhere, Dugin and other nationalists emphasized the significance of preserving Russia's "traditional" values and institutions, which are viewed as anti-Western, anti-market, and anti-democratic (Dugin, "Apologiya natsionalizma"; Alexandr Prokhanov and Shamil' Sultanov, "Izmenit'sya, chtoby vyzhit', *Den'*, March 6, 1991; Borodai, "Treti put'"). Dugin's philosophy is quite popular in today's Russia, particularly among the military, and his book *Geopolitics* (1997, 2d ed. 2000) is a standard reference in academic courses on geopolitics.

79. Baranov, "Doktrina Tofflera-Fukuiami-Huntingtona i realnost' mira." As if he intended to confirm the worst suspicions of Russia's nationalists, Fukuyama moved away from his original argument about institutional triumph of the West and closer to embracing the geopolitically based argument, according to which the West must be more proactive and use available capabilities for defending/promoting its values in non-Western parts of the world. For example in 1999, with Zbigniew Brzezinski, Robert McFarlane, and William Kristol, he signed the letter calling on President Clinton to use his authority and put pressure on Russia in order to stop the war in Chechnya (*Nezavisimaya gazeta*, November 5, 1999)

80. Narochnitskaya, "Natsional'nyi interes Rossiyi"; Pozdnyakov, "My sami razorili svoi dom" and "Geopoliticheski kollaps"; Dugin, *Osnovy geopolitiki;* Mitrofanov, *Shagi novoi geopolitiki;* Zyuganov, *Geografiya pobedy.*

81. Fon Kreitor, "Stoletiye novogo mira," 29.

82. Furman, "Vneshnepoliticheskiye oriyentiry Rossiyi"; Kapustin, "Natsional'nyi interes"; Gadzhiyev, *Geopolitika*, 259–276.

83. Kapustin, "Rossiya i Zapad," "Natsional'nyi interes"; Panarin, *Revansh istoriyi*, "Amerikanski global'nyi vyzov"; Mitropolit Kirill, "Norma very kak norma zhizni," *Nezavisimaya gazeta*, February 16, 2000.

84. Cited in Kortunov, "Imperskoye i natsional'noye," 78. This concept of national interests was developed more fully in Krasin, "O rossiyskikh natsional'nykh interesakh," *Natsional'nyiye interesy.*

85. Krasin, "O rossiyskikh natsional'nykh interesakh," 12. See similar remarks about global civil society in the making in Kapustin, "Natsional'nyi interes," 14–15; Panarin, *Revansh istoriyi*, 14; Shakhnazarov, "Miroporyadok tsivilizatsi," 82.

86. Kapustin, *Sovremennost'*, 103.

87. Mikhail Gorbachev, "V Kosovo Soiedineniye Shtaty oprobovali novuyu dotrinu," *Nezavisimaya gazeta*, July 8, 1999. See also Gadzhiyev, *Geopolitika*, 366–367.

88. The concluding chapter addresses Putin's views and policies after the September 11, 2001 terrorist attack on the United States.

89. In the early 1993, for example, one prominent intellectual wrote a sizable academic article to critique Fukuyama's belief that Western Liberalism is the only possible historical path (Kapustin, "Rossiya i Zapad," 85). However, in the book published in 1998, the same author writing on the same subject noted that, in the late 1990s, he didn't think it was worthwhile to seriously consider Fukuyama's thesis (Kapustin, *Sovremennost'*, 103).

90. Zudin, "'Oligarhiya' kak politicheskaya problema rossiyskogo post-kommunizma"; Simonia, "Economic Interests and Political Power in Post-Soviet Russia."

91. Zudin, "Neokorporativizm v Rossiyi?"

92. See, for example, Andranik Migranyan, "Avtoritarnyi rezhim v Rossiyi: kakovy perspektivy?" *Nezavisimaya gazeta*, January 1995; Brudny, "Neoliberal Economic Reform"; A. Tsygankov, "Manifestations of Delegative Democracy."

93. Antonenko, "Russia, NATO and European Security after Kosovo"; Tsygankov, "The Final Triumph of the Pax Americana?"

94. *Amerika: vzglyad iz Rossiyi*, 259. September 11 became an important turning point in Russian perceptions of the West and the world's strategic environment. I discuss this change in perception in greater detail in chapter 6.

95. Ibid., 137, 215.

96. A poll of over 1,600 Russians conducted in March by the All-Russian Center for Public Opinion Studies (VTsIOM), www.polit.ru/img/sys/pr_ver/pr_delim.gif, accessed on April 12, 2003.

CHAPTER 5 CLASH OF CIVILIZATIONS? THE RECEPTION OF SAMUEL HUNTINGTON'S PROJECT

The earlier versions of this chapter appeared as joint papers (with Pavel Tsygankov) in Russian ("Plyuralizm ili obosobleniye" tsivilizatsi?") and English ("Pluralism or Isolation of Civilizations").

1. O'Hagan, "Clash of Civilizations?" 3.

2. Ibid., 4.

3. Kaplan, "The Coming Anarchy."

4. Barber, "Jihad vs. McWorld."

5. Gurr, *Minorities at Risk*. Gurr's findings were published by the U.S. Institute of Peace, a think tank that is highly influential within both Washington policy circles and academia.

6. Huntington, *Political Order in Changing Societies*. In his generally more optimistic book about the worldwide spread of democracy, Huntington agreed with the unprecedented nature of the phenomenon, but emphasized many difficulties lying ahead of the Third World and post-communist societies (*The Third Wave*).

7. Huntington, "No Exit: The Errors of Endism."

8. O'Hagan, "Clash of Civilizations?" 1.

9. Alker, "If Not Huntington's 'Civilizations,' Then Whose?" 559; Dodds, *Geopolitics in a Changing World*, 15.

10. In 1997, Huntington wrote, "the Cold War fostered a common identity between American people and government. . . . The end of history, the global victory of democracy, if it occurs, could be a most traumatic and unsettling event for America" ("The Erosion of American National Interests," 31–32).

11. This point is documented in the previous chapter.

12. Huntington, "The Clash of Civilizations?" 23–25.

13. Ibid., 22, 23–25.

14. For elaboration on this point, see Huntington's "The West: Unique, Not Universal."

15. Other scholars also have argued that, despite some modifications, Huntington remained committed to a realist mode of thinking (Rubenstein and Crocker, "Challenging Huntington," 113–128; Alker, Amin, Biersteker, and Inoguchi, "How Should We Theorize Contemporary Macro-Encounters"; O'Hagan, "Clash of Civilizations?" 19).

16. Huntington, "The Clash of Civilizations?" 39.

17. Ibid., 29.

18. Ibid., 48.

19. Ibid., 26.

20. Ibid., 43. In his rebuttal, Huntington extended the point to the U.S. domestic scene by arguing that the policy and ideology of "multiculturalism" runs counter to the idea of individual equality and "color-blindness." In Huntington's view, promoting multiple cultural identities—"multiculturalism"—could disunite America ("If Not Civilizations, What?" 190).

21. Huntington, "The Clash of Civilizations?" 40, 48–49.

22. Huntington had in mind Fukuyama's "end of history" argument, according to which the end of communism signifies the emergence of a universal

Liberal era and worldwide Westernization. In his second article, Huntington explicitly stated, "History has not ended. The world is not one. Civilizations unite and divide humankind" (Huntington, "If Not Civilizations, What?" 194).

23. Huntington, "The Clash of Civilizations?" 49; Huntington, *Clash of Civilizations,* 241, 312.

24. My discussion is based mainly on analysis of publications that appeared in leading academic periodicals, such as *Politicheskiye Issledovaniya, Pro et Contra, Mirovaya Ekonomika i Mezhdunarodniye Otnosheniya,* and *Obshchestvenniye Nauki i Sovremennost'* during the 1994–1999 period. I also surveyed leading newspapers of Globalists and Nationalists and books published by Russia's most influential intellectuals and politicians.

25. The views of this school were similar to those of Gorbachev and Social Democrats. Although the two schools developed in different—the Soviet and post-Soviet—contexts, they defended a similar core of ideas and responded to the same opposing views on Liberal Westernizers, on the one hand, and Nationalists and Expansionists, on the other.

26. See, for example, Mirski, "'Stolknoveniye tsivilizatsi'?" 73; Pantin and Khoros' presentations in "'Tsivilizatsionnaya model'"; Trofimov and Chernikov in "'Stolknoveniye tsivilizatsi'"; Utkin, "Konflikt tsivilizatsi."

27. *Polis* (*Politicheskiye Issledovaniya*) is one of the top political science journals in Russia. It is published by the Institute of Comparative Politics, Russia's Academy of Science.

28. Such, in Pantin's opinion, was the criticism of most scholars, observers, and politicians whose response to Huntington was published by *Foreign Affairs.* Pantin called upon Russia's participants in the round table organized by Polis to move beyond the criticism provided by American discussants of the "Clash of Civilizations" (Pantin's presentations in "'Tsivilizatsionnaya model'," 122). Similar points were made by Igor Maksimychev ("Kuda idet Yevropa posle padeniya berlinskoi steny?" *Neza visimaya gazeta,* August 7, 1997) and Georgi Shakhnazarov ("Miro-poryadok tsivilizatsi," 149).

29. Among Globalists, Trofimov and Rashkowski provided particularly strong criticism of Huntington's inconsistency on this point. I will not go into the details of this criticism for two reasons. First, I am more interested in Russia's Globalists' conceptual criticism of the "Clash" thesis. Second, in identifying Huntington's inconsistency in defining civilizations, that is by using multiple definitions (religion/ethnic/geographic) for characterizing allegedly the same phenomenon across the world, Russia's intellectuals were not particularly original as compared to their American counterparts, and the reader can become familiar with the thrust of the argument from the *Foreign Affairs* articles.

30. Utkin, "Konflikt tsivilizatsi," 80.

31. As far as economic processes go, they emphasized the importance of fighting against poverty and inequality and the responsibility of the West as a technological leader for solving those problems (see, for example, Simonia, "Budet li sleduschaya voina stolknoveniyem tsivilizatsi?" 77; Zlobin in "'Stolknoveniye tsivilizatsi'"; Khoros in "'Tsivilizatsionnaya model'"; Shakhnazarov, "Miroporyadok tsivilizatsi," 159–161).

32. The idea of global Reason is borrowed from Russian scientist Vladimir Vernadski. Nikolai Zlobin referred to Vernadski's concept of Noosphera in his presentation (Zlobin in "'Stolknoveniye tsivilizatsi'," 133).

33. Shestopal in "'Stolknoveniye tsivilizatsi'."

34. Sydorov in "'Stolknoveniye tsivilizatsi'," 138. For similar points in writings of Russian Globalists, see Simonia, "Budet li sleduschaya voina," 77; Rashkowski in "'Tsivilizatsionnaya model'," 131; Panarin in "'Tsivilizatsionnaya model'," 129; Panarin, *Revansh istoriyi*.

35. Medovoi in "'Stolknoveniye tsivilizatsi'," 137. Simonia ("Budet li sleduschaya voina", 77–80) and Shakhnazarov ("Miroporyadok tsivilizatsi," 156), among other Globalists, also emphasized the point of Huntington's responsibility for further political development of the world.

36. Shestopal in "'Stolknoveniye tsivilizatsi'," 134.

37. Ibid.

38. Ironically, they referred to the United States as a generally successful example of such a community. The fact that Huntington overlooked the similarity of Russia and America at this point was, in the minds of Russian Globalists, an indicator of his "ideological bias" (see for example, Panarin in "'Tsivilizatsionnaya model'," 130).

39. See, for example, Shestopal's presentation in "'Stolknoveniye tsivilizatsi'," 134.

40. Khoros in "'Tsivilizatsionnaya model'," 123.

41. Zlobin in "'Stolknoveniye tsivilizatsi'," 133; Khoros in "'Tsivilizatsionnaya model'," 123–124.

42. Shakhnazarov made this point in his response to Huntington ("Miroporyadok tsivilizatsi," 158). This does not, however, imply that Russian Globalists would agree with the Western intervention in Yugoslavia, which in their view was conducted as an act of international aggression carried out with no respect for cross-civilizational negotiations (see A. Tsygankov, "The Final Triumph of the Pax Americana?"). Russian Globalists were similarly critical of American interventionism in the post–September 11 world (Aleksei Arbatov, "Irakskiye uroki," *Moscow News,* June 18–24, 2003; Gorbachev, *Grani globalizatsiyi*).

43. I continue to discuss the views of National Democrats. Unlike the pro-Western Liberals, this school was not fearful of Russia's interaction with

non-Western civilizations and perceived it as politically and culturally important. For fears of the non-West by Russia's Westernizers, see, for example, Yegor Gaidar, "Rossiya XXI veka," *Izvestiya,* May 15, 1995; Kara-Murza, "Na perekrestke politiki i nauki." One can speculate that the Westernizers' poor representation in discussing Huntington's thesis had to do with the conflict the thesis created in their worldview: the fear of non-Western civilizations, on the one hand, and the commitment to globalization and interdependence, on the other.

44. I return to this point in the following section.

45. Podtserob, "Konflikt dvukh tsivilizatsi ili ikh vzaimodeistviye?" 74.

46. For a more extensive historical perspective on Russia's Eurasianist discussions, see Hauner, *What Is Asia to Us?;* Orlova, *Yevraziyskaya tsivilizatsiya;* Paschenko, *Ideologiya yevraziystva.*

47. Khoros in "'Tsivilizatsionnaya model'," 124; Rashkowski in "'Tsivilizatsionnaya model'," 133.

48. It may sound paradoxical to those who were aware that Russia's Nationalists, as compared to Globalists, generally expressed much greater animosity toward the West.

49. This point was also made by Urban and Solovei, *Russia's Communists at the Crossroads,* 98; Patomäki and Pursiainen, "Western Models and the Russian Idea," 71.

50. This distinction is a modification of Jack Snyder's differentiation between aggressive and defensive realists (*Myths of Empire*).

51. Samuilov, "Neizbezhno li stolknoveniye tsivilizatsi?" 66.

52. Tsymburski in "'Tsivilizatsionnaya model'," 137.

53. Andrei Karagodin, "Otkroveniya mondialistov," *Den',* September 3, 1994.

54. Samuilov, "Neizbezhno li stolknoveniye tsivilizatsi?" 63.

55. See, for example, Samuilov, "Neizbezhno li stolknoveniye tsivilizatsi?" 61; Karagodin, "Otkroveniya mondialistov"; Tsymburski in "'Tsivilizatsionnaya model'," 142.

56. See, for example, Samuilov's examples from Yugoslavia's and the former Soviet region's experiences ("Neizbezhno li stolknoveniye tsivilizatsi?" 64–65).

57. Tsymburski in "'Tsivilizatsionnaya model'," 128, 136.

58. Ibid.

59. See, for example, Samuilov, "Neizbezhno li stolknoveniye tsivilizatsi?" 65.

60. Ibid., 60. See similar claims in Kaspe, "Rossiyskaya tsivilizatsiya," 76–83; Ismayil Aliyev, "Yevraziystvo kak natsionalnaya ideiya," *NG-Stsenariyi,* February 4, 1998. These points about Eurasia as an original civilization of a non-Western nature were emphasized by classical Eurasianists and are

developed by many contemporary Russian writers (see especially Dugin, *Osnovy geopolitiki;* Orlova, *Yevraziyskaya tsivilizatsiya*).

61. The argument, of course, goes back to the old Eurasianist movement of the 1920s that insisted on Russian cultural (*sliyaniye* or "fusion" and *vklyucheniye* or "inclusion") and geopolitical (*mestorazvitiye* or "space-development") unity with people and nations of Central Asia and the Far East (Orlova, *Yevraziyskaya tsivilizatsiya;* Paschenko, *Ideologiya yevraziystva*).

62. Vadim Tsymburski seemed to be the only observer who proposed a serious modification of Huntington's model by theorizing the areas in between Huntington's "civilizations" and referring to them as *Limitrof* ("Narody mezhdu tsivilizatsiyami"; "Geopolitika dlya 'yevraziyskoi atlantidy'"). However, he too was generally receptive of the idea and primarily challenged the notion of *civilizations,* but not their *clash* (see especially his "Narody mezhdu tsivilizatsiyami," 155–156).

63. See, for example, remarks on the necessity and inevitability of the integration of the newly independent states ("'Tsivilizatsionnaya model','" 153).

64. Tsymburski in "'Tsivilizatsionnaya model'," 145. Samuilov backed this point with the necessity for Russia to maintain its domestic stability. A Russo-Western alliance against the Muslim world would, in his view, "inevitably exacerbate the relations between people of Slav and Turkish nationality, thereby threatening Russia's territorial integrity and strengthening its domestic political instability" (Samuilov, "Neizbezhno li stolknoveniye," 62).

65. See especially Dugin, *Osnovy geopolitiki* and Zyuganov, *Geografiya pobedy.*

66. Mitrofanov, *Shagi novoi geopolitiki,* 221.

67. See Gennadi Zyuganov's interpretation of Huntington's article (*Rossiya i sovremennyi mir,* 70–73). See also Karagodin, "Otkroveniya mondialistov," and hints of Tsymburski in "'Tsivilizatsionnaya model'," 145–146.

68. The argument was only partially normative as Globalists identified what they called the "objective preconditions" for cooperation in the post–cold war world. See the preceding section on Russia's reception of Huntington's thesis.

69. Kara-Murza, Panarin, and Pantin, "Dukhovno-ideologicheskaya situatsiya," 10.

70. This point was particularly important for contemporary Russian Globalists who were fairly critical of the early version of Liberalism associated with Russia's first foreign minister Andrei Kozyrev and his philosophy of the country's strategic partnership with the West. While accepting some of the old Globalism's premises (such as increasing economic transnationalization

and globalization of the world), the new Globalists rejected its essentially pro-Western stance and minimal appreciation of world cultural diversity.

71. Ibid.

72. Shakhnazarov, "Miroporyadok tsivilizatsi," 156; Shakhnazarov, *Otkroveniya i zabluzhdeniya teoriyi tsivilizatsi.*

73. In the West, Hayward Alker also linked Huntington's view on civilizations with the Hegelian philosophical tradition (see Alker, "If Not Huntington's 'Civilizations,' Then Whose?").

74. Kara-Murza, Panarin, and Pantin, "Dukhovno-ideologicheskaya situatsiya," 10. This point was developed in books by Gadzhiyev (*Geopolitika* and *Vvedeniye v geopolitiku*), Kapustin (*Sovremennost'*), and Panarin (*Revansh istoriyi*).

75. Among more current intellectual supporters of the "pluralism of civilizations," contemporary Globalists sometimes pointed to philosopher Mikhail Gefter and linguist Yuri Lotman. The former put forward concepts of the "world of worlds" and of the "co-development through diversity," while the latter argued that there is nothing primordial about cultures and that a spontaneous transformation of one culture to another is quite possible. Zlobin mentioned both names in his discussion of the Huntington thesis in "'Stolknoveniye tsivilizatsi'," 132–133.

76. Kozyrev, *Preobrazheniye,* 24. Russia's Globalists organized a series of debates about Russia's optimal strategy of adjustment to the processes of global interdependence. See, for example, a discussion of Neklessa's article in *Vostok* (Neklessa, "Postsovremennyi mir," "Epilog istoriyi"; "Postsovremennyi mir") and discussion in *Otkritaya politika* (Mel'vil', "Liberal'naya vneshnepoliticheskaya alternativa dlya Rossiyi"; "Vneshnyaya politika"). See also a book by Kochetov (*Geoekonomika*), which contains a discussion on Russia's geoeconomic adjustment to the global economy.

77. At this point, the Globalists' response to Huntington coincided with their reaction to Zbigniew Brzezinski, another influential American writer and the author of *The Grand Chessboard.* Brzezinski is well known in Russian political and intellectual circles, and his book was widely discussed as another platform for developing Russia's geopolitical thinking.

78. Rogov, *Yevraziyskaya strategiya dlya Rossiyi;* see also Sergei Rogov, "Isoliatsiya ot integratsiyi," *NG-Dipkur'er,* December 7, 2000.

79. In addition, Rogov viewed such a design as a strong incentive for transforming the currently weak and disintegrated Commonwealth of Independent States into a more economically and politically stable and cohesive arrangement (Rogov, *Yevraziyskaya strategiya dlya Rossiyi,* 26, 50).

80. See Igor' Maksimychev ("Kuda idet Yevropa posle padeniya berlinskoi steny?" *Nezavisimaya gazeta,* August 7, 1997) on Russia's relations with Europe; Lomanov ("Na peripheriyi 'stolknoveniya tsivilizatsi'," 21–23) and

Dmitri Trenin ("Kitaiski faktor," *Nezavisimaya gazeta*, July 8, 1998) on relations with China; and Vitali Naumkin ("Rossiya i Iran v tsentralnoi Aziyi i Zakavkaz'e," *NG-Sodruzhestvo*, July 7, 1999) on Russo-Iranian relations.

81. See, for example, Dakhin, "Kontury novogo mira," 78–86; Tsymburski in "'Tsivilizatsionnaya model'," 145; Orlova, *Yevraziyskaya tsivilizatsiya*, 122; Nartov, *Geopolitika*, 8–21.

82. For example, Vadim Tsymburski used a substantial portion of his presentation to make a case that Huntington's piece was a manifestation of a gradual degradation of the Western liberal style of discourse into a fascistlike one and that upon closer inspection fascist ideology was simply another image of liberalism, not its alternative ("'Tsivilizatsionnaya model'," 144–146).

83. It is worth noting that before World War II there existed an influential intellectual movement called Eurasianists that emphasized the continuity between Soviet and prior Russian history. Eurasianists viewed Eurasia as a bridge between different cultures and civilizations, as a unit that played its geopolitical role while in different forms—the Great Russian Empire, the Soviet Union, or a post-Soviet Eurasian power. Contemporary Nationalists were especially attracted to this sense of difference and independence of Russian civilization and tried to build on Eurasianist theories (for a more extensive discussion, see A. Tsygankov, "Hard-Line Eurasianism").

84. See, for example, Kaspe, "Rossiyskaya tsivilizatsiya."

85. The contemporary external proletariat, as argued by Tsymburski, is the population of those territories that do not belong to any civilization in particular. The external proletariat emerged as the result of a degradation of Confucian, Muslim, and Indian civilizations under the influence of the West (see Tsymburski in "'Tsivilizatsionnaya model'," 141). For further development of this argument, see Tsymburski, "Narody mezhdu tsivilizatsiyami" and "Geopolitika dlya." For a more Globalist reaction, see Mezhuyev, "Review."

86. Depending on writers' defensive or aggressive political orientation, the degree of recommended integration and isolation from the world varied from moderate (Samuilov, "Neizbezhno li stolknoveniye"; Tsymburski in "'Tsivilizatsionnaya model'"") to extreme (Zyuganov, *Rossiya i sovremennyi mir*).

87. See Tsymburski in "'Tsivilizatsionnaya model'"; Samuilov, "Neizbezhno li stolknoveniye"; Samil' Sultanov, "Tretya mirovaya voyna uzhe nachalas'," *Zavtra* 18, 1995; Nikolai Ryzhkov, "Konfrontatsiya ili dialog?" *Nezavisimaya gazeta*, September 28, 1999. For an argument supportive of Russia's geopolitical alliance with Iran, see Aleksei Gromyko, "Rossiya i Iran," *Nezavisimaya gazeta*, June 26, 1998. See similar arguments for Russia's participation in integrating Caucasus (Ilya Maksakov, "Eshche odin general

stal politikom," *Nezavisimaya gazeta,* December 29, 1998), Siberia (Mikhail Nikolayev, "Vostochnyi potentsial," *Nezavisimaya gazeta,* January 21, 2000), and the former Soviet states (Vadim Balytnikov, "Ot soyuznogo gosudarstva k yevraziyskomu soyuzu," *Nezavisimaya gazeta,* January 26, 2000).

88. Tsymburski, "Geopolitika dlya."

89. "Rossiya i prostranstvo"; Fon Kreiter, "Stoletiye novogo mira," 28.

90. Mitrofanov, *Shagi novoi geopolitiki,* 221.

91. Dugin, *Osnovy geopolitiki,* 28.

92. Zyuganov, *Geografiya pobedy,* 172.

93. Ibid., 180. Alexei Mitrofanov went so far as to suggest that Russia must do everything possible to arm China by significantly expanding its weapons sales and—so as to establish a better geopolitical balance—even encourage Chinese expansion into the territories of southern Kazakhstan and some of the southern former Soviet republics (cited in Nartov, *Geopolitika,* 244). Russian Nationalists, however, were wary of China's rising threat to Russia and were far from united on the issue of strategic partnership with China (for critical views, see Dugin, *Osnovy geopolitiki,* 360–362; Nartov, *Geopolitika,* 240–249).

94. Nartov, *Geopolitika,* 269–270; Zyuganov, *Geografiya pobedy,* 202–203.

95. Panarin, "Amerikanski global'nyi vyzov," 58–59.

96. See my "Mastering Space in Eurasia" for a review of various Russian projects of providing peace and stability in the post-Soviet region.

97. Sergei Stankevich, "Derzhava v poiskakh sebya," *Nezavisimaya gazeta,* March 28, 1992.

98. In 1999, Huntington predicted a Sino-Russian war within ten to fifteen years (as cited in Trenin, *The End of Eurasia,* 318).

99. Vladimir Putin, "Rossiya: Novyye vostochnyye perspektivy," *Nezavisimaya gazeta,* October 14, 2000. Interestingly enough, in his earlier published book, Putin referred to Russia as a country of European, even Western European mentality (Putin, *First Person*). Apparently, Russia's president saw no conflict between the two statements and viewed Russia as a country that combined different identities.

100. Rogov, *Yevraziyskaya strategiya*; Yelena Lashkina, "Rossiya na perekrestke," *NG-Politekonomiya,* September 26, 2000. I summarized some of these proposals earlier in the chapter.

101. One expert noted that Russia's ties to China "have now drawn closer than at any time in the past 40 years" (Jim Munn, "Putin Turns Russia Eastward Again," *Los Angeles Times,* July 26, 2000).

102. I rely mostly on G. Smith, *Post-Soviet States,* chap. 6.

103. See more on various projects of Russia's nation-building in Tolz, "Forging the Nation."

104. Both were cited in G. Smith, *Post-Soviet States,* 143.

105. Ibid., 143–144.

106. Turovski, *Politicheskiye protsessy v regionakh Rossiyi.* Other experts argued that it was not so much the model of asymmetrical federalism that presented a problem, but the fact that the contemporary Russian Federation had three types of asymmetry—the constitutionally embedded, the extra-constitutionally negotiated, and the anticonstitutionally exercised (Stepan, "Russian Federalism in Comparative Perspective").

107. As Jeff Kahn has argued, Putin's reform included some extra-constitutional, if not non-constitutional, arrangements and presented serious concerns of executive overreach (Kahn, "What Is the New Russian Federalism?"). For a similar argument, see Chirikova and Lapina, "Political Power and Political Stability in the Russian Regions").

108. G. Smith, *Post-Soviet States,* 151–152.

109. Under Yeltsin, Russian federalism was often based on some doubtful and illegitimate arrangements. Not only were the center-region treaties not ratified by the federal or local legislatures, but they also sometimes included secret agreements which were not even published (Kahn, "What Is the New Russian Federalism?").

110. Samuel Huntington, "A Local Front of a Global War," *New York Times,* December 16, 1999.

111. Alexandr Dzasokhov, "Razvitiye sovremennogo mira idet po opasnomu puti," *Nezavisimaya gazeta,* December 10, 1999. For similar statements and the development of the argument about the uniqueness of Chechnya's case, see an article by the former deputy of Bashkortostan's parliament, Bulat Urazbayev ("Zapad i Vostok soidutsya v XXI veke," *Nezavisimaya gazeta,* July 14, 2000), and the minister of the Republic of Dagestan (Zagir Arukhov, "Tak li uzh neizbezhen 'konflikt tsivilizatsi'?" *HG-Religiyi,* April 11, 2001).

112. As constructivist and post-structuralist studies argue, a unit's identity is never fixed, but is rather constituted by its external environment and is constantly negotiated and renegotiated through a process of interaction with the environment (see, for example, Wendt, "The Agent-Structure Problem in International Relations Theory"; Neumann, "Self and Other in International Relations").

113. Other scholars reached similar conclusions (see Ruggie, *Winning Peace,* 163; Ikenberry, "The West: Precious, Not Unique"; Urban and Solovei, *Russia's Communists at the Crossroads,* 98; Walt, "Building Up New Bogeyman," 189).

114. Trenin, *The End of Eurasia,* 319–320.

115. See especially Alker, Amin, Biersteker, and Inoguchi, "How Should We Theorize Contemporary Macro-Encounters?"

CHAPTER 6 THE WORLD ORDER AFTER SEPTEMBER 11

1. Putin, "Zayavleniye Prezidenta Rossiyskoi Federatsiyi," September 24, 2001.

2. Ibid.; Michael Wines, "Putin Offers Support to U.S. for Its Antiterrorist Efforts," *New York Times,* September 25, 2001.

3. See Putin, "Rossiya: Novyye vostochnyye perspektivy." Since 1999, Russia's president has visited key states of the region—the former Soviet area, China, India, Mongolia, North Korea, and Brunei—and signed some agreements of key significance, such as a strategic treaty with China. Putin even visited Cuba, from where he made a characteristic statement supportive of a multipolar world and critical of "unipolar hegemonic tendencies" in the world.

4. Domestically, only 15 percent of the membership of the Russian Duma supported Putin's move, and it was equally controversial in the army ("Putin policy shift is bold but risky," *Financial Times Survey,* April 15, 2002).

5. Although Putin has signed the 2000 Foreign Policy Concept, in which the notion of a multipolar world was used ("Kontseptsiya Vneshnei Politiki"), he subsequently distanced himself from the term. In Putin's April 2002 state of the nation address, the term was not mentioned at all. Russian Foreign Minister Igor' Ivanov also spoke of a new pragmatism in Russia's policies: "Today, our foreign policy resources are relatively limited. And they will be concentrated in fields that are vital for Russia" (as cited in Robyn Dixon, "Russia to Follow New Pragmatism in Its Foreign Policy," *Los Angeles Times,* July 11, 2000).

6. According to Putin, "the norm of the international community and the modern world is a tough competition—for markets, investments, political, and economic influence . . . nobody is eager to help us. We alone have to fight for a place under the 'economic sun'" (Putin, "Poslaniye Prezidenta," 4–5).

7. In his April 2002 state of the nation address, Putin emphasized international factors of economic significance and Russia's need to survive economically in the new world (Putin, "Poslaniye Prezidenta," 3–4, 14–15). The emphasis on geoeconomics builds on earlier discussions of Russian intellectuals about optimal strategies of adjustment to the processes of global economic interdependence (see Neklessa, "Postsovremennyi mir v novoi sisteme koordinat"; "Postsovremennyi mir"; Rogov, *Yevraziyskaya strategiya;* Kochetov, *Geoekonomika*). The influential Council for Foreign and Defense Policy summarized the new liberal-nationalist vision in the document untitled "Strategy for Russia: Agenda for President—2000." The authors of the document criticized Primakov's concept of a multipolar world as outdated, financially expensive, and potentially confrontational. Instead, they offered

the concept of "selective engagement," which they compared to Russia's nineteenth-century policy of "self-concentration" after its defeat in the Crimean war and with China's policy since Deng Xioping (*Strategiya dlya Rossiyi: povestka dlya prezidenta — 2000*). For analyses of Putin's Pragmatist philosophy see Tretyakov, "Pragmatizm vneshnei politiki Putina"; Meshkov, "Aktual'niye aspekty vneshnei politiki Rossiyi."

8. On this point, see Bill Keller, "A Beautiful Friendship," *New York Times,* May 18, 2002.

9. Putin proclaimed his commitment to Russia's traditional identity in his programmatic speech "Russia at the Turn of the Millennium," in which he emphasized patriotism, a strong state, and social solidarity as his country's core values (Putin, "Russia at the Turn of the Millennium"). During the presidential campaign in March 2000, he stated that, "from the very start, Russia was created as a supercentralized state. This is part of its genetic code, tradition and people's mentality" (CNN, March 26, 2000, www.cnn.com).

10. Some Muslim leaders called for a jihad or holy war against the United States, and Putin cited concern for the nation's Islamic minority as a major factor in the government's decision to oppose military action in Iraq (Michael Wines, "Two Leaders of Russia's Muslims Split over Jihad against U.S.," *New York Times,* April 4, 2003).

11. Given the West's considerable role in world affairs, its own quarrels can only weaken Russian globally oriented forces. As one Russian observer wrote during the war in Iraq, "with the West absorbed in the war and its own internal squabbles it has ceased to be a factor that could push Russia toward more radical transformation" (Liliya Shevtsova, "Iraq's Impact on Russia," *Moscow Times,* April 10, 2003).

12. The word for "alliance" (*soyuz*) in Russian sounds the same as that for "union," which makes the proposed rapprochement, or *soyuz,* with the West sound almost like political and cultural unification.

13. Grigori Yavlinski, "Druzhba na vremya ili soyuz navsegda?" *Obschaya gazeta,* January 24, 2002.

14. Ibid.; see also Grigori Yavlinski, "Dver' v Yevropu nahoditsya v Vashingtone," *Obschaya gazeta,* May 16, 2002.

15. Kara-Murza, "Na perekrestke politiki i nauki."

16. Ibid. Dmitri Trenin, another influential voice within the Russian Liberal foreign policy community, came out critical of Putin's Pragmatist philosophy as being insufficiently pro-Western. He also insisted that Russia must make a "civilizational" choice in favor of "integration into contemporary Europe" because "for Russia, Europeanization means modernization" (Trenin, "Vladimir Putin's Autumn Marathon").

17. It seems that Bush uses the "pure evil" terminology because he lacks a rational explanation for why American values are criticized in Muslim and

other countries. At a press conference on October 12, 2001, the leader of the "free world" stated: "How do I respond when I see that in some Islamic countries there is vitriolic hatred for America? I'll tell you how I respond: I'm amazed. I just can't believe it because I know how good we are" (as cited in Ali, *The Clash of Fundamentalisms,* ix).

18. Thomas Friedman, "World War Three," *New York Times,* September 13, 2001. For similar arguments made by Western conservatives, see Fukuyama, "Their Target: The Modern World"; Margaret Thatcher, "Advice to a Superpower," *New York Times,* February 11, 2002.

19. The terminology comes from Kara-Murza, "Na perekrestke politiki i nauki." For a similar culturally essentialist language as used by Liberals such as Kara-Murza and Boris Grushin, see "Slabost', kotoruyu ne pobedit' siloi," *Obschaya gazeta,* September 20, 2001.

20. Buzgalin, "Russia and America: A New Twist in the Confrontation?"

21. Valeri Fedorov, "Vperyed, k ideologiyi?" *Nezavisimaya gazeta,* February 18, 2002.

22. Dmitri Furman argued that Putin's pro-Western choice might help to preserve the essentially non-democratic regime in Russia, just as an American alliance with Central Asian states and Pakistan does not mean to make these states more human rights friendly (Dmitri Furman, "Polyet dvuglavogo orla," *Obschaya gazeta,* May 30, 2002).

23. See, for example, Graham Allison, Karl Kaiser, and Sergei Karaganov, "The World Needs a Global Alliance for Security," *International Herald Tribune,* November 21, 2001; Kortunov, "Stanovleniye novogo myrovogo poryadka."

24. Putin, "Zayavleniye Prezidenta Rossiyskoi Federatsiyi," September 24, 2001.

25. Putin, speech to the German Parliament, September 25, 2001.

26. Several leaders of parliamentary factions have emphasized the role of the U.N. in authorizing international actions against terrorism (as cited in Marina Volkova, "Putin sozyvayet politelitu," *Nezavisimiya gazeta,* September 25, 2001).

27. Putin stated, "We have to firmly proclaim our priorities in the European direction." He went on to define Russia's policy priorities in relations with Europe and America as those of "integration" and "maintenance of constant dialogue," respectively (Putin, "Poslaniye Prezidenta," 18). Earlier, the view was elaborated in other official foreign policy documents and speeches (see "Kontseptsiya vneshnei politiki"; Meshkov, "Aktual'niye aspekty vneshnei politiki Rossiyi").

28. Lydiya Andrusenko, "Poidyet li Rossiya v soyuzniki SshA," *Nezavisimiya gazeta,* September 21, 2001.

29. For example, State Duma speaker Gennadi Seleznev announced, "The United States cannot stay in the Central Asian states more than six months because that was the agreed term under which they went there." He went on to argue that the United States could not set up military bases in the region without a U.N. mandate (*RFE/RL Newsline*, January 25, 2002).

30. On the other hand, Liberal parties continued to lose their appeal. For example, the Union of Right Wing Forces (which holds 9 percent of seats in the Duma) saw its rating fall to 4 percent by the beginning of 2002 (Buzgalin, "Russia and America").

31. Milrad Fatullayev, "Voina idyet v Rossiyu," *Nezavisimaya gazeta,* November 10, 2001.

32. Katrina Vanden Heuvel and Stephen F. Cohen, "Endangering U.S. Security," *Nation,* April 15, 2002. For a warning about the narrow domestic support for Putin's agreement to cooperate with Washington's military campaign against terrorism, see also Stephen F. Cohen, "Second Chance with Russia," *Nation,* November 5, 2001.

33. *RFE/RL Newsline,* January 16, 2002.

34. Sergey Ptichkin and Aleksey Chichkin, "From Where Russia Is Clearly Visible," *Rossiyskaya Gazeta,* January 22, 2002 (as translated by *CDI Russia Weekly,* no. 190, January 25, 2002). The American presence in the region, argued another source, resembled post–World War II events, when the Americans quickly turned from allies into enemies (Evgeny Mikhilov, "The Art of Wiping Things Out," *Versty,* January 24, 2002, as translated by *CDI Russia Weekly,* no. 190, January 25, 2002).

35. *Amerika: vzglyad iz Rossiyi,* 27.

36. Ibid., 124. At the same time, Russians continued to show strong support for Putin's decision to side with the West (ibid., 34, 124; "Rossiyani podderzhivayut sozdaniye soyuza RF i SshA v bor'be s mezhdunarodnym terrorizmom," *Nega-Set,* November 18, 2001).

37. "Most Statists shared the verdict that the tragedy was the result of Washington's hegemonic policies" (see Boris Poklad, "Ekho s Atlantiki. Amerikanskaya tragediya i Rossiya," *Nezavisimaya gazeta,* January 30, 2002).

38. Some Statists begin to question the notion of a "multipolar world" and revise it in favor of developing international law and collective security mechanisms centered on the United Nations Security Council (see especially the views of influential Statist Sergei Kortunov, "Stanovleniye novogo myrovogo poryadka"). Here, their views are similar to those of National Democrats. The similarity in the two groups' views was also notable in their perceptions of Western intervention in Yugoslavia in 1999 and Russia's most appropriate response to it. (See A. Tsygankov, "The Final Triumph of Pax Americana?")

39. Tsymburski, "Eto tvoi posledni geokul'turnyi vybor, Rossiya."

40. Ibid.

41. See, for example, his articles on Russia's national interests (Kortunov, "Imperskoye i natsional'noye v rossiiskom soznaniyi").

42. Kortunov, "Rossiysko-Amerikanskoye partnerstvo," 69.

43. Ibid., 78.

44. Ibid., 79–80.

45. Panarin, "Ontologiya terrora," 46. For other similar statements, see Aleksandr Prokhanov, "Ameriku potseloval angel smerti," *Zavtra,* September 18, 2001; Dugin, "Terakti 11 Sentyabrya: economicheski smysl."

46. Dugin, "Terakty 11 sentyabrya"; Zyuganov, "Politicheski doklad"; Leonid Ivashev, "Global'naya provokatsiya," *Nezavisimaya gazeta,* October 10, 2001.

47. Panarin, "Ontologiya terrora," 48–49.

48. Ibid., 49.

49. Zyuganov, "Politicheski doklad"; Marina Volkova, "Putin sozyvayet politelytu," *Nezavisimaya gazeta,* September 25, 2001.

50. See, for example, a statement by Dugin ("Lider 'yevraziytsev' predskazyvayet mirovuyu voinu," *Prima,* September 17, 2001).

51. See, for example, Held, "Violence and Justice in a Global Age"; Kortunov, "Stanovleniye novogo myrovogo poryadka."

52. Fukuyama, "Their Target."

53. Ibid.

54. Ibid.

55. Ibid.

56. For instance, Egyptian scholar Abdel Monem drew our attention to Fukuyama's contradiction with his earlier views, and argued for their self-fulfilling quality (Monem, "A Self-Fulfilling Prophecy"). And the mainstream *Washington Post* observed that "Fukuyama has been on defensive," whereas "Huntington has been in ascendancy since September 11" and "his book, five years after publication, has rocketed onto the bestseller lists" (Achenbach, "The Clash"). Even before September 11, the Russian foreign minister had in one of his speeches referred to the "end of history" argument as something that "today may seem merely odd," given "the real scale of new threats and challenges during the era of globalization" (Ivanov, "Rossiya v mirovoi politike," 4).

57. Abdel Monem also noticed the similarity of Fukuyama's new reasoning with that of the old Huntington (Monem, "A Self-Fulfilling Prophecy"), and Tariq Ali even wrote that Fukuyama was now "much closer to Huntington's original thesis than Huntington" (Ali, *The Clash of Fundamentalisms,* 283).

58. Naim, "Why the World Loves to Hate America."

59. Fukuyama, "Their Target."

60. As cited by Ali, *The Clash of Fundamentalisms*, 272.

61. The public has certainly given the "clash of civilization" thesis a new currency, as his 1996 book returned to the list of bestsellers. Several commentators noticed and analyzed Huntington's departure from his earlier views (Achenbach, "The Clash"; Ali, *The Clash of Fundamentalisms*, 283).

62. Huntington, "The Age of Muslim Wars."

63. Ibid.

64. Ibid.

65. For example, Akbar Ahmed, a professor of Islamic studies at American University, reported that when he interviewed people in Morocco and Pakistan after the appearance of Huntington's original article, he kept hearing that "the West wants a war with Islam." "I would say, how do you come to this conclusion? And they would say, the leading Harvard professor wants a war with Islam," Ahmed recalled. "It was becoming dangerously self-fulfilling" (as cited in Achenbach, "The Clash"). Muslims felt stereotyped and homogenized by Huntington outside Morocco and Pakistan, too. In this book, I have also reported reactions from Iran and Russia (see especially chapters 1 and 5). For other reactions, see Monem, "A Self-Fulfilling Prophecy" and Said, "Clash of Ignorance."

66. Fukuyama said, "I think it's not just wrong, it's also not helpful to world politics. It gives aid and comfort to people who want to reject Western values" (as cited in Achenbach, "The Clash").

67. Kaplan, "Looking the World in the Eye."

68. As cited in Said, "The Clash of Ignorance." Another conservative commentator wrote of Huntington's "clash of civilizations" argument, "again and again, and in so many words, Huntington successfully predicts the future. Repeatedly, Huntington tells us that we're in for a long-term struggle (including periods of intense violence) with the Muslim world. But these generalized predictions are the least of it. Not only is Huntington right, he is right for all the right reasons—and correct in depth and detail as well" (Kurtz, "The Future of 'History'").

69. "For Huntington, a clash of civilizations was a worst-case scenario. For bin Laden it was a game plan," argued Barber. Barber was referring especially to bin Laden's videotape aired in October, in which bin Laden said, "These events have divided the whole world into two sides, the side of believers and the side of infidels" (as cited in Achenbach, "The Clash"). See a similar assessment of the editor of *New Left Review*, Tariq Ali, in *Clash of Fundamentalisms*, 273.

70. Ali, *Clash of Fundamentalisms*, 283.

71. Achenbach, "The Clash."

72. Huntington didn't sound as unilateral as Fukuyama and wasn't supportive of a prolonged military response. He predicted: "The longer and the more intensely the United States and its allies use military force against their opponents, the more widespread and intense will be the Muslim reaction" (Huntington, "The Age of Muslim Wars").

73. Mead, *Mind, Self, and Society*, 271.

74. Scholars of East Asian and Muslim cultures often arrive at the same conclusion. For example, summarizing results of a collective study on China, Thomas J. Christensen concluded that "foreign pressure fuels nationalism, not Liberalism, in China and actually makes public opinion and elite politics more conservative than they would otherwise be" ("Pride, Pressures, and Politics," 248). And Richard Falk concluded from his study of the impact of Western exclusionary discourse on Islam that such discourse "weakens democratic forces in existing Islamic states in their efforts to uphold a secular conception of relations between religion and the state, and to protect the freedoms and autonomy of individuals" ("False Universalism and the Geopolitics of Exclusion," 20). For similar observations, see Salla, "Political Islam and the West," 731; Hashmi, "Islamic Ethics in International Society," 234.

75. Said, *Culture and Imperialism*, 216.

76. In formulating these guidelines, I follow the lead of those who have been concerned with a truly global world order scholarship. My thinking was especially affected by work of Hayward R. Alker, Tahir Amin, Thomas Biersteker, and Takashi Inoguchi (see especially their "How Should We Theorize Contemporary Macro-Encounters").

77. For a recent development of this point, see Crawford and Jarvis, *International Relations—Still an American Social Science?*

78. Exceptions do exist—one can only remember the methodologically diverse and ethically sensitive scholarship of Karl Deutsch, Richard Falk, and Rob Walker (see Deutsch, *Political Community*; Falk, *The End of World Order* and *Human Governance*; Walker, *Culture, Ideology, and World Order* and *Inside/Outside*)—but they continue to be marginalized by realist scholarship of various brands.

79. On this point, see especially, Alker and Biersteker, "The Dialectics of World Order." See also Inayatullah and Blaney, "Knowing Encounters."

80. Connoly, "Cross-State Citizen Networks," 351–352.

BIBLIOGRAPHY

Achenbach, Joel. "The Clash." *The Washington Post,* December 16 (2001).
Afanasyev, Yu., ed. *Inogo ne dano.* Moskva: Progress, 1988.
———. *God posle Avgusta.* Moskva: Progress, 1992.
Agurski, M. *The Third Rome: National-Bolshevism in the USSR.* Boulder, Colo.: Westview, 1987.
Ali, T. *The Clash of Fundamentalisms. Crusades, Jihads and Modernity.* London: Verso, 2002.
Alker, Hayward R. "Dialectical Foundations of Global Disparities." *International Studies Quarterly* 25, 1 (1981).
———. "Dialectical Thinking about World Order: Ten World Hypotheses That Have Made My Days." Paper delivered at the Anaheim Meeting of the International Studies Association, 1986.
———. "If Not Huntington's 'Civilizations,' Then Whose?" Review. *Fernand Braudel Center* 18, 4 (1995).
———. *Rediscoveries and Reformulations. Humanistic Methodologies for International Studies.* Cambridge: Cambridge University Press, 1996.
Alker, Hayward R., Tahir Amin, Thomas Biersteker, and Takashi Inoguchi. "How Should We Theorize Contemporary Macro-Encounters: In Terms of Superstates, World Orders, or Civilizations?" A paper presented to the thematic panel "Encounters among Civilizations," Third Pan-European International Relations Conference, SGIR-ISA, Vienna, Austria, September 16–19, 1998.
———. "Twelve World Order Debates Which Have Made Our Days." A paper presented at the founding meeting of the Russian International Studies Association, MGIMO University, Moscow, April 20–21, 2000.

177

Alker, Hayward R., and Thomas J. Biersteker. "The Dialectics of World Order: Notes for a Future Archeologist of International *Savior Faire*." *International Studies Quarterly* 28, 2 (1984).

Alker, Hayward R., Thomas J. Biersteker, and Takashi Inoguchi. "From Imperial Power Balancing to People's Wars." In *International/ Intertextual Relations,* edited by J. Der-Derian and M. J. Shapiro. Lanham: Lexington Books, 1989.

Amerika: vzglyad iz Rossiyi. Do i poslye 11 sentyabrya. Moskva: Institut fonda "Obschestvennoye mneniye," 2001.

Amin, T. *Nationalism and Internationalism in Liberalism, Marxism, and Islam.* Islamabad: International Institute of Islamic Thought, 1991.

Anderson, B. *Imagined Communities.* London: Verso, 1983.

Anderson, P. *A Zone of Engagement.* London: Verso, 1992.

Antonenko, Oksana. "Russia, NATO, and European Security after Kosovo." *Survival* 41, 4 (1999).

Arab-Ogli, Eduard A. "Yevropeiskaya tsivilizatsiya i obschechelovecheskiye tsennosti." *Voprosy filosofiyi* 8 (1990).

Arbatov, G. A. *Zatyuanuvsheyesya vyzdorovleniye (1955–1985): svidetel'stvo sovremennika.* Moskva: Mezdunarodniye otnosheniya, 1991.

Aron, Leon. "The Foreign Policy Doctrine of Postcommunist Russia and Its Domestic Context." In *The New Russian Foreign Policy,* edited by Michael Mandelbaum. New York: Council on Foreign Relations, 1998.

Ashley, Richard. "The Geopolitics of Geopolitical Space: Toward a Critical Social Theory of International Politics." *Alternatives* 12, 4 (October 1987).

Attali, J. *Millennium. Winners and Losers in the Coming World Order.* New York: Times Books, 1991.

Baburin, S. *Territoriya gosudarstva.* Moskva: Moskovski Universitet, 1997.

Badie, B. *The Imported State. The Westernization of the Political Order.* Stanford: Stanford University Press, 2000.

Baranov, Vladimir. "Doktrina Tofflera-Fukuiami-Huntingtona i realnost' mira." *Nepogoda,* www.smi.ru:8081/nepogoda/, accessed on June 26, 2000.

Barber, Benjamin R. "Jihad vs. McWorld." *Atlantic Monthly* 269, 3 (1992). http://www.theatlantic.com/politics/foreign/images, accessed on November 3, 1999.

Batalov, Eduard Ya. "Yedinstvo v mnogoobraziyi—printsip zhivogo mira." *Voprosy filosofiyi* 8 (1990).

Batkin, Leonid. "Stat' Yevropoi." In *Vozobnovleniye istoriyi.* Moskva: Moskovski Rabochi, 1991.

Beloborodov, Dmitri. "Konets istoriyi kak torzhestvo 'liberalnoi demokratiyi'?" *Polyarnaya Zvezda* (2000), http://zvezda.ru/2000/01/27, accessed on June 26, 2000.

Berger, P. J., and T. Luckmann. *The Social Construction of Reality. A Treatise in the Sociology of Knowledge.* New York: Doubleday, 1966.

Biersteker, Thomas J. "Eroding Boundaries, Contested Terrain." *International Studies Review* 1, 1 (1999).

Blaney, David L., and Naeem Inayatullah. "Neo-Modernization? IR and the Inner Life of Modernization Theory." *European Journal of International Relations* 8, 1 (2002).

Bloom, William. *Personal Identity, National Identity, and International Relations.* Cambridge: Cambridge University Press, 1990.

Bobrow, D. B., ed. "Prospects for International Relations: Conjectures about the Next Millennium." A special issue of *International Studies Review* 1, 2 (1999).

Bogaturov, Alexei D. "Iskusheniye yasnostyu." *Kosmopolis* (1997).

Borodai, Yuri. "Treti put'." *Nash sovremennik* 9 (1991).

———. "Totalitarizm." *Nash Sovremennik* 7 (1992).

Boroujerdi, Mehrzad. "Iranian Islam and the Faustian Bargain of Western Modernity." Syracuse University, 1997. http://web.syr.edu/~mborouje/jpr.html, accessed on May 19, 2001.

Bozeman, Adda. "The International Order in a Multicultural World." In *The Expansion of International Society,* edited by Hedley Bull and Adam Watson. Oxford: Clarendon Press, 1984.

Breton, A., et al., eds. *Nationalism and Rationality.* Cambridge: Cambridge University Press, 1995.

Breton, Albert, and Margot Breton. "Nationalism Revisited." In *Nationalism and Rationality,* edited by Albert Breton et al. Cambridge: Cambridge University Press, 1995.

Brewer, M. B., and D. T. Campbell. *Ethnocentrism and Intergroup Attitudes. East African Evidence.* New York: John Wiley & Sons, 1976.

Brown, Chris. "International Political Theory and the Idea of World Community." In *International Relations Theory Today,* edited by Stephen Smith and Ken Booth. University Park, Penn.: Pennsylvania State University Press, 1995.

———. "History Ends, Worlds Collide." *Review of International Studies* 25, 1 (1999).

Brown, M. E., S. M. Lynn-Jones, and S. E. Miller, eds. *Debating the Democratic Peace.* Cambridge, Mass.: MIT Press, 1996.

Brubaker, R. *Nationalism Reframed.* Cambridge: Cambridge University Press, 1996.

Brudny, Yitzhak M. "Neoliberal Economic Reform and the Consolidation of Democracy in Russia." In *The International Dimension of Post-Communist Transition in Russia and the New States of Eurasia,* edited by Karen Dawisha. Armonk, London: M. E. Sharpe, 1997.

————. *Reinventing Russia. Russian Nationalism and the Soviet State, 1953–1991.* Cambridge, Mass.: Harvard University Press, 1998.

Brzezinski, Z. *The Grand Failure. The Birth and Death of Communism in the Twentieth Century.* New York: Charles Scribner's Sons, 1989.

————. *Out of Control. Global Turmoil on the Eve of the Twenty-First Century.* New York: Charles Scribner's Sons, 1993.

————. "Premature Partnership." *Foreign Affairs* (1994).

————. *The Grand Chessboard.* New York: Basic Books, 1998.

Bull, Hedley. *The Anarchical Society: A Study of Order in World Politics.* New York: Columbia University Press, 1977.

————. "Martin Wight and the Theory of International Relations." In *International Theory: The Three Traditions,* edited by Martin Wight. New York: Holmes and Meier, 1992.

Bull, H., and A. Watson, eds. *The Expansion of International Society.* Oxford: Clarendon Press, 1984.

Bunce, Valerie. "The Political Economy of Postsocialism." *Slavic Review* 58, 4 (1999).

Buzan, B., C. Jones, and R. Little. *The Logic of Anarchy: Neorealism to Structural Realism.* New York: Columbia University Press, 1993.

Buzgalin, Aleksandr. "Russia and America: A New Twist in the Confrontation?" *Prism* 8, 3 (2002). http://www.jamestown.com accessed on April 2, 2002.

Campbell, D., and M. J. Shapiro, eds. *Moral Spaces: Rethinking Ethics and World Politics.* Minneapolis: University of Minnesota Press, 1998.

Chaadaev, Petr. "Apology of a Madman." In *Readings in Russian Civilization,* edited by Thomas Riha. 2d ed. Chicago: University of Chicago Press, 1969.

Chirikova, Alla, and Natalya Lapina. "Political Power and Political Stability in the Russian Regions." In *Contemporary Russian Politics,* edited by Archie Brown. Oxford: Oxford University Press, 2001.

Christensen, Thomas J. "Pride, Pressures, and Politics: The Roots of China's Worldview." In *In the Eyes of the Dragon. China Views the World,* edited by Yong Deng and Fei-Ling Wang. Lanham: Rowman & Littlefield, 1999.

Clover, Charles. "Dreams of the Eurasian Heartland." *Foreign Affairs* 78, 2 (1999).

Connoly, William E. "Cross-State Citizen Networks: A Response to Dallmayr." *Millennium* 30, 2 (2001).

Cortell, Andrew P., and James W. Davis, Jr. "Understanding the Domestic Impact of International Norms." *International Studies Review* 2, 1 (2000).

Cox, Robert W. "Civilizations: Encounters and Transformations." *Studies in Political Economy* 47, 3 (1995).

Cox, R. W., with T. J. Sinclair. *Approaches to World Order.* Cambridge: Cambridge University Press, 1996.

Crawford, R. M. A., and D. S. L. Jarvis, eds. *International Relations—Still an American Social Science? Toward Diversity in International Thought.* New York: State University of New York Press, 2001.

Dakhin, Vladimir. "Kontury novogo mira." *Svobodnaya mysl'* 4 (1995).

Dallmayr, Fred R. "Globalization from Below." *International Politics* 36, 9 (1999).

Deng, Yong. "Conception of National Interests: Realpolitik, Liberal Dilemma, and the Possibility of Change." In *In the Eyes of the Dragon. China Views the World,* edited by Yong Deng and Fei-Ling Wang. Lanham: Rowman & Littlefield, 1999.

Der-Derian, J., and M. J. Shapiro, eds. *International/Intertextual Relations.* Lanham: Lexington Books, 1989.

Deutsch, K. W. *Political Community and the North Atlantic Area.* New York: Greenwood Press, 1969.

Diligenski, German G. "'Konets istoriyi' ili smena tsivilizatsi?" *Voprosy filosofiyi* 3 (1991).

Diligenski, German, and Vladislav Lektorski. "Problemy tselostnogo mira." *Voprosy filosofiyi* 12 (1990).

Dodds, K. *Geopolitics in a Changing World.* New York: Prentice Hall, 2000.

Donaldson, R. H., and J. L. Nogee. *The Foreign Policy of Russia: Changing Systems, Enduring Interests.* Armonk: M. E. Sharpe, 1998.

Doyle, Michael. "Liberalism and World Politics." *American Political Science Review* 80 (1986).

Dugin, Alexandr. "Konservativnaya revolyusiya." In his *Konservativnaya revolutsiya.* Moskva: Arktogeya, 1994.

———. "Apologiya natsionalizma." In his *Konservativnaya revolutsiya.* Moskva: Arktogeya, 1994.

———. *Osnovy geopolitiki.* Moskva: Arktogeya, 1997.

———. "Terakty 11 sentyabrya: ekonomicheski smysl." In *Geopolitika terrora.* Moskva: "Arktogeya tsentr," 2002.

Dunlop, J. B. *Faces of Contemporary Russian Nationalism.* Princeton, N.J.: Princeton University Press, 1983.

———. *The New Russian Nationalism.* New York: Praeger, 1985.

English, R. D. *Russia and the Idea of the West. Gorbachev, Intellectuals, and the End of the Cold War.* New York: Columbia University Press, 2000.

Evangelista, M. *Unarmed Forces. The Transnational Movements to End the Cold War.* Ithaca, N.Y.: Cornell University Press, 1999.

Falk, R. *The End of World Order: Essays on Normative International Relations.* New York and London: Holmes & Meier, 1983.

———. *Human Governance: Toward a New Global Politics.* University Park, Penn.: Pennsylvania State University Press, 1995.

———. "False Universalism and the Geopolitics of Exclusion: The Case of Islam." *Third World Quarterly* 18, 1 (1997).

Fon Kreitor, Nikolai. "Stoletiye novogo mira: pluralizm protiv universalizma." *Molodaya gvardiya* 6 (1998).

"Formatsiyi ili tsivilizatsiyi?" *Voprosy filosofiyi* 10 (1989).

Friedman, T. L. *The Lexus and the Olive Tree.* New York: Farrar, Straus, Giroux, 1999.

"From Civilizational Clash to Inter-Civilizational Dialogue." Tehran: The Organization for Defending Victims of Violence, 2000. http://www.neda.net.ir/odvvweb, accessed on May 19, 2001.

Fukuyama, Francis. "The End of History?" *The National Interest* 16, Summer (1989).

———. *The End of History and the Last Man.* New York: Free Press, 1992.

———. "Capitalism and Democracy." *The Journal of Democracy* (1992).

———. "Neyasnost' natsional'nogo interesa." *Nezavisimaia Gazeta* 1992.

———. "The Modernizing Imperative. The USSR as an Ordinary Country." *The National Interest* 20, Spring (1993).

———. "Reflections on the End of History, Five Years Later." In *After History? Francis Fukuyama and His Critics,* edited by Timothy Burns. Lanham: Rowman & Littlefield, 1994.

———. *Trust. The Social Virtue and the Creation of Prosperity.* New York: Free Press, 1995.

———. "The Primacy of Culture." *Journal of Democracy* 6, 1 (1995)

———. "Social Capital and the Global Economy." *Foreign Affairs* (1996).

———. "Their Target: The Modern World." *Newsweek,* January 2002. http://www.msnbc.com/news/ accessed on May 30, 2002.

Furedi, Frank. *The New Ideology of Imperialism.* London: Pluto Press, 1994.

———. "The Enthronement of Low Expectations: Fukuyama's Ideological Compromise for Our Time." In *Has History Ended? Fukuyama, Marx, Modernity,* edited by C. Bertram and A. Chitty. London: Avebury, 1994.

Furman, Dmitri. "Vneshnepoliticheskiye oriyentiry Rossiyi." *Svobodnaya mysl'* 8 (1995).

Gadzhiyev, K. S. *Geopolitika.* Moskva: Mezhdunarodniye otnosheniya, 1997.

———. *Vvedeniye v geopolitiku.* Moskva: Logos, 1998.

Garton Ash, T. *The Magic Lantern.* New York: Random House, 1990.

Gefter, M. Ya. *Iz tekh i etikh let.* Moskva: Progress, 1991.

Gellner, E. *Nations and Nationalism.* Oxford: Blackwell, 1983.

Giddens, A. *The Nation-State and Violence.* Berkeley: University of California Press, 1985.

Gilligan, C. *In a Different Voice.* Cambridge, Mass.: Harvard University Press, 1982.

Goble, Paul A. "Can We Help Russia Become a Good Neighbor?" *Demokratizatsiya. The Journal of Post-Soviet Democratization* 2, 1 (1994).

Goldstein, J., and R. O. Keohane, eds. *Ideas and Foreign Policy: Beliefs, Institutions, and Political Change.* Ithaca, N.Y.: Cornell University Press, 1993.

Gorbachev, M. *Perestroika. New Thinking for Our Country and the World.* New York: Harper and Row, 1987.

———. *The Search for a New Beginning: Developing a New Civilization.* San Francisco: HarperSanFrancisco, 1995.

———. *On My Country and the World.* New York: Columbia University Press, 2000.

Gorbachev, M., ed. *Grani globalizatsiyi: Trudnyye voprosy sovremennogo razvitiya.* Moskva: Alpina, 2003.

Gurr, T. *Minorities at Risk.* Washington, D.C.: United States Institute of Peace, 1993.

Haan, N., R. N. Bellah, P. Rabinow, and W. M. Sullivan, eds. *Social Science as Moral Inquiry.* New York: Columbia University Press, 1983.

Haas, Peter. "Introduction: Epistemic Communities." *International Organization* 46, 2 (1992).

Habermas, J. *Theory and Practice.* Boston: Beacon Press, 1973.

Hall, P., ed. *The Political Power of Economic Ideas.* Princeton, N.J.: Princeton University Press, 1989.

Harding, S. *Is Science Multicultural? Postcolonialism, Feminism, and Epistemologies.* Bloomington: Indiana University Press, 1998.

Hashmi, Sohail H. "Islamic Ethics in International Society." In *International Society. Diverse Ethical Perspectives,* edited by David R. Marpel and Terry Nardin. Princeton, N.J.: Princeton University Press, 1998.

Hassan, Hassan Bakr A. "Islamic Revivalism and Its Impact on the Middle East and the Superpowers." In *Culture and International Relations,* edited by Jongsuk Chay. New York: Praeger, 1990.

Hauner, M. *What Is Asia to Us? Russia's Asian Heartland Yesterday and Today.* Boston: Unwin Hyman, 1986.

Held, David. *Democracy and Global Order.* Oxford: Polity Press, 1995.

———. "The Changing Contours of Political Community: Rethinking Democracy in the Context of Globalization." In *Global Democracy,* edited by Barry Holden. London: Routledge, 2000.

———. "Violence and Justice in a Global Age." October 2001. http://www.openDemocracy.net accessed on November 30, 2001.

Herman, Robert G. "Identity, Norms, and National Security: The Soviet Foreign Policy Revolution and the End of Cold War." In *The Culture of*

National Security, edited by Peter J. Katzenstein. New York: Columbia University Press, 1996.

Hoffmann, Stanley. "An American Social Science: International Relations." *Daedalus* 106, 3 (1977).

Holsti, K. J. *The Dividing Discipline. Hegemony and Diversity in International Theory.* Boston: Unwin Hyman, 1985.

Hughes, Christopher. "Globalization and Nationalism: Squaring the Circle in Chinese International Relations Theory." *Millennium* 26, 1 (1997).

Huntington, Samuel P. *Political Order in Changing Societies.* New Haven, Conn.: Yale University Press, 1968.

————. "No Exit: The Errors of Endism." *The National Interest* Fall (1989)

————. *The Third Wave. Democratization in the Late Twentieth Century.* Norman and London: University of Oklahoma Press, 1991.

————. "The Clash of Civilizations?" *Foreign Affairs* 72, 4 (1993).

————. "If Not Civilizations, What? Paradigms of the Post-Cold War World," *Foreign Affairs* 72, 6 (1993).

————. *The Clash of Civilizations and the Remaking of World Order.* New York: Simon & Schuster, 1996.

————. "The West: Unique, Not Universal." *Foreign Affairs* 75, 6 (1996).

————. "The Erosion of American National Interests." *Foreign Affairs* 76, 5 (1997).

————. "Lonely Superpower." *Foreign Affairs* 78, 2 (1999).

————. "The Age Of Muslim Wars." *Newsweek,* January 2002. http://www.msnbc.com/news/672440.asp accessed on May 30, 2002.

Ikenberry, G. John. "The West: Precious, Not Unique." *Foreign Affairs* 76, 2 (1997).

————. *After Victory: Institutions, Strategic Restraint, and the Rebuilding of Order after Major Wars.* Princeton, N.J.: Princeton University Press, 2000.

Inayatullah, Naeem, and David L. Blaney. "Knowing Encounters: Beyond Parochialism in International Relations Theory." In *The Return of Culture and Identity in IR Theory,* edited by Yosef Lapid and Friedrich Kratochwil. Boulder, Colo.: Lynne Rienner, 1996.

————. "Toward an Ethnological IPE: Karl Polanyi's Double Critique of Capitalism." *Millennium* 28, 2 (1999).

"International Relations Theory and the New World Order. The Forum." *Mershon International Studies Review* 40, 1 (1996).

Isaac, Jeffrey C. "The Meanings of 1989." In *The Revolutions of 1989,* edited by Vladimir Tismaneanu. London: Routledge, 1999.

Ivanov, Igor' S. "Rossiya v mirovoi politike." *Mezhdunarodnaya zhizn'* 5 (2001).

Izbiratel'noye ob'edineniye "Vybor Rossiyi": Programma. Moskva: Vybor Rossiyi, 1993.

Iz-pod glib: Sbornik statei. Moskva: Russkaya kniga, 1992.

Jervis, Robert. "Hypotheses on Misperception." In *International Politics. Enduring Concepts and Contemporary Issues,* edited by Robert J. Art and Robert Jervis. New York: HarperCollins, 1968 [1992].

———. *Perception and Misperception in International Politics.* Princeton, N.J.: Princeton University Press, 1976.

Jonas, H. *The Imperative of Responsibility: In Search of an Ethics for the Technological Age.* Chicago: University of Chicago Press, 1985.

Jones, W. S. *The Logic of International Relations.* Boston: Little Brown, 1985.

Kahn, Jeff. "What Is the New Russian Federalism?" In *Contemporary Russian Politics,* edited by Archie Brown. Oxford: Oxford University Press, 2001.

Kaplan, Robert D. 1994. "The Coming Anarchy." *Atlantic Monthly* 271 (1994). http://www.theatlantic.com/politics/foreign/images accessed on November 3, 1999.

———. "Looking the World in the Eye." *Atlantic Monthly* December (2001).

Kapustin, Boris. "Rossiya i Zapad na puti k miru mirov." *Kentavr* 1, 2 (1993).

———. "Natsional'nyi interes kak konservativnaya utopiya." *Svobodnaya mysl'* 3 (1996).

———. *Sovremennost' kak predmet politicheskoi teoriyi.* Moskva: ROSSPEN, 1998.

Karagodin, Andrei. "Otkroveniya mondialistov." *Zavtra* 36 (1994).

Kara-Murza, Alexei. "Na perekrestke politiki i nauki." *Polis* 6 (2001). http://www.politstudies.ru/universum/esse/8kmz.htm#17 accessed on February 14, 2002.

Kara-Murza, Alexei, Alexandr Panarin, and Igor' Pantin. "Dukhovno-ideologicheskaya situatsiya v sovremennoi Rossiyi: perspektivy razvitiya." *Polis* 4 (1995).

Kaspe, Svatoslav. "Rossiyskaya tsivilizatsiya i ideiyi A. Dzh. Toynbi," *Svobodnaya mysl'* 2 (1995).

Kaufman, Stuart J. "Approaches to Global Politics in the Twenty-first Century: A Review Essay." *International Studies Review* 2 (1999).

Keohane, R. O., and J. S. Nye, eds. *Transnational Relations and World Politics.* Cambridge, Mass. Harvard University Press, 1972.

Kerr, David. "The New Eurasianism: The Rise of Geopolitics in Russia's Foreign Policy." *Europe-Asia Studies* 47, 6 (1995).

Khatami, Mohammed. "Empathy and Compassion: Believing in Dialogue Paves the Way for Hope." Speech at the U.N.-sponsored Conference of Dialogue among Civilizations. *The Iranian,* September 8, 2000. http://www.iranian.com accessed on May 20, 2001.

Khorev, Boris. *Rossiyu pribirayut k rukam.* Moskva: Paleia, 1996.

Kochetov, E. G. *Geoekonomika.* Moskva: BEK, 1999.

Kohn, H., ed. *The Mind of Modern Russia. Historical and Political Thought of Russia's Great Age.* New York: Harper & Row, 1955.

"'Konets istoriyi' ili konets ideologiyi?" *SshA: Ekonomika, Politika, Ideologiya* 6 (1990).

"Kontseptsiya vneshnei politiki Rossiiskoi Federatsiyi." *Nezavisimaya gazeta,* July 7, 2000.

Kortunov, Sergei. "Imperskoye i natsional'noye v rossiiskom soznaniyi." *Mezhdunarodnaya zhizn'* 5, 6 (1998).

———. "Rossiysko-Amerikanskoye partnerstvo?" *Mezhdunarodnaya zhizn'* 4 (2002).

———. "Stanovleniye novogo myrovogo poryadka," *Mezhdunarodnaya zhizn'* 6 (2002).

Kovalev, O. "Russian 'Realism': Theory and Policy Preferences." Doctoral dissertation, University of Delaware, 1997.

Kozyrev, A. V. *Preobrazheniye.* Moskva: Mezhdunarodniye otnosheniya, 1995.

Krasin, Yuri A., ed. "Vzaiomodeistviye obschestvennykh sistem v tselostnom mire." *Voprosy filosofiyi* 8 (1990).

———. "O rossiyskikh natsional'nykh interesakh." *Svobodnaya mysl'* 3 (1996).

———. *Natsional'nyiye interesy.* Moskva: Gorbachev-fond, 1996.

Krasner, S., ed. *International Regimes.* Ithaca, N.Y.: Cornell University Press, 1983.

Krauthammer, Charles. "The Unipolar Moment." *Foreign Affairs: America and the World* (1990/1991).

Kupchan, Charles A. "After Pax Americana: Benign Power, Regional Integration, and the Sources of a Stable Multipolarity." *International Security* 23, 2 (1998).

Kurginyan, S. E. et al. *Postperestroika.* Moskva: Politizdat, 1990.

Kurtz, Stanley. "The Future of 'History': Francis Fukuyama and Samuel P. Huntington, post–September 11." *Policy Review* 113 (2002), http://www. hoover.org accessed on July 20, 2002.

Lapid, Y., and F. Kratochwil, eds. *The Return of Culture and Identity in IR Theory.* Boulder, Colo.: Lynne Rienner, 1996.

Layne, Christopher. "From Preponderance to Offshore Balancing: America's Future Grand Strategy." *International Security* 22, 1 (1997).

Leander, Anna. "Betrand Badie: Cultural Diversity Changing International Relations?" In *The Future of International Relations. Masters in the Making?* edited by Iver Neumann and Ole Weaver. London: Routledge, 1997.

Lepor, K. P., ed. *After the Cold War: Essays on the Emerging World Order.* Austin: University of Texas Press, 1996.

LeVine, Robert A. "Socialization, Social Structure, and Intersocietal Images." In *International Behavior. A Social-Psychological Analysis,* edited by Herbert C. Kelman. New York: Holt, Rinehart and Winston, 1965.

LeVine, R. A., and D. T. Campbell. *Ethnocentrism: Theories of Conflict, Ethnic Attitudes, and Group Behavior.* New York: John Wiley & Sons, 1972.

Light, Margot. *Marxism and Soviet International Relations.* Sussex: Wheatsheaf Books 1988.

———. "Foreign Policy Thinking." In *Internal Factors in Russian Foreign Policy,* edited by Neil Malcolm et al. Oxford: Oxford University Press, 1996.

Linklater, A. *Men and Citizens in the Theory of International Relations.* New York: St. Martin's Press, 1982.

———. *The Transformation of Political Community.* Oxford: Polity Press, 1998.

Lomanov, Alexandr. "Na peripheriyi 'stolknoveniya tsivilizatsi'." *Pro et Contra* 3, 1 (1998).

Lukin, Vladimir P. "Russia and Its Interests." In *Rethinking Russia's National Interests,* edited by Stephen Sestanovich. Washington, D.C.: Center for Strategic and International Studies, 1994.

Lynch, A. *The Soviet Study of International Relations.* Cambridge: Cambridge University Press, 1987.

Lynch, Marc. "The Dialogue of Civilizations and International Public Sphere." *Millennium* 29, 2 (2000).

MacFarlane, Neil S. "Democratization, Nationalism, and Regional Security in the Southern Caucasus." *Government and Opposition* 10 (1997).

MacIntyre, A. *After Virtue.* Notre Dame, Ind.: University of Notre Dame Press, 1981.

———. *Whose Justice? Whose Rationality?* Notre Dame, Ind.: University of Notre Dame Press, 1987.

Mahbubani, Kishore. "The Dangers of Decadence. What the Rest Can Teach the West." *Foreign Affairs* 72, 5 (1993).

Mannheim, K. *Ideology and Utopia. An Introduction to the Sociology of Knowledge.* New York, London: A Harvest-HBJ Book, 1936.

Mapel, D. R. and T. Nardin, eds. *International Society. Diverse Ethical Perspectives.* Princeton, N.J.: Princeton University Press, 1998.

Mead, G. H. *Mind, Self, and Society from the Standpoint of a Social Behaviorist.* Chicago: University of Chicago Press, 1967.

Mel'vil', Andrei. "Liberal'naya vneshnepoliticheskaya alternativa dlya Rossiyi?" *Otkritaya politika* 6 (1998).

Meshkov, Aleksei. "Aktual'niye aspekty vneshnei politiki Rossiyi." *Mezhdunarodnaya zhizn'* 4 (2002).

Meyer, John W., et al. "World Society and the Nation-State." *American Journal of Sociology* 103, 1 (1997).

Mezhuyev, Boris. "Review of Tsymburski's book *Rossiya—zemlya za Velikim Limitrofom.*" *Pro et Contra* 5, 2 (2000).

Migranyan, Andranik. "Rossiya i blizhneye zarubezhiye." *Nezavisimaya gazeta,* January 12, 1994.

Miliukov, P. *Russia and Its Crisis.* London: Collier-Macmillan, 1962.

Milliken, Jennifer. "The Study of Discourse in IR." *European Journal of International Relations* 5, 2 (1999).

———. "Discourse Study: Bringing Rigor to Critical Theory." In *Constructing International Relations,* edited by Karin M. Fierke and Knud Erik Jorgensen. Armonk: M. E. Sharpe, 2001.

Mirski, Georgi. "'Stolknoveniye tsivilizatsi?'—debaty na Zapade." *Mirovaya ekonomika i mezhdunarodniye otnosheniya* 11 (1994).

Mitrofanov, A. V. *Shagi novoi geopolitiki.* Moskva: unknown publisher, 1997.

Mohanty, Chandra Talpade. "Under Western Eyes: Feminist Scholarship and Colonial Discourses." In *Comparative Political Culture in the Age of Globalization,* edited by Hwa Yol Jung. Lanham: Lexington Books, 2002.

Moiseyev, Nikita N. "Universal'nyi evolyutsionizm." *Voprosy filosofiyi* 3 (1991).

Monem, Abdel. "A Self-Fulfilling Prophecy." *Worldlink. The Magazine of the World Economic Forum* (2002). http://www.worldlink.co.uk/stories storyReader$1103 accessed on May 2002.

Morrice, David. "The Liberal-Communitarian Debate in Contemporary Political Philosophy and Its Significance for International Relations." *Review of International Studies* 26, 2 (2000).

Muravchik, J. *Exporting Democracy. Fulfilling America's Destiny.* Washington, D.C.: The American Enterprise Institute, 1992.

Naim, Moises. "Why the World Loves to Hate America." *Foreign Policy.* December (2001)

Narochnitskaya, Natalya. "Natsionalnyi interes Rossiyi." *Mezhdunarodnaya zhizn'* 3–4 (1992).

Nartov, N. A. *Geopolitika.* Moskva: Yuniti, 1999.

Neklessa, Alexandr I. "Postsovremennyi mir v novoi sisteme koordinat." *Vostok* 2 (1997).

———. "Epilog istoriyi." *Vostok* 5 (1998).

Neumann, Iver B. *Russia and the Idea of Europe. A Study in Identity and International Relations.* London: Routledge, 1996.

———. "Self and Other in International Relations." *European Journal of International Relations* 2, 3 (1997).

Odell, J. S. *U.S. International Monetary Policy: Markets, Power, and Ideas as Sources of Change.* Princeton, N.J.: Princeton University Press, 1982.

O'Hagan, Jacinta. "Clash of Civilizations?" In *Contesting Images of World Politics*, edited by Greg Fry and Jacinta O'Hagan. London: Macmillan Press, 2000.

Onuf, N. G. *The World of Our Making: Rules and Rule in Social Theory and International Relations*. Columbia: University of South Carolina Press, 1989.

Oren, Ido. "Is Culture Independent of National Security? How America's National Security Concerns Shaped 'Political Culture' Research." *European Journal of International Relations* 6, 4 (2000).

———. "The Subjectivity of the 'Democratic' Peace: Changing U.S. Perceptions of Imperial Germany." *International Security* 20, 2 (1995).

Orlova, I. A. *Yevraziyskaya tsivilizatsiya*. Mosvka: Norma, 1998.

O Tuathail, G., and S. Dalby, eds. *Rethinking Geopolitics*. London: Routledge, 1998.

Panarin, Aleksandr. "Yevraziyski proyekt v mirosistemnom kontekste." *Vostok* 3 (1995).

———. *Revansh istoriyi*. Moskva: Logos, 1998.

———. *Rossiya v tsyklakh mirovoi istoriyi*. Moskva: MGU, 1999.

———. "Amerikanski global'nyi vyzov." *Rossiyskaya federatsiya* 8 (1999).

———. "Ontologiya terrora." In *Geopolitika terrora*. Moskva: "Arktogeya tsentr," 2002.

Paschenko, A. Ia. *Ideologiya yevraziystva*. Moskva: MGU, 2000.

Patomäki, Heikki, and Christer Pursiainen. "Western Models and the Russian Idea: Beyond 'Inside/Outside' in Discourses on Civil Society." *Millennium* 28, 1 (1999).

Pfaff, William. "Redefining World Power." *Foreign Affairs* 70, 1 (1999).

Plattner, Marc. "The Democratic Moment." In *The Global Resurgence of Democracy*, edited by Larry Diamond and Marc Plattner. Baltimore: Johns Hopkins University Press, 1992.

Podtserob, Alexei. "Konflikt dvukh tsivilizatsi ili ikh vzaimodeistviye?" *Mezhdunarodnaya zhizn'* 3 (1998).

Porter, Bruce. "Russia and Europe." In *The Sources of Russian Foreign Policy*, edited by Celeste Wallander. Boulder, Colo.: Westview Press, 1996.

Posen, Barry R. "The Security Dilemma and Ethnic Conflict." *Survival* 35 (1993).

"Postsovremennyi mir: novaya systema koordinat: Forum." *Vostok* 1 (1998).

Pozdnyakov, El'giz A. "Natsional'noye i internatsional'noye vo vneshnei politike." *Mirovaya ekonomika i mezhhdunarodniye otnosheniya* 5 (1989).

———. "Vneshnyaya i vnutrenyaya politika: Paradoksy vzaimosvyazi." *Mirovaya ekonomika i mezhhdunarodniye otnosheniya* 10 (1989).

———. "Mirovoi sotsial'nyi progress: mify i real'nost." *Mirovaya ekonomika i mezhhdunarodniye otnosheniya* 11 (1989).

———. "Formatsionnyi i tsivilizatsionnyi podkhody i mezhdunarodniye otnosheniya." In *SSSR v mirovom soobschestve*, edited by Nodar A. Simoniya. Moskva: Progress, 1990.

———. "My sami razorili svoi dom, sami dolzhny i podnyat' yego." *Mezhdunarodnaya zhizn'* 3–4 (1992).

———. "Geopoliticheski kollaps i Rossiya." *Mezhdunarodnaya zhizn'* 8–9 (1992).

"Preobrazhennaya Rossiya v novom mire." *Mezhdunarodnaya zhizn'* 3–4 (1992).

Primakov, Yevgeni. "Mezhdunarodniye otnosheniya nakanune XXI veka: problemy, perspektivy." *Mezhdunarodniya zhizn'* 10 (1996).

———. "Rossiya v mirovoi politike." *Mezhdunarodniya zhizn'* 5 (1998).

"Problemy tselostnogo mira." *Voprosy filosofiyi* 12 (1990).

Proektor, D. M. *Noviye izmereniya rossiyskoi politiki bezopasnosti na rubezhe stoletiy.* Moskva: IMEMO, 1997.

Putin, Vladimir V. "Russia at the Turn of the Millennium, 1999." http://www.government.gov.ru/government/minister/article-vvp1.html accessed in May 2002.

———. *First Person: An Astonishingly Frank Self-Portrait by Russia's President.* New York: Public Affairs, 2000.

———. Rossiya: novyye vostochnyye perspektivy. *Nezavisimaya gazeta,* October 1, 2000.

———. "Zayavleniye Prezidenta Rossiyskoi Federatsiyi V.V. Putina." September 24, 2001. http://www.kremlin.ru/events/311.html accessed on December 5, 2001.

———. Speech to the German parliament, September 25, 2001.

———. "Poslaniye Prezidenta Rossiyskoi Federatsiyi V.V. Putina Federal'nomu Sobraniyu Rossiyskoi Federatsiyi." *Mezhdunarodnaya zhizn'* 5 (2002).

Rahr, Alexander. "'Atlanticists' versus 'Eurasians' in Russian Foreign Policy." *RFE/RL Research Report* 1, 22 (1992).

Rajaee, F. *Globalization on Trial. The Human Condition and the Information Civilization.* West Hartford, Conn.: Kumarian Press, 2000.

Rengger, Nicholas J. "A City Which Sustains All Things? Communitarianism and International Society." *Millennium* 21, 3 (1992).

Risse-Kappen, Thomas. "Ideas Do Not Float Freely." *International Organization* 48, 3 (1994).

Rogers, E. M. *Diffusion of Innovations.* 4th ed. New York: Free Press, 1995.

Rogov, S. *Yevraziyskaya strategiya dlya Rossiyi.* Moskva: Institut SshA i Kanady, 1998.

"Rossiya i prostranstvo," *Elementy* 4 (1993).

"Rossiya i Zapad: vzayimodeistviye kul'tur." *Voprosy filosofiyi* 6 (1992).

Rubenstein, Richard E., and Jarle Crocker. "Challenging Huntington." *Foreign Policy* 96, Fall (1997).

Ruggie, John Gerard. "International Regimes, Transactions, and Change: Embedded Liberalism in the Postwar Economic Order." *International Organization* 36, 2 (1982).

————. "Continuity and Transformation in the World Polity: Toward a Neorealist Synthesis." *World Politics* 35, 2 (1983).

————. "At Home Abroad, Abroad at Home: International Liberalization and Domestic Stability in the New World Economy." *Millennium* 24, 3 (1994).

————. *Winning the Peace. America and World Order in the New Era.* New York: Columbia University Press, 1996.

————. "What Makes the World Hang Together." *International Organization* 52, 3 (1998).

Ruiz, Lester Edwin J. "Culture, Politics, and the Sense of the Ethical: Challenges for Normative International Relations." In *Principled World Politics,* edited by Paul Wapner and Lester Edwin J. Ruiz. Lanham: Rowman & Littlefield, 2000.

Said, Edward W. *Culture and Imperialism.* New York: Alfred A. Knopf, 1993.

————. "The Clash of Ignorance." *Nation.* October 22 (2001).

Salla, Michael E. "Political Islam and the West: A New Cold War or Convergence?" *Third World Quarterly* 18, 4 (1997).

Samuilov, Sergei M. "Neizbezhno li stolknoveniye tsivilizatsi?" *SShA: Ekonomika, Politika, Ideologiya* 1, 2 (1995).

Sautman, Barry. "The Devil to Pay. The 1989 Debate and the Intellectual Origins of Yelstin's 'Soft Authoritarianism'." *Communist and Post-Communist Studies* 28, 1 (1995).

Sergounin, Alexander A. "Russian Post-Communist Foreign Policy Thinking at the Cross-roads." *Journal of International Relations and Development* 3, 3 (2000).

Shakhnazarov, Georgi. "Miroporyadok tsivilizatsi?" *Pro et Contra* 3, 4 (1998).

————. *Otkroveniya i zabluzhdeniya teoriyi tsivilizatsi.* Moskva: Sovremennyi gumanitarnyi universitet, 2000.

Shenfield, S. *The Nuclear Predicament: Explorations in Soviet Ideology.* London: Routledge, 1987.

Shlapentokh, Vladimir. "'Old,' 'New' and 'Post' Liberal Attitudes towards the West: From Love to Hate." *Communist and Post-Communist Studies* 31, 3 (1998).

Simonia, Nodari. "Budet li sleduschaya voina stolknoveniyem tsivilizatsi?" *Mirovaya ekonomika i mezhdunarodniye otnosheniya* 11 (1994).

————. "Economic Interests and Political Power in Post-Soviet Russia." In *Contemporary Russian Politics*, edited by Archie Brown. Oxford: Oxford University Press, 2001.

Siniyavski, Andrei. "Intelligentsiya i vlast'." In *Osnovy Sovetskoi tsivilizatsiyi*. Moskva: Agraf, 2001.

Smith, G. *The Post-Soviet States. Mapping the Politics of Transition*. London: Arnold, 1999.

Smith, Michael Joseph. "Moral Reasoning and Moral Responsibility in International Affairs." In *Ethics and International Relations*, edited by Kenneth W. Thompson. New Brunswick: Transaction Books, 1985.

Snyder, J. *Myths of Empire*. Ithaca, N.Y.: Cornell University Press, 1991.

Sogrin, Vladimir. "Zapadnyi liberalizm i rossiyskiye reformy." *Svobodnaya mysl'* 1 (1996).

Sorokin, K. E. *Geopolitika sovremennosti i geostrategiya Rossiyi*. Moskva: ROSSPEN, 1996.

"Sotsial'nyi progress v sovremennom mire." *Kommunist* 3 (1988).

Spasski, Nikolai. "Novoye mishleniye po amerikanski." *Mirovaya ekonomika i mezhdunarodniye otnosheniya* 6, 7 (1992).

Stankevich, Sergei. "Toward a New 'National Idea'." In *Rethinking Russia's National Interests*, edited by Stephen Sestanovich. Washington, D.C.: Center for Strategic and International Studies, 1994.

Steger, Manfred B. "Of Means and Ends: 1989 as Ethicopolitical Imperative." In *After the Fall: 1989 and the Future of Freedom*, edited by George Katsiaficas. London: Routledge, 2001.

Stepan, Alfred. "Russian Federalism in Comparative Perspective." *Post-Soviet Affairs* 16, 2 (2000).

"'Stolknoveniye tsivilizatsi': Perspektivy i alternativy." *Obschestvenniye nauki i sovremennost'* 4 (1995).

Strategiya dlya Rossiyi: Povestka dlya prezidenta—2000. Moskva: Sovet po vneshnei i oboronnoi politike, 2000. www.svop.edu accessed in July 2000.

Taylor, C. *Sources of the Self: The Making of the Modern Identity*. Cambridge, Mass.: Harvard University Press, 1983.

————. *The Ethics of Authenticity*. Cambridge, Mass.: Harvard University Press, 1991.

Taylor, C., et al. *Multiculturalism and "The Politics of Recognition."* Princeton, N.J.: Princeton University Press, 1992.

Tibi, Bassam. "Post-Bipolar Order in Crisis: The Challenge of Politicised Islam." *Millennium* 29, 3 (2000).

Tivnan, E. *The Moral Imagination. Confronting the Ethical Issues of Our Day*. New York: Simon & Schuster, 1995.

Tolz, Vera. "The Burden of Imperial Thinking." *RFE/RL Research Report* 1, 49 (1992).

———. "Forging the Nation: National Identity and Nation Building in Post-Communist Russia." *Europe-Asia Studies* 50, 6 (1998).

———. *Russia: Inventing the Nation.* London: Arnold, 2001.

Torbakov, Igor. "The 'Statists' and the Ideology of Russian Imperial Nationalism." *RFE/RL Research Report* 1, 49 (1992).

Trenin, Dmitri. *The End of Eurasia: Russia on the Border between Geopolitics and Globalization.* Moscow: Carnegie Moscow Center, 2001.

———. "Vladimir Putin's Autumn Marathon: Toward the Birth of a Russian Foreign Policy Strategy." Carnegie, Moscow, Briefing Paper, 11 (2001).

Tretyakov, Vitali. "Pragmatizm vneshnei politiki Putina." *Mezhdunarodnaya zhizn'* 5 (2002).

"'Tsivilizatsionnaya model' mezhdunarodnykh otnosheni i yeye implikatsiyi." *Polis* 1 (1995).

Tsygankov, Andrei P. "From Liberal Internationalism to Revolutionary Expansionism: The Foreign Policy Discourse of Contemporary Russia." *Mershon International Studies Review* 41, 2 (1997).

———. "Hard-line Eurasianism and Russia's Contending Geopolitical Perspectives." *The East European Quarterly* 32, 3 (1998).

———. "Manifestations of Delegative Democracy in Russian Local Politics—What Does It Mean for the Future of Russia?" *Communist and Post-Communist Studies* 30, 4 (1998).

———. "The Final Triumph of the Pax Americana? Western Intervention in Yugoslavia and Russia's Debate on the Post-Cold War Order." *Communist and Post-Communist Studies* 33, 3 (2001).

———. "The Culture of Economic Security. National Identity and Politico-Economic Ideas in the Post-Soviet World." *International Politics* 39, 2 (2002).

———. "Rediscovering National Interests after the 'End of History': Fukuyama, Russian Intellectuals, and a Post–Cold War Order." *International Politics* 39, 4 (2002).

———. "Mastering Space in Eurasia. Russia's Geopolitical Thinking after the Soviet Break-Up." *Communist and Post Communist Studies* 35, 1 (2003).

Tsygankov, Pavel A. "Identifikatsiya Yevropy vo vneshnei politike Rossiyi: ot ideologiyi 'yestestvennogo partnerstva' k pragmatike natsional'no gosudarstvennykh interesov." *Sotsial'no-Politicheski Zhurnal* 6 (1995).

Tsymburski, Vadim. "Narody mezhdu tsivilizatsiyami." *Pro et Contra* 2, 3 (1997).

———. "Geopolitika dlya 'yevraziyskoi Atlantidy'." *Pro et Contra* 4, 4 (1999).

———. "Eto tvoi posledni geokul'turnyi vybor, Rossiya." *Polis* 1 (2001). http://www.politstudies.ru/universum/esse/8kmz.htm#17 accessed on February 24, 2002.

Turovski, R. ed. *Politicheskiye protsessy v regionakh Rossiyi.* Moskva: Tsentr politicheskikh tekhnologi, 1998.

Urban, J. B., and V. D. Solovei. *Russia's Communists at the Crossroads.* Boulder, Colo.: Westview Press, 1997.

Utkin, Anatoli. "Konflikt tsivilizatsi?" *Novaya Rossiya* 2 (1997).

Van der Dennen, Johan M. G. "Ethnocentrism and In-group/Out-group Differentiation: A Review and Interpretation of the Literature." In *The Sociobiology of Ethnocentrism. Evolutionary Dimensions of Xenophobia, Discrimination, Racism, and Nationalism,* edited by Vernon Reynolds, Vincent Falgar, and Ian Vine. London & Sydney: Croom Helm, 1987.

Vekhi: Sbornik statei. Moskva: Molodaya gvardiya, 1991.

Vernadski, V. I. *Nauchnaya mysl' kak planetarnoye yavleniye.* Moskva: Nauka, 1991.

Vitalis, Robert. "The Graceful and Generous Liberal Gesture: Making Racism Invisible in American International Relations." *Millennium* 29, 2 (2000).

"Vneshnyaya politika: trebovaniya nauki i opasniye igry." *Otkrytaya politika* 5 (1998).

Vucinich, A. *Darwin in Russian Thought.* Berkeley: University of California Press, 1988.

———. *Einstein and Soviet Ideology.* Stanford: Stanford University Press, 2001.

Waever, Ole. "The Sociology of a Not So International Discipline: American and European Developments in International Relations." *International Organization* 52, 4 (1998).

Walker, R. B. J., ed. *Culture, Ideology, and World Order.* Boulder, Colo.: Westview Press, 1984.

———. *Inside/Outside: International Relations as Political Theory.* Cambridge: Cambridge University Press, 1993.

Wallerstein, I. *Geopolitics and Geoculture.* Cambridge: Cambridge University Press, 1991.

Walt, Stephen M. "Building Up New Bogeymen." *Foreign Policy* 106, Spring (1997).

———. "Fads, Fevers, and Firestorms." *Foreign Policy* 109, Spring (2000).

Waltz, K. N. *Theory of International Politics.* Reading: Addison-Wesley, 1979.

Walzer, M. *Just and Unjust Wars.* New York: Basic Books, 1977.

Warner, D. *An Ethic of Responsibility in International Relations.* Boulder and London: Lynne Rienner, 1991.

Weller, Christoph. "Collective Identities in World Society." In *Civilizing World Politics. Society and Community beyond the State,* edited by Mathias Albert, Lothar Brock, and Klaus Dieter Wolf. Lanham: Rowman & Littlefield, 2000.

Wendt, Alexander. "The Agent-Structure Problem in International Relations Theory." *International Organization* 41 (1987).

————. "Anarchy Is What States Make of It: The Social Construction of Power Politics." *International Organization* 46, 2 (1992).

————. "Constructing International Politics." *International Security* 20 (1995).

————. *Social Theory of International Politics.* Cambridge: Cambridge University Press, 1999.

Wiarda, Howard J. "The Ethnocentrism of the Social Science. Implications for Research and Policy." *The Review of Politics* 43, 2 (1981).

Wiatr, Jerzi J. "Central Europe in the World Order." *Central European Political Science Review* 1, 1 (2000).

Wight, M. *International Theory. The Three Traditions,* edited by Gabriele Wight and Brian Porter. New York: Holmes & Meier, 1992.

Wolfe, A. *Whose Keeper? Social Science and Moral Obligation.* Berkeley: University of California Press, 1989.

Woods, Ngaire. "Economic Ideas and International Relations: Beyond Rational Neglect." *International Studies Quarterly* 39 (1995).

Yee, Albert S. "The Causal Effects of Ideas on Policies." *International Organization* 50, 1 (1996).

"Z" (anonymous). "To the Stalin Mausoleum." *Daedalus* January (1990).

Zagladin, Nikita, and Boris Kapustin. "Al'ternativy i imperativy v mirovoi politike." *Mirovaya ekonomika i mezhhdunarodniye otnosheniya* 3 (1990).

Zagorski, Andrei V. "Monopolyarnost': novoie kachestvo mezhdunarodnykh otnosheni." *Kosmopolis* (1997).

Zamoshkin, Yuri A. "'Konets istoriyi': ideologizm i realizm." *Voprosy filosofiyi* 3 (1990).

Zimmerman, W. *Soviet Perspectives on International Relations, 1956–67.* Princeton, N.J.: Princeton University Press, 1969.

————. *The Russian People and Foreign Policy: Russian Elite and Mass Perspectives, 1993–2000.* Princeton, N.J.: Princeton University Press, 2002.

Zudin, Alexei. "'Oligarhiya' kak politicheskaya problema rossiyskogo postkommunizma." *Obschestvenniye nauki i sovremennost'* 1 (1999).

————. "Neokorporativizm v Rossiyi? (Gosudarstvo i biznes pri Vladimire Putine)." *Pro et Contra* 6, 4 (2001).

Zyuganov, Gennadi A. *Rossiya i sovremennyi mir.* Moskva: Informatsion-noizdatel'skoye agentstvo "Obozrevatel'," 1995.

————. *Geografiya pobedy.* Moskva: an unknown publisher, 1998.

————. "Politicheski doklad Sovyeta SKP-KPSS XXXII syezdu." October 2001. http://www.kprf.ru/tribuna/dokladckpkhcc.html accessed on February 24, 2002.

INDEX

ANDREI P. TSYGANKOV
is assistant professor of international relations and political science
at San Francisco State University.

www.ingramcontent.com/pod-product-compliance
Lightning Source LLC
Chambersburg PA
CBHW071740270326
41928CB00013B/2752